A Student's Guide to

First-Year Writing

2009–2010

Marlowe Daly-Galeano
Marissa Juárez
Jacob Witt

University of Arizona

30th Edition

HAYDEN
HM
McNEIL

Printed in the United States of America

10 9 8 7 6 5 4 3 2 1

ISBN 978-0-7380-3308-2

Hayden-McNeil Publishing
14903 Pilot Drive
Plymouth, MI 48170
www.hmpublishing.com

HallA 3308-2 F09

Acknowledgements

As always, the editors are supported and encouraged by their colleagues at the University of Arizona and by the wonderful staff at Hayden-McNeil. This year's revision of the *Guide* would not have been possible without the help of many individuals. We would like to thank Anne-Marie Hall, director of the Writing Program, for her invaluable encouragement, advice and support throughout the year. We are especially grateful for the care with which she read and commented on this year's *Guide*. We would also like to thank course directors Patrick Baliani, Carol Nowotny-Young, D. R. Ransdell, and Erec Toso as well as Chris Minnix, Vicki Mills, and the UA library staff for their input and contributions. For their administrative support, we thank Penny Gates, Monica Vega, Chris Minnix, and Sara Vickery, along with Lourdes Canto for her assistance with the essay contest.

We thank and congratulate *Student's Guide* Cover Art Contest winner Colin Darland for creating the unique and professional cover and text illustrations for the 30th edition of the *Guide*.

We are indebted to the judges of our annual essay contest for their valuable service (they are mentioned by name in Appendix E of this book). Without their time and thoughtful feedback, we could not so publicly recognize and reward the efforts of our many first-year students.

Most importantly, we wish to thank the students who have generously shared their work. Many of their contributions are published in these pages, while others are available online at <http://english.arizona.edu/index_site. php?id=588&preview=1>. Their work will serve as samples for new students to study and discuss.

We are deeply appreciative of the many writing instructors and others who have given us assignments, students' essays, comments on essays, critiques of last year's edition, and other materials. We also want to extend our thanks to all those instructors who contributed chapter sections that provide new or fresh perspectives on the materials in this book.

We are grateful for the outstanding editorial team at Hayden-McNeil Publishing, particularly Lisa Wess and Michele Ostovar. They are always a pleasure to work with, and their enthusiasm for the project is an integral part of the *Guide's* success.

As a 30th edition, this book is the result of three decades of contributions, help, and advice from innumerable people whose influence can still be seen in these pages. Without all of you, this book would not be where it is now—a reflection of a collaborative Writing Program comprised of dedicated and caring instructors. We would like to extend our thanks to our predecessors and colleagues throughout the years.

A Student's Guide to First-Year Writing editors,

Marlowe Daly-Galeano

Marissa Juárez

Jacob Witt

Table of Contents

PART II Strategies and Concepts

PART IV Sample Essays

Introduction to First-Year Writing

1

Introduction to First-Year Writing

1.1 Writing at the University of Arizona: An Overview

Welcome to the University of Arizona! During your stay here, you'll do a lot of writing, and your first-year writing class is a place to begin the journey toward becoming a stronger, more confident writer. What does it mean to be a "writer" anyway? This chapter will explore this question not only in a university context, but also within all of the communities to which we belong.

Being a "writer" means different things to different people. The kind of writing you do depends on several factors. One of these factors is your *purpose*. In other words, why are you writing and what do you hope to accomplish with your writing? Another factor is your *audience*. You might ask yourself, "Who is going to read my writing?" You will make choices that correspond to the answers of these questions. That's why a reporter who works at the *Arizona Daily Star*, for example, writes an article for the newspaper using a journalistic style. If that reporter were asked to write a formal report for her boss, she would use a different writing style, and still a different one if she were writing a letter to her grandmother or an email to a friend. Even if the reporter sought to put the same story into an article, a report, a letter, and an email, these texts would look quite different depending on her purpose for relaying the information and the particular audience that she had in mind when writing. What type(s) of writing do you do? Why do you write certain things (emails, diaries, essays, and so on)? It might be helpful to think of the kinds of writing you'll do here at the university, as well as in your community and in your career (reports, blogs, emails, memos, letters to the editor, and so on). Your first-year writing courses are designed to guide you to **evaluate** writing situations and respond accordingly. As a result, you'll be better prepared for the challenges in both your university and professional careers, as well as in your pursuit of social and political interests. In addition to providing the tools to succeed in academic writing, the University of Arizona's first-year writing curriculum stresses critical analysis, a skill that allows you to adapt your writing style and persona to whatever type of writing you need or want to pursue outside of the classroom.

Keyword: evaluate

In order to help you achieve your own writing goals and to ensure that your first-year composition courses prepare you well for university expectations, the Writing Program has developed the following **outcomes** for first-year writing classes:

By the end of the first-year composition sequence, you will be able to engage in a writing process that includes the following:

1. Assess the rhetorical strategies writers use to achieve their purposes.

2. Write persuasive documents that provide appropriate and effective evidence for various audiences, situations, and purposes.

3. Develop critical analyses of personal, public, and scholarly issues based on research, observations, and reflections from their own experiences.

4. Revise their drafts in response to feedback from readers and offer useful feedback to other writers on how to revise their writing.

5. Produce research and writing using appropriate academic conventions.

Our program brings together students and teachers from a variety of cultures and languages as well as academic disciplines. Writing courses are designed to challenge you to explore such diversity. You will discuss the differences and inequalities that exist within our community, and consider the common traits shared by diverse members of our society. Instructors in the program come from various programs in English, such as creative writing, literature, applied linguistics, and rhetoric and composition. In addition, your peers represent the many possible majors across the curriculum. Both teachers and students come from across the country and around the world. All of these sources of difference lead to an exciting variety in materials, class activities, discussions, and assignments. Consider student Naohiro Wada's advice. Although this student specifically directs her advice to Japanese speakers, the general sentiment of her recommendations is equally important for all students, regardless of language or nationality:

> I have some advice for new international students, especially for Japanese speakers. First of all, Japanese speakers may not always be good at listening and speaking in English because of the differences between English and Japanese. It is not possible to get these skills in a short term, so you just have to be patient for a while. As time goes on, you will be relieved. Next, the writing styles of English and Japanese are different in many ways. You should put your Japanese writing style aside while writing in English. Finally, in college classes you have to read a lot. When you read books, you will come across unknown words. However, these may be too many to look up in the dictionary. So you should get only the important points from an article without using the dictionary all the time.

In your composition course(s), you will read challenging material on wide-ranging subjects, explore self-selected topics from different angles, and express your ideas in college-level essays. Instructors may encourage you to explore issues or topics that are challenging or even troublesome in order to push you to examine your ideas in writing. You might find that some texts or class discussions make you uncomfortable. Sometimes you might struggle with the material because it conflicts with your personal belief system, but working with controversial issues can help you define and articulate your own position in relation to the complex context surrounding those issues.

The Writing Program sets your English writing class size much lower than that of your other general education classes, which means that you will have the opportunity to get to know your instructor and classmates on a more personal level. Many instructors make use of full-class and small-group discussion. In this setting, your responsibilities as an individual student will be more clearly defined. We find student Ray Hum's advice especially pertinent here:

> The true value of an English composition class is largely dependent on the student. If the student approaches the class with high motivation, then the class will certainly be enjoyable and valuable to him or her. If, on the other hand, the student approaches the class with a disinterested attitude, then the class will inevitably be a waste of time to him or her.

While the small size of your composition class may mean that your teacher has high expectations for your participation and work, there are many benefits to the smaller group, including the opportunity to receive feedback and assistance from your instructor and your peers. Chris Clark provides the following advice to fellow students:

> The most important thing all freshmen should know in order to succeed is that you have to go to class. English is probably the most common course at UA, and success later starts in the beginning. You will find that the majority of students taking English 101 and 102 are freshmen just like yourself, and going through the same things you are. It's a good chance for you to make friends while starting college out on the right foot. English 101 and 102 teachers are also well aware that you are going through a big adjustment and are sensitive to that. Not only have I found that the English teachers go out of their way to help accommodate new students, but they also act as advisors if you need help.
>
> In addition to helping your transition to college go smoothly, they teach you a variety of techniques in writing and composition that will help you immensely in other classes up until the time you graduate. These techniques will aid you in your NATS classes, your TRAD classes, even upper-division classes. By attending class, doing the work, and applying it elsewhere, you are setting yourself up for a successful career at UA. Good luck!

1.2 A Guide to the *Guide*

The *Student's Guide* offers useful information specific to the University of Arizona's first-year writing program. Information about formatting, grammar, integrating sources, and other such general writing guidelines can be found in writing handbooks such as Diana Hacker's *Rules for Writers*, which we use in first-year writing. This book focuses on writing processes, revision, analysis, and the types of assignments you will encounter in your writing courses—it's intended to complement what your instructor teaches in class.

Part I of the *Guide* gives an overview of first-year writing. This first chapter is a general introduction and examines some assumptions that underlie college writing. It also discusses grades and gives an overview of each course in the first-year writing sequence, including its goals and major assignments.

Part II introduces you to various strategies and concepts in writing. It guides you through various components of the writing process you'll need to know to write a successful essay. Here you will learn what to do even before you begin writing, how to engage in the process of research at the university, how to get started writing, and how to use feedback to improve your writing.

Part III shows you how to apply the strategies discussed in Part II to the specific assignments you will encounter in first-year writing. Each chapter has subsections that outline different ways to think about an assignment or paper, as well as different strategies that you may choose to employ.

Part IV provides a collection of sample essays written by students in the Writing Program over the last few years.

Appendix A describes the many resources available at the University of Arizona to help you with your writing. It tells what to expect from their services. Some are open to all students and are free of charge, whereas others are restricted or charge a fee.

Appendix B lists various campus resources and their contact information.

Appendix C lists the computing centers on campus.

Appendix D provides information specifically for students whose first language is not English. It includes tips from instructors and other ESL students, as well as a list of resources that may be of help.

Appendix E explains the *Student's Guide* Essay Contest, the Jan Lipartito Historical Remembrance Essay Contest, the Difference and Equality Essay Contest, and the annual *Guide* Cover-Design Contest. It also lists the winners and judges for 2009.

We hope the student sample essays will serve as a springboard for discussion in your classroom. They are here to give you an idea about what an essay might look like, but also to give you the opportunity to critique strengths and weaknesses of the content, organization, evidence, language, or style of different essays. We believe our selections will give you ideas about different kinds of writing, help you brainstorm about your own projects, and make your experience in first-year writing more manageable and rewarding.

In short, this book will introduce you to the world of college writing. We hope that, like us, you'll find that you enjoy writing and believe that writing well is a vital way to learn and communicate effectively. Finally, we welcome your comments on this *Guide* and encourage you to submit your essays for future editions! Please feel free to e-mail us at wpguide@u.arizona.edu.

1.3 Using Written Response and Grades to Improve Your Writing

Your grades help you learn about your writing and improve your writing strategies. In deciding upon a grade, your instructor evaluates how well all the various elements of your essay work together to achieve its goals. Remember that your instructor's comments and grades evaluate your essay, not you. You should read the final comments with an eye to how they'll help you with your future writing. At the same time, also keep in mind that the letter grades used in writing courses at the UA reflect the general grading standards of the Writing Program. Recently several writing instructors at the University of Arizona developed the following "Manifesto on Written Feedback":

A Manifesto on Written Feedback

From The University of Arizona Writing Instructors to Our Students
In collaboration with Professor Nancy Sommers, during her recent visit to UA, the following UA writing instructors thoughtfully and respectfully submit the following objectives and opinions on how to read and use comments on written assignments: Rosanne Carlo, Anne-Marie Hall, Faith Kurtyka, Rachel Lewis, Jessica Shumake, Cassie Wright.

1. We would like you to understand that our comments are part of the teaching and learning process. We write comments not just to evaluate your essay, but to help you see how the lessons about writing from class emerge in your writing. One way to better understand the purpose of our comments is to actively participate in class and carefully read the rubric and the assignment sheet. These are the ways we communicate with you ahead of time about what we are looking for in your writing.

2. We would like you to know that we intend our comments to be constructive. We value your ideas and want to learn from you and hope that you will use our comments to learn from us as well.

3. We would like you to approach each essay not as an independent unit, but as a brief moment in your overall development as a writer. Our comments are meant to be useful to you in this assignment and your future writing.

4. We would like you to accept responsibility for using our comments in the revision process. We also expect you to share your strengths as a writer in commenting on your peers' papers.

5. We would like you to understand comments are both descriptive and evaluative. Writing a letter grade is perhaps the least interesting thing we do as writing instructors. Take the time to re-read the entire essay alongside our comments to understand the grade in context. We invite you to use our comments as an opportunity to talk further about your writing.

This manifesto should give you a better understanding of how instructors generate written responses to your writing and how they hope you will use these responses. The manifesto also reflects the fact that there is a relationship between the instructor's comments and the letter grade you will ultimately receive in the class, but it encourages you to use both the grades and the comments as tools for improving your writing throughout the semester.

Below, Stephanie Gonsalves, a UA student, reflects upon the differences between what is expected in high school and college writing courses:

> Compared to high school writing, college writing is more complicated. For example, whereas in high school, one draft was enough to get you by with an "A" or "B," in college you may rewrite your paper three or more times and still receive only a "C." Also, in college, you are asked to write in various classes, such as chemistry, philosophy, and physics. In different classes, you need to write on different topics, create different tones, and use specialized vocabulary. The most important thing for you as a writer is to be aware of the different writing situations and revise, revise, revise for the different audiences.

An **A essay** has a well-defined sense of purpose. This purpose is consistently developed and supported throughout the essay and is suited to the form of essay assigned—for example, the essay may be intended to develop an analysis, narrate an event, or develop a persuasive argument. The writer specifically addresses the audience's values, beliefs, and assumptions. The writer's persona is appropriate to the purpose and audience. An A essay, then, conveys a sense of complexity not just in the discussion of the topic but also in the audience, purpose, and persona that are evident in the organization and expression of the text. There are no mechanical features that distract the reader, and the style is not just clear but vivid. An A essay is excellent in that it fulfills all criteria of the assignment.

A **B essay** also contains a sense of the complexity of the rhetorical situation by meeting the needs of readers and effectively achieving its purpose, but the essay might be less specific in addressing the audience's values, beliefs, and assumptions. Again, the writer clearly articulates and supports the purpose throughout the essay, as evident in the content and expression, although the purpose might be less developed than in an A essay. The writer also successfully conveys a persona that is appropriate to the purposes of the text, and the language and content persuade the audience to accept the writer in that role. A B essay is very good in that it fulfills most aspects of the assignment, is factually correct, and contains few mechanical errors.

A **C essay** is a competent essay, one whose content is simple and fairly clear, but which might have less of a sense of the complexity of the rhetorical situation. The writer develops the purpose throughout the essay in ways that are clear yet obvious. The writer might still be struggling with some of the interplay of content or expression. A C essay minimally fulfills the assignment.

A **D essay** is weak in one or more of the areas of purpose, audience, and persona, as reflected in the content, organization, expression, and mechanics. The purpose of the essay might be unclear or inconsistent. The author might have chosen an inappropriate audience, might have switched audiences within the essay, or might have ignored the question of audience altogether by writing in a style and at a depth that suggest only the author will understand the essay.

An **E** will be assigned when the requirements for the assignment have clearly not been met.

On the following page, we have included a sample grading rubric that indicates the standards of the Writing Program for the four broadly defined areas of an essay: content, organization, expression, and mechanics. Remember that this is just one possible approach to grading. Each instructor will devise and use specific sets of grading criteria for a given essay assignment based on those and other standards. Some instructors may even work with their classes to develop rubrics appropriate for particular assignments in order to be sure that students fully understand the instructor's expectations. Ask your instructor for a detailed explanation of grading criteria for each writing assignment before the essay is due so you'll have a clearer goal in mind.

Additional Information Regarding Grades and Policies

Incomplete Grades

You may be awarded the grade of I (Incomplete) *only* at the end of a semester and *only if you have completed at least 70 percent of the coursework*. Your instructor will fill out the required form, which specifies the work to be completed and the due dates. You and your instructor must sign the form, stating agreement to the terms.

Sample Essay Grading Rubric

	Superior	Strong	Competent	Weak	Unacceptable
Content	Exceptionally clear sense of purpose; extremely well-suited to needs of assignment; strong audience awareness.	Clear sense of purpose; generally well-suited to needs of assignment; relatively consistent audience awareness.	Some sense of purpose; moderately well-suited to needs of assignment; some awareness of audience.	Weak or inappropriate sense of purpose; inconsistent or unclear response to needs of assignment; little audience awareness.	No discernable sense of purpose; does not respond to needs of assignment; no awareness of audience.
Organization	Extremely well-ordered and effectively developed; unified and coherent; smooth transitions.	Mostly well-ordered and developed; generally well-unified and coherent; clear transitions.	Some order and development; some sense of coherence and unity; functional transitions.	Insufficient development; order unclear; little coherence or unity; absent or very awkward transitions.	Lack of order and development; no coherence or unity; absence of transitions.
Expression	Varied and forceful sentences; smooth, fluent, and precise diction; tone appropriate for audience.	Correct sentences with some variety; clear diction; tone mostly appropriate for audience.	Mostly correct sentences but with little variety; generally correct diction; tone sometimes appropriate for audience.	Frequently incorrect or repetitive sentences; vague or confusing diction; tone inappropriate for audience.	Incorrect sentences; nonstandard diction; problematic tone.
Mechanics	No errors in standard grammar, spelling, or punctuation to distract readers.	Very few errors in standard grammar, spelling, or punctuation to distract readers.	Occasional errors in standard grammar, spelling, or punctuation that may distract readers.	Frequent errors in standard grammar, spelling, or punctuation that distract readers.	Serious problems with grammar, spelling, or punctuation.

Grade Appeals

The Writing Program is committed to providing you with fair, clear, and useful responses to your writing, and we will process grade appeals in an efficient and objective fashion. A grade appeal is based on the quality of the writing and the grades awarded to that writing. If you disagree with a specific grade or with the grading policy outlined in the course syllabus, speak immediately with your instructor. You may also speak with your instructor's faculty teaching advisor or the Course Director, but they will not become involved in considering changes in grades until after the semester when you file a grade appeal.

If you believe your *final course grade* in a writing course was unfairly or incorrectly given, you should first meet with the instructor of the class and then with the Course Director. Go to ML 380 for complete instructions.

1.4 Overview of English 101/107

Goals
In English 101/107, you should learn how to: • Analyze texts through close reading. • Develop strategies for analyzing texts for particular purposes, audiences, and situations. • Analyze the ways in which authors use textual conventions to achieve their purposes in specific contexts. • Write essays that develop analyses with evidence drawn from the texts you read. • Incorporate other writers' interpretations into the analyses you write. • Practice research, reading, writing, and revision strategies that can be applied to work in other courses and in different professions. • Create multiple, meaningful revisions of your writing and suggest useful revisions to other writers. • Analyze and reflect on your progress as an academic writer.

Overview of the Course

You probably learned a lot about writing in high school English, and this course will build upon what you learned, asking you to think about writing and reading in ways that you may not have experienced before. This semester you'll read a variety of texts closely and carefully, and you'll write essays that analyze those texts. Your instructor will ask you to design clear, complex thesis statements for your essays and to support them with specific details and evidence from the text(s) you're working with. You'll also work on expressing your own ideas and opinions in writing.

One thing you'll often hear is that reading and writing never take place in a vacuum but always within a specific context or situation. In other words, the way you read and interpret a text will be influenced by your personal beliefs and values, your upbringing, your social, cultural, and economic background, and so on. The students in your class will "see" a text from their own unique perspectives, opening up the possibility for numerous interpretations of the text. Likewise, the texts you will read in English 101/107 are informed by the authors who write them, as well as the social, historical, and political contexts in which they are created.

This course asks you to read and interpret texts within particular contexts and to support your claims with specific evidence. To do this, you will question texts in ways you might not have considered before. For example, you might ask why an author represented a character or event in a particular way, whom the intended audience might be, how the details of the text are effective with that audience, and why you responded as you did. Such questions will help you make important discoveries about the texts you'll read and write about this semester. Your voice, experience, and particular viewpoint will help shape your essays. Your task will be to read as a writer, take charge of the material you read, and follow up with research and further analysis. You will design and develop essays that articulate your ideas in the context of specific writing situations. Although you will have some latitude in designing your essays, you will be encouraged to consider the needs of your readers and reflect upon how you can better communicate your ideas to them.

This course will also help you learn how to integrate sources correctly into your paper to support your arguments. You need to follow bibliographic conventions to be able to write as a member of the academic community. To this end, you'll follow the guidelines of one commonly used style of documentation, the format used by the Modern Language Association (MLA). Other professional organizations may require different formats for references, but

The information in "Chapter 3: Close Reading and Interacting with the Text," "Chapter 4: Writing as a Process," "Chapter 7: Research as Part of the Writing Process" and "Chapter 8: Analysis" will be useful for you over the course of the semester.

the MLA guidelines, widely used in English and related disciplines, will give you a model to work from. Another step in writing for academic audiences is learning how to share your own ideas about texts and effectively using feedback from other students and from instructors. This course will give you the chance to practice these things. Gradually, you'll become more skilled at constructing focused and compelling pieces of writing. In the midst of this work, you will refine your writing style by paying more attention to mechanics, grammar, and usage.

You'll have the opportunity to analyze a variety of texts, which will help you develop an even broader perspective on how authors use language and images to communicate their ideas. In analyzing this array of texts, you'll gain proficiency in writing and reading that will help you in your other courses and outside college.

Essential Terms

Text. A text in this course may refer to written, visual, or aural artifacts. A text can mean a piece of writing, a photograph or film, an event or place, or even sounds that can be analyzed.

Context. By context, we mean the circumstances surrounding the creation and reception of a text. In this course you'll examine texts in various contexts—for example, the personal associations of readers, the biographical backgrounds of writers, related historical events, and political purposes. The best contexts to study are those that illuminate the meanings and uses of the text.

Audience. Just as all texts are written in a particular situation for a specific audience, you should keep your own audience in mind as you write essays for this course. Unless your instructor specifies otherwise, you should write for a general academic audience. This means that your readers are likely to have read the text you are discussing (or ones similar to it) and will require only a brief summary of the text and only the most pertinent details on its context or the writer. Your audience will appreciate a clear focus, a complex argument grounded in specific supporting details, a careful reading of the text, and a thesis that includes qualifications that anticipate opposing arguments.

Purpose/Thesis. As you construct your essays, you'll define your purpose to meet the needs of a particular audience, academic and otherwise. You'll join complex conversations with readers who are committed to exploring diverse opinions for the purpose of developing new ideas. This community generally expects that the purpose of a piece of writing will be stated in a *thesis* that briefly summarizes the basic argument of an essay. A thesis usually becomes apparent to a reader in the introduction to the essay, although it may be stated in a later part of an essay or even remain unstated or implied.

The Assignments

In this course, you'll practice three types of analysis by writing three major essays, each with two or more drafts. Short in- and out-of-class writing assignments will help you prepare for these essays. You will also prepare a Final Exam Portfolio.

Note that your instructor might vary the specific nature and order of the essay assignments. Sample essays appear in Part IV of the *Guide*. All essays require analysis, argument, and revision. Some essays require research.

- **Analysis Essays** focus closely on the text itself in a limited context. For instance, you might analyze the writer's rhetorical strategies or the literary, textual, or cultural features that shape your response to the text. You might also compare the strategies or features evident in two different texts or explore your reactions to the text(s). Some of your instructors may assign literacy narratives as a form of analysis. In all cases, however, your analysis will depend on a close reading of the text(s).

- **Text-in-Context Essays or Contextual Essays** focus on a text and its relationship to a larger context, such as the author's biography, the historical or cultural situation surrounding the text, a particular theoretical approach such as feminism or psychoanalysis, the literary tradition to which the work belongs, or a related set of texts. Contextual analysis depends on close reading, research, argument, revision, and synthesis. Research for this paper will be limited in focus; your instructor may even provide a few sources for you to use. These essays emphasize your ability to evaluate and incorporate sources effectively.

- **Writer's Journals or Reading Journals** focus on your responses to what you read, see, write, and hear over the entire semester, in and out of class. They can include spontaneous entries and responses to formal prompts. These short texts will help you synthesize and reflect on your reading and writing experiences and prepare you for writing your essays.

- **Final Exam Portfolios** focus on specific aspects of writing you have learned or practiced over the course of the semester. Your portfolio will consist of revised essays and an essay that explains your revisions and reflects on your writing process.

The series of assignments you will work through in this course build from close reading to analyses of broader contexts, to an expanded analysis that takes your own context into account culminating in a portfolio that showcases your work throughout the semester. In summary, English 101/107 will give you the skills to analyze texts in a specific context, build arguments about texts, conduct detailed and relevant research on texts and their contexts, and revise your work and reflect on your revisions. Student Adrian Sotomayor offers the following testament to the emphasis and importance of analysis:

> Get ready for a year full of analysis! Whether you like it or hate it, you will have to analyze everything you read. The first essay, textual analysis, was both the easiest and the hardest to write. It was easy because I had the option of choosing a story that interested me from several that were presented; thus, it helped me form a relatively strong argument about the text. On the other hand, I had previously taken English 100 but had taken a semester break from English. This created my initial struggle in which I was lost and forgot most, if not all, of what I had learned. To get by, I started to read the *Student's Guide* to see what other students had to say (yep, the same thing you are reading now). It helped me see that I wasn't alone and actually helped with the tips that some students gave.

> For the text-in-context essay, research proved to be more tedious than it could have been. Since I live so far from the U of A and I had no gaps between classes, I found it hard to actually set apart some time to go to the library and research a topic. So my tip to you is, do your research early! You will find that sometimes you will have to change your thesis or you will not have enough evidence. Finding this out early gives you more time to go back and look up information. If you write this paper the night before, you will find yourself struggling to find information due to the large amount of time that research requires. Good luck, and don't procrastinate!

Developing different methods or styles of reading will help you deal with the large amount of reading you'll be asked to do in college and in the workplace. For more on close reading strategies, see "Chapter 3: Close Reading and Interacting with the Text."

You can find sample essays for each of these assignments in Part IV of the *Student's Guide*. As you browse through the sample essays, keep in mind that the specific essays you produce will vary depending on your instructor's emphasis and on whether you are enrolled in 101 or 107.

Essential Readings for English 101/107

Part II: Strategies and Concepts

- Chapter 2: Academic Discourse as Writing for Specific Audiences and Purposes

- Chapter 3: Close Reading and Interacting with the Text

- Chapter 4: Writing as a Process

- Chapter 5: Re-Visioning Your Work

- Chapter 7: Research as Part of the Writing Process

Part III: Assignments

- Chapter 8: Analysis

- Chapter 9: Text-in-Context (requires focused research)

- Chapter 12: Personal and Reflective Writing

Part IV: Sample Essays

1.5 Overview of English 101/197B with a Writing Studio Component

Goals
In addition to the goals indicated on pp. 10–11, you will learn how to: • Identify concepts and functions of "story" and how they relate to literacy and critical awareness in writing, reading, language, and education. • Analyze literacy practices as artifacts that are inseparable from culture, economy, and social politics. • Engage in weekly writing workshops where you will practice writing and revising your work.

Overview of the Course

English 101 with a writing studio focuses on the same goals and skills as English 101, only it carries an additional one credit "studio" course. This fourth credit, English 197B, is a required part of the course and is intended to help you improve your writing by giving you extra practice working on and revising your assignments in class.

Like English 101/107, English 101 with a studio component focuses on close reading and analysis. Thus you might also want to read the Overview of English 101/107, located on pages 10–12 of *A Student's Guide* for more information about how close reading and analysis inform the course.

Aside from the studio component of 101/197B, this course varies a bit in terms of the types of texts you'll be reading and the assignments you'll be writing. For example, English 101/197B focuses on the concept of literacy and the ways in which it is practiced, so you will primarily be reading texts that deal with such subjects as writing, reading, language, and education. As you read these texts, you will work to locate the ways in which literacy practices become embedded with cultural, historical, economic, and sociopolitical meaning. You will also consider the ways in which access to education is affected by race, gender, social class, and other factors.

For instance, before the abolition of slavery, African-Americans were prevented from learning to read and write because those in power, white men of higher class standing, felt that such access to education would empower African-Americans to challenge their social positions. During this historical period, a man named Frederick Douglass wrote about his experiences as a slave who was learning to read and write, and he describes his acquisition of literacy in ways that illustrate the social inequalities he faced in doing so. Because he did not have access to the same resources as those in power—pen, paper, and books, for example—Douglass had to use what he had available to him. He learned to write by marking on wooden logs and fences; he read newspapers he found on the street. In short, the ways in which he achieved literacy were shaped by the social, political, and historical climate of that time.

In examining the ways in which literacy practices are informed by contextual factors, as in the example above, you will begin to develop a critical understanding of writing, reading, language, and education. You will also be able to consider your own literacy practices and how they are shaped by your individual experiences and the social context in which you live.

Essential Terms

Narrative. Any story that describes events or experiences, whether fictional or factual, can be considered narrative. Thus newspaper articles that describe recent events or novels that describe a character's journey follow a narrative structure. When you are telling a group of friends about your most recent camping trip, you are telling a narrative as well.

Literacy Narrative. A personal narrative that focuses on an event or events in the author's acquisition of literacy. Literacy narratives can explore a specific, significant experience with writing, reading, and/or language, or they can discuss how writing, reading, and/or language have played a role in the author's past experience.

1.6 Overview of Honors English Composition (English 109H)

Goals
In Honors English Composition, you should strengthen your ability to: • Analyze texts through close reading and critical thinking.   • Develop strategies for analyzing texts for particular purposes, audiences, and contexts.   • Analyze the ways in which authors use textual conventions to achieve their purposes in specific contexts.   • Write essays that develop analyses with evidence drawn from the texts you read.   • Locate and analyze evidence to develop an argument.   • Practice research, reading, writing, and revision strategies that can be applied to work in other courses and in different professions.   • Use the conventions of scholarly research, analysis, and documentation; practice research as a *process*.   • Create multiple, meaningful revisions of your writing and suggest useful revisions to other writers.   • Analyze and reflect on your progress as an academic writer.

This course will build upon the skills you developed in your high school English classes. Honors English Composition has as its emphases close reading, critical thinking, analytical writing, and the understanding of the importance of context. The course will help you to achieve and effectively use the recursive processes of active reading, writing, researching, providing feedback to other writers, and doing all steps of revision. You will learn the process of doing research, which will include finding your own sources as well as learning how to incorporate them into a complex and well-developed argument. In Honors English Composition you may be asked to write either a text-in-context essay or a rhetorical analysis essay, since both types of essays place texts in context. You will read a variety of texts of different types. For example, you may be assigned to read literary texts (of fiction, poetry, or nonfiction), films, visual arts, or a combination of these genres. In this course you should attain all of the goals of first-year composition listed on page 2.

Assignments

- **Poetics Essay:** In this paper you will perform a literary analysis or a close reading of a text. You will engage in a variety of reading and writing related exercises culminating in an essay demonstrating superior critical reading, thinking, and writing skills. You will be prompted to deepen and refine your relative given strengths as critical thinkers and writers.

- **Rhetorical Concerns Essay:** In this assignment you will address rhetorical concerns through the construction of a text-in-context essay, a rhetorical analysis essay, *or* a cultural analysis essay. You will again perform individual scrutiny of texts, but this time you will be considering your ideas in broader contexts. Your instructor may choose to emphasize historical, sociological, cultural, aesthetic, and interdisciplinary issues when guiding you to write this essay.

- **Research Process Assignment:** This assignment may take many forms but is designed around the idea of research as a *process*. Emphasis is given to accessing and incorporating library and internet resources as well as incorporating other forms of research (like interviews or case studies) into an analytical essay. You may be asked to work in groups while developing projects and to share available campus resources. In some classes, you will have the opportunity to present your findings to the class.

- **The Final Exam:** You will write a reflective essay that synthesizes the concerns of the course. A theoretical text may function as a lens to help you make connections to themes and concepts. Your teacher will choose the best final exam format for your particular class. You may have an in-class essay, a take home exam, an in-class presentation to other students, or even a reflective introduction to your research project.

Essential Readings for Honors English Composition

Part II: Strategies and Concepts
- Chapter 2: Academic Discourse as Writing for Specific Audiences and Purposes

- Chapter 3: Close Reading and Interacting with the Text

- Chapter 4: Writing as a Process

- Chapter 5: Re-Visioning Your Work

- Chapter 7: Research as Part of the Writing Process

Part III: Assignments
- Chapter 8: Analysis

- Chapter 9: Text-in-Context (requires focused research)

- Chapter 10: Rhetorical Analysis

- Chapter 11: Exploring a Controversy and Writing a Public Argument

Part IV: Sample Essays

1.7. Using *Rules for Writers* to Improve Your Writing

Rules for Writers by Diana Hacker is a text that, along with English 197W and your *Student's Guide*, will help you to achieve the goals of your first-year writing courses. All good writers need a good writing handbook. It's a quick reference to the **rules and strategies** currently valued in academic and professional writing. It's not really a textbook to use in one class and then discard at the end of the semester. Rather, a writing handbook is a continuing guide for most of the writing questions you'll have during your entire college career and beyond in your personal and professional life. In fact, many of your professors here at the university can show you the one handbook they've been referencing for many years. They wouldn't even think about writing anything important without that handbook by their side.

Keyword:
rules and strategies

Take a quick tour of *Rules for Writers* to see all that it has to offer you.

- Glance at the "Brief Menu" inside the front cover or the "Detailed Menu" inside the back cover.

- Fan through the pages to see how the book is organized and how easy it is to find what you're looking for.

- Read the "How to Use This Book and Its Web Site" section starting on page xv.

- Try one or more of the book's tutorials starting on page xix.

- Try a few exercises to get your feet wet.

- If you're an ESL writer, turn to the "ESL Menu" on page 618 for specific ESL hints throughout the book and separate sections on the most common ESL transfer errors.

Turn to the handbook whenever you have any questions about writing. Your writing instructors might assign pages for you to read and digest, especially sections about the writing or research processes, or guidelines for writing a successful academic argument. Your instructors might also assign a few exercises to help you with grammar (*Should I say "The number of children is" or "The number of children are"?*), style (*Can I use "lots of" in my research paper?*), or punctuation skills (*Should I use a comma before this "and"?*). Your handbook can answer all these questions.

Your handbook will also help you understand and respond to your instructors' feedback. Your instructors might mark your texts with a simple symbol or refer to a specific page or section in the handbook. For example, if you're having problems expressing *parallel ideas*, your instructors might mark your text with the parallel symbol //, with a reference to the handbook page number or section that discusses parallelism. The list of revision symbols on page 619 shows a shorthand system that your teacher may use—with handy references to sections in the handbook. So, think of *Rules for Writers* as a friend to turn to for good advice, for all those writing questions you'll face not only in first-year writing, but also throughout your undergraduate studies and perhaps in your professional career.

1.8 Overview of English 102/108

Goals

In English 102/108, you should learn how to:

- Read texts to assess how writers achieve their purposes with their intended audiences.

- Devise writing strategies suited to various rhetorical situations.

- Develop an argument with persuasive appeals to your audience.

- Locate and analyze evidence to develop an argument.

- Develop ideas with observations and reflections on your experience.

- Revise in response to feedback from readers to improve drafts.

- Use the conventions of scholarly research, analysis, and documentation.

- Use the conventions of academic writing, including how to write clear, convincing prose.

Overview of the Course

The purpose of first-year writing is to introduce students to university-level writing. As a student you are here to learn, to expand your knowledge, to contribute new perspectives, and to develop new ways of thinking. As you learned in your first-semester writing course, we read, write, and do research in differing ways as contexts and cultures vary. Your instructors will ask you to go beyond simply communicating knowledge. They'll want you to go further to revise or expand upon existing knowledge. As a member of the university community, you're encouraged to contribute to current knowledge and ideas through your own process of discovery, insight, research, and revision.

In your first-year writing classes you'll learn that all writing is persuasive because all writers use strategies to persuade their readers. Even creative writing is persuasive; novelists, for example, have to keep their readers interested in the story and make characters and their actions believable. Academic writing is particularly persuasive because scholars have to put forth arguments that build on previous arguments to develop new knowledge. The job of scholarly and professional writing is to persuade readers to accept the new argument and the new knowledge. However, in academic and professional communities, an argument is not typically a "fight" which the participants strive to win by overpowering their opponents. Instead, an argument arises from a difference in views and, as such, is an opportunity for further inquiry. An interesting argument in your major or on the news may provide you with the opportunity to investigate what the controversy is about. Why do people disagree? What underlying values and assumptions underlie their various viewpoints? By investigating various positions on an issue, you'll come to understand more fully where you stand and why you feel as you do. The personal can in fact be a valuable part of persuasion. You will encounter strategies in your first-year writing course to make your writing more personal through the effective use of word choice, tone, content, organization, and voice.

Essential Terms and Concepts

Rhetoric. You may have heard this term used in a negative sense; for example, to describe a manipulative political speech as simply "empty rhetoric." However, in first-year writing we use this term in its classical sense as **the art of persuasion**. This sense of *rhetoric* includes the various strategies an author or speaker uses to accomplish his or her purpose for a specific audience. A **rhetorical analysis** is concerned with how writers and speakers use words in particular situations to achieve definite goals.

Inquiry. You might have first heard this term in the sense of "investigation," as in a policy inquiry. At the university this definition still applies. An inquiry is a line of investigation into an issue, topic, or problem. Focusing on a particular line of inquiry helps academics and professionals narrow the scope of their efforts, and in this class, it can help you carry your work forward from one assignment to the next.

Rhetorical Situation. As you learned in your first-semester writing class, the production of texts takes place within contexts—"the circumstances surrounding and influencing the creation and reception of a text." Context is one of the elements of a rhetorical situation; the others are the intended audience and the author's purpose. When analyzing the rhetoric of a text, you should take into account these elements of the rhetorical situation.

Rhetorical Strategies. These are the methods an author chooses to construct the text, develop ideas, and write persuasively. They can include the types of evidence used to support the argument, the author's voice, even the format of the text. When you analyze the rhetoric of a text, you will look at these choices in terms of the rhetorical situation and determine how well they work in that situation.

The Assignments

- **Rhetorical Analysis:** You will begin the semester by critiquing the argument of others. This type of analysis goes beyond the work you did in English 101/107, by focusing on and evaluating arguments. Rhetorical Analysis comes in many different forms which are communicated in Chapter 10, the 102 text, and your instructor's lectures.

- **Controversy Analysis:** The next assignment still focuses on different arguments, but your task is to research a controversy and present an analysis of the emerging arguments surrounding the controversy. This assignment also challenges you to perform academic research to support your claims about the controversy you are analyzing.

- **Public Argument:** Following your research assignment, you'll be asked to take a side on the issue you've researched and present a public argument. Public arguments can come in various forms (speeches, editorials, posters, etc.), but all use the rhetorical devices you learned during the first assignment to persuade an audience in some way.

- **Reflection and Revision:** You'll reflect on your writing over the course of the term and write a critical assessment of it. This reflection seeks to track the improvements you've made over the course of the semester or your entire first-year writing course.

Essential Readings for English 102/108

PART II

Strategies and Concepts

2
Academic Discourse as Writing for Specific Audiences and Purposes

2.1 Academic Discourse: An Overview

In Chapter One of this book, you learned some of the many different ways you can think about the act of writing. You probably write daily, from emailing friends to making out grocery lists to taking notes in a class, but in your first-year writing classes, you will be asked to consider an expanded concept of what it means to be a "writer" in an academic context. For instance, academic writing, or "discourse," generally requires that you utilize sources according to certain citation guidelines, make use of a writing "voice" that is reasoned rather than strident, and maintain a certain level of formality in your diction. More specifically, academic writing means:

• writing for specific purposes and for specific audiences;

• following discipline-specific style guidelines and genre conventions; and

• incorporating credible research to support arguments and/or observations.

Academic writing is writing for specific audiences and purposes. It follows discipline-specific style guidelines and genre conventions and incorporates credible research to support arguments and/or observations.

To get a sense of what it means to write in an academic context, you can think about the different forms of writing you have been asked to do in the past. For example, in your chemistry lab, you might have been asked to write a lab report detailing your observations of an experiment. In this case, your target audience would be your chemistry lab teacher and other students in your lab, while your purpose would be to detail what you found out from the experiment. In writing a lab report, you would be expected to write in an objective (non-biased) tone, to follow the genre conventions of a lab report (which might include sections like an introduction or overview of the experiment, materials, methods, observations, and conclusions), and to avoid using "I" in the narrative of your report. Finally, you would be expected to provide concrete, specific details about the things you observed during the experiment, and you would likely use these details to support your conclusions (your analysis of what you observed).

These conventions are common in the sciences, but are quite different from the kind of writing you would do in a literature class, where you might be asked to write an analytic essay about a character in a novel. In that case, you would closely read the novel, noting the character's progression over the course of the novel, particularly how he or she changed as a result of the novel's climax. You might also incorporate research on the historical context in which the novel takes place, including the political climate or the societal values that characterize the time period. Your observations in this case would not come from watching an experiment in action, but rather from what you notice as you read. Like in a lab report, you would be expected to support your analysis with specific details about the character, but unlike a lab report, your interpretation would likely come in the form of a thesis statement. Your evidence would come in the form of textual citations—that is, you would cite key points in the novel, historical sources, or literary theorists to support your reading of the character.

In a business class, you might be asked to write formal letters, memos, resumes, recommendation reports, or project proposals. These genres all have their own particular style and formatting conventions as well. For example, project proposals usually begin by providing an evidence of the need for the completion of the project and detailing the potential consequences of not moving forward. It would also include thorough descriptions of the proposed project, a step-by-step plan for carrying out the project, and a budget estimating the total cost. As a writer working within this context, you would need to consider these genre conventions, and you would need to adapt your writing to match the communication practices most valued within the field of business. Being an effective academic writer thus requires that you always consider the purpose of your writing, your target audience, and the context in which you are writing (for example, the genre you're working in and the style conventions of the academic discipline in which you're writing).

Considering your audience, purpose, and other contextual factors is a crucial part of becoming an effective writer because, as the above examples illustrate, each academic discipline has its own way of writing and communicating with people inside the discipline. You can think of these unique ways of communicating as **discourse communities,** or communities of people who share a discipline-specific set of writing practices, as well as specialized vocabulary that is understood by members of the group. As a college student, you likely belong to several different discourse communities, from your major field of study to each extracurricular group to which you belong. For example, if you're a chemistry major, then you have a specific way of talking and communicating with others who study and teach chemistry; you all share a set of common vocabulary and communication practices. The same would be true if you belong to a student organization like Animal AdvoCATS, where members of the group also have communication practices that are unique to the group. Take a moment to jot down the various discourse communities to which you belong. What are the communication practices of each group? How do these practices differ across groups? How does your writing and speech change from one group to the next? Thinking about these things will enable you to understand the concept of discourse community and to recognize the ways in which academic writing means different things in different situations.

> A **discourse community** is a group of people who share discipline-specific ways of writing and communicating.

The most important thing to note about academic writing, then, is that it changes from one discipline to the next. While all academic writing shares some common features—formality in tone, for example—there are major differences as well. Your job as a writer will be to note the written conventions within the academic disciplines you encounter and to apply them in your own writing. You may sometimes find that writing "academically" is a challenge, since it often demands that you learn to step back from your usual writing processes and reflect on the attitudes and habits that have shaped who you are. Success in college, however, requires that you learn to master the conventions of academic discourse across disciplines and in your major course of study.

If your first language is not English, however, the university experience will also include a process of learning how written language differs from speech, how cultural expectations shape writing conventions, and how classroom environments and learning styles can be affected in a multitude of culturally-specific ways. In this chapter, Neil Johnson and Shawn Steinhart address some of the specific considerations important for both ESOL (English for Speakers of Other Languages) students and native English speakers who are working to master the conventions of academic discourse.

For instance, Johnson and Steinhart discuss academic discourse as a particular type of "genre" or category of writing, with unique rules and guidelines that even native speakers of English may not have considered in detail.

Attention to word usage and sentence construction, for example, is especially helpful for every writer during the revision process. Regardless of how proficient you already are in writing in English, you can use this chapter throughout your first-year writing courses as you draft, revise and reflect on your writing.

In the following section, Stephen Sweat discusses the transferable skills you will learn in first-year writing—skills that will help you become an effective writer in a variety of academic disciplines. While academic writing is taught in first-year composition courses given through the English department, the skill of engaging in academic discourse is necessary across disciplines and will be useful to you both inside and outside the English classroom.

2.2 Donkeys, Daisies, and Dancing: Critical Thinking and Composition Across Disciplines

By Stephen Sweat

I have never particularly liked the course title "Freshman Composition." I always thought it something of a misnomer because it seems to suggest that the English 100 series focuses solely on writing. Granted, the courses are designed, in part, to teach techniques for crafting and refining clear, expository prose, but this is only one of the objectives. The other primary objective is the development of critical thinking skills. Writing is only as strong as the thought it contains, and if writing is not founded upon insightful and well-reasoned thought, it just won't be good writing. Remember, a donkey in a tuxedo is still a donkey. Sure, he looks nice, but he's still an ass. Thus, I propose that from now on the English 100 series instead be labeled something like "Critical Thinking and Written Expression" or, perhaps, "Critical Thought and Composition." After all, this is what the series is really about.

But even if we did change the course title, I suspect that students would still question the relevancy of the courses in the English 100 series. Really, what does English have to do with Business or Dance or Biosystems Engineering? To be honest, I don't really know. So first things first, let's determine the courses and disciplines for which English Composition is and is not relevant. Do the courses in which you are enrolled require you to remember, comprehend, analyze, evaluate, apply, or synthesize information? Does the discipline you study require reading, listening, writing or thinking? If you answered no to both of these questions, then the English 100 series is not the place for you. However, if you answered yes to either of these questions, then the English 100 courses are abundantly relevant to your studies. In fact, they are fundamental.

For those of you who remain skeptical, I have composed a list of the top five reasons why everything you need to know for your discipline begins with the English 100 series—the collegiate equivalent of "Everything I Need to Know I Learned in Kindergarten."

1. **English Composition aims to make you a more sensitive and acrobatic reader.**

   No, this does not mean that you will cry more easily when reading poems or that you will be able to participate in more complex yoga poses. What it does mean is that the readings and work you do in English Composition will help you be more receptive to how texts create meaning and influence readers. Whether you are reading a scientific journal or a short story, you need to be aware of the rhetorical techniques the author uses to persuade you, so you can make informed judgments about those texts. And when I say texts, I don't just mean print texts. Everything is text, from people, to film, to data, to architecture, and everything is readable. Every discipline "reads" something, interprets something, and this is why the English 100 series is as much about reading as it is about writing. The interpretive skills you develop here make you a better interpreter in other contexts, like the study of Grizzly Bear migratory patterns or how matter behaves when approaching absolute zero. Furthermore, by exposing you to a variety of texts, English Composition helps you develop the cognitive flexibility to read different genres of texts well, so when you register for TRAD 104, RELI 220A, and BNAD 302, you will have the cognitive litheness and sophistication to jump from one subject matter to another with relative ease. Good readers are not just good readers in one discipline, but in many.

2. **English Composition helps develop higher order thinking skills (analysis, synthesis, application, and evaluation).**

   When you are reading Charlotte Perkins Gilman's "The Yellow Wallpaper" or Sherman Alexie's "Because My Father Always Said He Was the Only Indian Who Saw Jimi Hendrix Play," you are not merely looking for the "point" of the story or essay. What you are doing is making sense of the whole through the analysis of the parts. Furthermore, you are trying to put the parts together in ways that allow for the creation of new meaning and interpretation. Thomas Edison failed over two-thousand times when trying to invent the light bulb. What eventually led to his success was his ability to analyze past experiments, synthesize that information, and apply it to come up with new ways of approaching his task. You show me an attorney, a doctor, or an engineer who does not do these things well, who cannot analyze, synthesize, and evaluate, and I'll show you a misdiagnosed patient who has no chance of winning his lawsuit as he sits in a courtroom that may collapse on him at any moment.

3. **English Composition helps provide you with the means to extend and develop thought.**

English philosopher and economist Bertrand Russell wrote that "Most people would rather die than think; and most people do." Call me a cynic but, for the most part, I believe this to be true. Why? Because thought is hard and it takes time, application and revision, and it involves doubt and perplexity and experimentation. But the English 100 series provides you with strategies and opportunities for the extension of thought. This is what the writing process, if you approach it as a process, does. It allows you, to borrow an overwrought metaphor, to germinate and cultivate ideas, and allow them to grow. Great ideas take time to develop. So often we dismiss ideas if they don't seem brilliant at first, but what we forget is that daisies often spring from manure. Freewriting allows us to spread the manure, the compost, so to speak, and see what daisies begin to spring up. Drafting and peer-reviewing essays help us to weed out those things that choke or occlude our best ideas. And believe me, this process, which we label the writing process, is really a process of thinking and is applicable not only to all majors, but all professions.

4. **English Composition helps you become a stronger writer and communicator.**

"All words," wrote nineteenth-century orator Henry Ward Beecher, "are pegs to hang ideas on." Good communicators are thoughtful and precise when choosing the pegs for their ideas, and this is precisely what English Composition wants to instill in you—a more conscious consideration of the words you choose, their connotations, and how you arrange them in relation to one another. Once again, I am hard pressed to think of a single class or major that does not require strong communication skills. By the way, if you want to become better at writing or speaking, this is the place to do it because your first-year English course is all about practice: "True ease in writing comes from art, not chance / Those move easiest who have learned to dance" (Alexander Pope). There aren't many courses that afford you the opportunity to become a better dancer, if you catch my drift. Furthermore, I've seen a number of written assignments from a variety of courses over the years and not a single assignment sheet asked for a poorly supported argument with an ambiguous focus and confusing organization. If you can refine your ability to craft strong theses, garner relevant support, and organize your ideas logically in your English classes, you will be better served in approximately 95.6% of your classes.[1]

5. **English Composition will help you better understand grammar and mechanics.**

No longer will you be mystified by the use of hieroglyphics and inscrutable symbols such as ; or [ ]. Understanding proper punctuation and applying it correctly allows one to appear, in the words of Jonathan Swift, "a scholar and wit, without the fatigue of reading or thinking." But then again, if there is no thought in your writing (see points 1–3), then all you've done is made certain the donkey's tie is straight and his shirt is pressed.

In the end, I have changed my mind. How about that? Through writing, I have not only extended my thought, but arrived at a new idea. I no longer think the term "composition" should be removed from the course description. After all, while composition can be interpreted as the act of writing, it is also the act of combining parts or elements to form a whole, and this is essentially what the English 100 series does. It combines all elements necessary for academic and professional success into a single series of courses. All of the foundational reading, writing, and thinking skills that will be required of you at university are combined/compounded (pay attention to the prefixes) into a single unified series. Ultimately, the composition of all courses and all disciplines have at their foundation English Comp.

Works Cited

Beecher, Henry Ward. *Proverbs from Plymouth Pulpit.* 1887. Print.

Pope, Alexander. "Essay on Criticism." 1711. Print.

Russel, Bertrand. Unknown Source.

Swift, Jonathan. *A Tale of a Tub.* 1704. Print.

2.3 Entering into the Conversation: An Introduction to Genre

By Neil Johnson and Shawn Steinhart

Sociolinguists (scholars who study how language is used) often use the term **communicative competence** when talking about what a person needs in order to successfully communicate in a language. Grammar is, of course,

---

[1] This datum has no statistical foundation whatsoever, but it can't be too far from the mark.

important, but a speaker must know a lot more about the culture and expectations of the community he or she wishes to join. In this chapter, we introduce the concept of **genre** as a way of understanding these expectations, in particular as they relate to developing communicative competence in the American academic community.

What is Genre?

You are probably familiar with the term **genre** from talking about such things as film and music. Most people know that there are several common genres for both of these things. Film genre includes categories such as horror, science fiction, romance, western and action. As far as music goes, the labels such as jazz, hip-hop, and rock actually refer to different genres of music. These labels and names are all around us and perform an important function.

Genre, then, is *a type of something* and these types are defined by similarity. If we think about an action film, for example, before the film has even started, we can make some assumptions about what we're going to see. We know there will be a hero and a villain and expect that the action will revolve around conflict between the two. It is also likely that the hero will be involved in some romantic interest, and that both partners will be attractive. If the film follows the standard action movie conventions, the hero will defeat the villain and win the girl, and everyone will be happy in the end.

For more information about reading and writing about film as a genre, see Chapter 8 pages 173–78.

This kind of predictability sounds boring. Why bother seeing a movie if we know how it's going to end? However, Thomas Sobchack (1995), an expert on film, argues that this predictability is actually part of a kind of social contract between the filmmaker and the audience. Audiences expect a film to follow certain conventions, and filmmakers know they must follow these conventions in order to tell their stories.

Where does genre come from?

As Sobchack explains, genre is an unwritten agreement between the writer and audience that has developed over time as more and more texts of a certain type are produced. In this sense then, we can think of genre as a repeated social action—created by people in a certain community over time as they interact together. In the case of film, genres are created over many years by different filmmakers working to produce a code that the audience understands and can use to understand the text being produced. For example, by convention a *bad guy* in a certain kind of action film may typically wear black and be physically unattractive. This is a kind of code so that the audience, when they see this figure on the screen, immediately understands that this person is not to be trusted. This code only works because the filmmaker understands that this is how the audience will react. So genre is really a form of communication.

Genre and Writing

Genre is also very important when it comes to writing. There are, of course, many famous genres of writing with which we are all familiar. Detective stories or romances are two genres that have their own codes, expectations and conventions. However, there are many other kinds of writing that also belong to a genre that we use daily without thinking about: letter, business letter, email, note, resume, job application. Each of these texts is shaped by genre conventions in very important ways, including the structure, or how the text is organized, and also the style in which it is written. These features and expectations have been created as a result of a particular situation and communicative need within a particular community of people, as in a discourse community. Genres develop as a result of the repeated ways people get things done in their social groups.

An example:

One such discourse community is the business community. In any given country, and even internationally, there are companies and businesses that must communicate with each other to achieve their goals. Over time, because of the nature of how these people communicate and what they do, a certain code or *genre* for business communication has developed. In a business letter in America, for example, it is accepted that within the first two sentences, the writer will state what the purpose of the letter is. There is a reason for this convention—people who read and answer these letters are very busy and deal with many such texts at one time; therefore, this community has developed a very direct and clear organization and style. If a letter in this community does not follow these conventions, it may not communicate its intent and there may be a breakdown in communication. So to communicate effectively with a discourse community a writer needs to know the conventions and expectations that have developed within that community.

Now that you are students at a university in the United States, you belong to a specific discourse community. The purpose of any writing that you do in this context is to effectively communicate your ideas with that community. That community, depending upon which specific one you are writing for, has very specific expectations and conventions about how you will communicate with them. If you fail to follow important aspects of these conventions, as with a business letter that does not inform the reader of its main idea right away, you will not communicate effectively.

In a sense this is what you are going to learn in your writing classes at the University of Arizona: how to effectively organize your ideas and how to write in an appropriate style for a particular community. We know what the expectations are because we are able to study many examples of successful academic writing to identify the unwritten rules. Awareness of these conventions and expectations will help improve your own writing.

2.4 Academic Writing Conventions at the Word Level

Research in the field of linguistics has highlighted a number of very important differences between formal (written) and less formal (spoken) language in English. One of these differences involves verbs. In many situations, English has two or more options to express an action or occurrence. The choice is often between a multiple-word verb and a single verb. Often in spoken English, a multiple-word verb is used; however, for academic written English, generally a single verb is preferred.

Here is an example:

1. According to some government scientists, *coming up with* clear proof of global warming has been difficult.

2. According to some government scientists, *providing* clear proof of global warming has been difficult.

Notice that the verb in the second sentence is a single word instead of three words when a phrasal verb is used. This indicates that the meaning of the sentence is being communicated by fewer words. This is an important feature of academic writing—there is little redundancy and the text is more concise.

Work in linguistics has also shown that certain verbs appear more frequently in academic writing than others. The following list of verbs has been shown to be among the most important for academic style:

abandon	accelerate	access	accompany
accomplish	accumulate	achieve	address
advocate	assert	assume	aid
cause	characterize	comply	conclude
connect	construct	constitute	contrast
decrease	define	denote	develop
determine	dramatize	eliminate	emphasize

enable	enact	establish	evaluate
formulate	guarantee	identify	illustrate
imply	interpret	investigate	juxtapose
maintain	posit	portray	presume
present	prevail	process	reach
require	restrict	specify	suggest

Each of the words in the above list has at least one synonym, and often these synonyms are used more frequently in speech. For example, in spoken English, one is more likely to say "*I gave up* the project and went home" than to say "I *abandoned* the project and went home." Consider these "academic verbs" and their synonyms:

Verb in academic writing	vs.	Verb in spoken English
accelerate		speed up
investigate		look into
accompany		go with
eliminate		get rid of
endure		put up with
explore		think about
research		find out about

2.5 Style Conventions in First-Year Writing

In your first-year writing courses, you will learn a set of conventions particular to these classes. Of course, these conventions go beyond the word level, and you are already familiar with many of them. The thesis statement, for example, is a writing convention you might have learned about in your high school English classes, as are topic sentences. Because these conventions are not universal (i.e., they don't apply in every writing situation), they can seem strange to those who have not been exposed to them. For example, Fan Shen, a Chinese-born scholar, writes about his struggles to adjust to Western writing conventions, and he argues that elements such as topic sentences reflect Western values (topic sentences appear at the beginning of paragraphs because Western readers are too busy to wade through a paragraph to find its meaning). This may be an unfair generalization, but it illustrates the importance of knowing your audience's expectations.

Another writing convention you'll learn in your first-year writing deals with your ability to craft arguments that are supported with concrete details. When you make an academic argument, for example, your audience expects you to have carefully considered all the facts before coming to a conclusion.

For more on rhetorical conventions in academic writing, refer to the Academic English boxes on pages 2, 23, and 359 in *Rules for Writers*.

37

Keyword: hedging

If you make an argument that relies on generalizations or makes sweeping assertions, your audience may find it difficult to agree with your points. This is why **hedging** is often used in academic writing. Hedging is sometimes also called "qualifying" your argument. Hedging means avoiding unequivocal statements of opinion, or making such statements as if they were fact. Instead, hedging requires that you try to use more open-ended phrasing that acknowledges the existence of different viewpoints.

There are **two main functions** of hedging: 1) giving the writer more credibility by appearing more balanced, and 2) creating a more appropriate stance for the writer in terms of audience reactions.

After reading the following sample sentences, discuss these two functions of hedging.

Sample sentences:

What are the differences in meaning for these sentences? Which sentence sounds the most informed and credible? Why?

1. People are totally against genetic engineering, but it provides benefits for humankind.

Using "Academic Verbs"

By Neil Johnson and Shawn Steinhart

Select an academic verb from the list below to create a more academic tone by replacing the italicized words in each of the seven sentences that follow:

List of academic verbs:

maintain   increase   cause   suggest

investigate   decrease   constitute

1. The most common causes of death in the U.S., such as heart disease and diabetes, are mainly *brought on* by lack of exercise and overeating.

2. Scientists are *looking into* innovative ways to combat AIDS.

3. The purpose of this paper is to try and *come up with* some ideas to help the major problems international students have in the United States.

4. Rice and fish *make up* a major part of the Japanese diet.

5. Worldwide consumption of McDonald's food has *gone up to* 526 million units per day.

6. Although fraternity houses have been able to *keep up* their membership numbers, some are beginning to question the future of these organizations.

7. The number of mature female turtles who are able to return to nest sites has *gone down* to only 145 today.

2. Some people are totally against genetic engineering, but it can provide benefits for humanity.

3. Some people are against genetic engineering, but it may provide many benefits for humanity in the future.

Some useful hedging words:

usually	essentially	perhaps	may
actually	apparently	often	some
likely	broadly	somewhat	somehow
potentially	normally	theoretically	maybe

Active vs. Passive Voice

Another stylistic convention you'll learn about in your first-year writing classes centers on the use of verb tenses. Recall earlier in the chapter when you read about some of the conventions you might follow if you were writing a chemistry lab report—the use of the personal "I" in the report, in particular. Many scientific disciplines avoid using the personal "I" in their forms of writing because they want to emphasize the action being performed, not the person responsible for the action. This is the main difference between the active and the passive voice: passive constructions focus on the action performed while active constructions give emphasis to the agent, or performer, of the action.

Passive Voice

Many academic genres (particularly experimental science) make use of the passive voice for the reasons noted above. Experimental scientists deem the actions performed—the meat of the experiment—most important, not necessarily the scientists who perform the experiment. Whereas English typically follows the Subject-Verb-Object (or SVO) order, passive constructions follow an Object-Verb-Subject (or OVS) order. Essentially, a **passive construction** moves the object of a sentence to the subject position.

For example:

SVO Order (Active voice)			OVS Order (Passive voice)		
John	threw	the ball	The ball	was thrown by	John
Subject	**Verb**	**Object**	**Object**	**Verb**	**Subject**

Notice that in the passive voice, the verb is made up of two components: a form of the verb "to be" (was) and the past participle (thrown).

Use passive voice to:

- Call attention to the receiver of the action rather than the performer:

  The bear was hit with buckshot.

- Point out the receiver of the action when the performer is unknown:

  A wallet was stolen from the library.

- Point out the receiver of the action when you want to avoid calling attention to the performer. There can be good reasons why a writer might want to do this! Consider:

  The factory workers were fired yesterday and the factory was closed.

  Nike fired the factory workers yesterday and then the Multinational closed the factory.

For more on forming the passive voice, see *Rules for Writers*, page 232.

What are the political implications of these statements? Who might prefer to use each one in such an announcement?

Active Voice

The active voice provides more clarity for the reader. It shows us exactly who did what to whom. That said, choosing active over passive is not always the best idea. One thing to consider is what you want to emphasize in your sentence—what you want your readers to recognize as the primary focus of a sentence. And is it important to know who is doing what? Is it obvious? Does it matter who is doing the action? Put those characters in the subject position even if you must use a passive verb.

Consider these sentences:

1. People grow rice in India (active: it is clear people are doing the growing).

2. Rice **is grown** in India (passive: Rice is now in the subject position).

In the passive construction, rice is given the attention, and because it is what's important, the use of the passive voice makes sense.

Now consider these sentences:

1. I took the seeds and planted them in the Petri dishes with 5 mm of water and then I measured the growth of the seeds every two days.

2. The seeds were planted in Petri dishes with 5 mm of water and growth was measured every two days.

For more advice on using active voice, see *Rules for Writers*, pages 80–83.

The second sentence, written in the passive voice, is more typical of scientific writing than the first sentence. What's important isn't who planted the seeds or measured them but the actual measurements themselves.

While these examples do not cover every stylistic convention of writing in academic contexts, they will help you get started. Whether to write in active or passive voice, whether to use "endure" instead of "put up with," or whether to use "usually" versus "always"—these are all choices you will make as a writer. More than anything, the examples of style conventions in this chapter should encourage you to think about the stylistic choices you make, since these choices should be informed by the audience to whom you are writing and your purpose for writing.

Academic discourse can sometimes be intimidating for students who are just beginning to learn the conventions that shape academic disciplines, but if you are attentive to these conventions, you will learn to apply them. As this chapter shows, different discourse communities have their own ways of writing and communicating, and your job as a writer will be to write in ways that are appropriate for your audience and purpose. Any genre, whether it is a lab report or a business letter, can be broken down into manageable pieces, but your writing will only be successful if you form it to meet your audience's needs and expectations. As you grow as a writer, think about the ways that the conventions of academic discourse serve you, but also begin to consider thoughtful, creative ways to transcend the rules you learn and pave new roads in your writing.

3

Close Reading and Interacting with the Text

3.1 Close Reading: An Overview

Before you summarize and analyze texts, you must read them closely. When we read texts, we often just read them once or scan for relevant or important information. For example, you might skim the "Arts & Leisure" section of the newspaper to find film times, or you might read an encyclopedia entry about the *Mona Lisa*. You might also scan a chapter in a biology textbook, looking for important terms that will be on your next exam. But such one-time reading for information is insufficient for the tasks you'll perform in your writing courses. In addition to reading a text for information, you'll need to read texts strategically by examining them with a particular focus on your purpose for reading. For example, you may be reading a text for your entertainment, for information on a topic that interests you, or for an assignment. You should plan on at least two readings of any text, especially those you write about, because you will need to get a feel for how language is being used in the piece and review specific elements of the text in order to develop your analysis.

For more on close reading, see *Rules for Writers*, pages 346–47.

When you read strategically, you focus your attention on the aspects of the texts that seem most important. One common way to think about the strategies you use when you read is to divide the process into three phases: consider the strategies you use before you read, the strategies you use as you read, and those you use to review your reading. To read more efficiently and effectively, you should first scan a text to get a basic sense of the text and its purpose. Then, in the second phase of the process, you should read more closely for content and meaning, considering how the text is constructed. In addition, you should consider your reactions to the text. How does it affect you emotionally and intellectually? During your second reading, engage your text in a dialogue. Ask it questions and pick out the most important points. In the third phase of the process, you should review the text and your responses to form some general conclusions. If you take a moment to review your reading, you will remember it more effectively; you will be better prepared to write and talk about it because you will have reduced the reading to some main ideas, rather than leaving yourself with a confusing jumble of details.

In this process, you should read strategically with an eye to why you are reading what your instructors assign. There is generally a good reason for what they have asked you to read, and if you consider how the reading fits into what you have discussed and read previously in the course, you will be more effective at achieving the purpose for which the reading was assigned. Remember that in first-year writing classes, all reading could lead to writing, and that good reading often leads to interesting writing. Ask these questions before and during your reading:

- Why might you be interested in this material?
- How might this information relate to your goals for the assignment and for the course as a whole?
- How does this information connect to other knowledge you have and to other texts you are reading?
- What can you *do* with this information?

Before Reading

Remember, previewing a text is about making the reading easier and more focused. This process does not need to take a lot of time. Spending as little as a minute or two on previewing can still be beneficial.

Before you start reading, consider some basic questions about the text. Reflecting on elements such as the title, subject matter, author, and organization will help you to understand the text more completely and save you time in the long run. For example, if you look at a book and see that the author's name is Stephen King, you'll have certain expectations and will therefore read it differently than you would read a book by, say, Albert Einstein. You should also keep in mind where the text is published (for instance, in an anthology required for the course or in a weekly periodical) and why the teacher might have assigned it. Some questions you might want to ask at this stage include:

- What assumptions do you have about the text after reading the title?
- What is the subject?

- Who is the author, and what is at stake in this topic for him or her?

- Have you read other work by this author? What?

- What experience or expertise does the author have to address this topic?

- When was the text originally published? Are you encountering it in a different context, such as in a classroom textbook? Who are the possible audiences?

- Look at the opening to the article, essay, or story—just the first paragraph or even just the first few sentences. What does it suggest to you?

- What are headings of chapters and major sections? What can you learn from these?

- Scan the conclusion to the text: What does the author consider most important, and why is it important?

Examining these larger elements of a text does not take a long time, but doing this will prepare you to understand the material in the body of the text. By studying the structural features before reading the main text, you'll better understand the organization of the text and will therefore read more effectively, spending less time wondering where ideas are heading.

Active Reading

Now that you have scanned the text, you're ready to begin reading it in detail. When you read, you should think of yourself as an active participant in what you get out of the material; you want to make the text your own. Reading actively will make it easier for you to remember what you have read and will enable you to use it effectively in your writing. This strategy will help you connect ideas in the text to ideas in other texts. Think of yourself as *active* in the reading process, which means you want *always* to raise questions about what is happening and how it is significant. After all, active reading implies action. You are continually performing the actions discussed here while you are reading. If you're reading a short story, for instance, talk back to that story (by **annotating** and/or writing in your journal), noting your thoughts about the narrative, the characters, the plot. How do you feel about what is happening in the story? Where is the story headed? Why is it headed in that direction? After reading, you may want to return to specific events in the text to see what in the story causes you to feel as you do. Also consider what in your own background might cause you to like or dislike a character or the story itself. To provide you with a concrete example on strategies for active reading, later in the chapter we'll apply these techniques to Stephen Crane's story entitled "The Snake" (page 47), "You're," a short poem by Sylvia Plath (page 53), and Martin Luther King's famous speech, "I Have a Dream" (page 54).

3.2 Annotation and Active Reading

By Annie Holub

No one really reads anything passively. Anytime you actually read something, you are engaging with it in some way, even if it's just following the words and sentences as they link together to form some kind of logical thread. Sometimes when you read, it reminds you of something you've read before, or something you've seen before, or it reminds you of something similar that has happened to you or someone you know. This is called active reading, and active reading goes hand in hand with the topic for this section: annotation.

What Is Annotation?

When you read more complex texts, you need to interact with the text so that you don't miss things that might be hard to see. By interacting with the text, we mean one simple thing: write on it. Annotation is the process of writing notes and comments about a text. Back in high school, you were more than likely told specifically NOT to write in your textbooks, but in college, they're yours—you paid for them—so feel free to make as much use of them as you'd like. Write in the margins. Underline things. Take notes on the pages. You can also annotate texts by having a piece of paper handy for notes if you're borrowing books or planning on selling them back in a more pristine condition—just remember to keep track of the page numbers and/or lines from the text you're annotating so you can find things again later.

What Am I Supposed to Look For or Write Down?

Here are some steps that will help you annotate any text that you're reading:

1. Underline words or phrases that confuse you or seem important.

2. Circle words you don't know or words that pop up more than once. Look up the words you don't know, and write the definition next to them.

3. Write ideas and comments in the margin that come to you as you read. If something in a text reminds you of something, write down what that line reminds you of and why.

4. If something surprises you or seems funny, put an exclamation point by it.

5. If something completely confuses you or doesn't make sense, put a question mark there so you know where to go back and re-read more closely.

6. What kind of feeling or tone are you getting from the text as you read? Try to jot down a couple of words that describe the tone. If the tone changes, mark where it happens.

7. Who is talking? What do you know about the speaker/narrator?

8. Who is the speaker/narrator talking to? What do you know about the addressee?

9. What is the speaker/narrator trying to tell the addressee?

10. Are there certain images that stand out, or that seem to reoccur? Keep track of these somehow (I use stars in the margin for this).

We may all be brilliant, but often we don't remember everything we thought of five minutes after reading a text, so it helps to have notes. And that's all annotation is: your notes about the text you're reading.

The following is an annotation of Stephen Crane's short story "The Snake."

Where the path wended across the ridge, the bushes of huckleberry and sweet fern swarmed at it in two curling waves until it was a mere winding line traced through a tangle. There was no interference by clouds, and as the rays of the sun fell full upon the ridge, they called into voice innumerable insects which chanted the heat of the summer day in steady, throbbing, unending chorus.

Wended = winding?

Oppressive heat, cicadas, like a summer day in the Sonoran desert. Not a very picturesque scene?

A man and a dog came from the laurel thickets of the valley where the white brook brawled with the rocks. They followed the deep line of the path across the ridges. The dog—a large lemon and white setter—walked, tranquilly meditative, at his master's heels.

Ridge is also sort of like "rift."

Tranquilly meditative = really, really calm—why both words?

The brook is fighting with the rocks—maybe more things will fight with each other?

Why this specific detail about the dog?

Suddenly from some unknown and yet near place in advance there came a dry, shrill whistling rattle that smote motion instantly from the limbs of the man and the dog. Like the fingers of a sudden death, this sound seemed to touch the man at the nape of the neck, at the top of the spine, and change him, as swift as thought, to a statue of listening horror, surprise, rage. The dog, too—the same icy hand was laid upon him, and he stood crouched and quivering, his jaw dropping, the froth of terror upon his lips, the light of hatred in his eyes.

Ominous

Assonance makes this sound ominous

Also ominous

Even the dog is scared

Slowly the man moved his hands toward the bushes, but his glance did not turn from the place made sinister by the warning rattle. His fingers, unguided, sought for a stick of weight and strength. Presently they closed about one that seemed adequate, and holding this weapon poised before him the man moved slowly forward, glaring. The dog with his nervous nostrils fairly fluttering moved warily, one foot at a time, after his master.

Seems instinctual—he's in hunting mode

The snake's body or the man's? Could be both? Why call attention to what his body does as opposed to what his mind does? Also instinctual—snake-like, even?

But when the man came upon the snake, his body underwent a shock as if from a revelation, as if after all he had been ambushed. With a blanched face, he sprang forward and his breath came in strained gasps, his chest heaving as if he were in the performance of an extraordinary muscular trial. His arm with the stick made a spasmodic, defensive gesture.

Snakes also muscular

The snake had apparently been crossing the path in some mystic travel when to his sense there came the knowledge of the coming of his foes. The dull vibration perhaps informed him, and he flung his body to face the danger. He had no knowledge of paths; he had no wit to tell him to slink noiselessly into the bushes. He knew that his implacable enemies were approaching; no doubt they were seeking him, hunting him. And so he cried his cry, an incredibly swift jangle of tiny bells, as burdened with pathos as the hammering upon quaint cymbals by the Chinese at war—for, indeed, it was usually his death-music.

Snake is mystical, other-worldly

This sounds like what happens to the man in the previous paragraph—snake and man have similar insticts?

Lots of emotion in the snake's rattle—why liken to Chinese at war? Makes the snake more exotic?

instinct

"Beware! Beware! Beware!"

Man and snake share same emotions

The man and the snake confronted each other. In the man's eyes were hatred and fear. In the snake's eyes were hatred and fear. These enemies maneuvered, each preparing to kill. It was to be a battle without mercy. Neither knew of mercy for such a situation. In the man was all the wild strength of the terror of his ancestors, of his race, of his kind. A deadly repulsion had been handed from man to man through long dim centuries. This was another detail of a war that had begun evidently when first there were men and snakes. Individuals who do not participate in this strife incur the investigations of scientists. Once there was a man and a snake who were friends, and at the end, the man lay dead with the marks of the snake's caress just over his East Indian heart. In the formation of devices, hideous and horrible, Nature reached her supreme point in the making of the snake, so that priests who really paint hell well fill it with snakes instead of fire. The curving forms, these scintillant coloring create at once, upon sight, more relentless animosities than do shake barbaric tribes. To be born a snake is to be thrust into a place a-swarm with formidable foes. To gain an appreciation of it, view hell as pictured by priests who are really skilful.

instinctual again!

What's with this parable? Why an East Indian? Exotic, strange—the snake caresses with his body, he has no hands, the caress = death

What is Crane saying about Nature here if the snake is the "supreme point?" Snakes are hellish, worse than fire...

Tone Biblical, but then "really skilful" seems out of place

As for this snake in the pathway, there was a double curve some inches back of its head, which, merely by the potency of its lines, made the man feel with tenfold eloquence the touch of the death-fingers at the

Death-fingers again—see third paragraph

nape of his neck. The reptile's head was waving slowly from side to side and its hot eyes flashed like little murder-lights. Always in the air was the dry, shrill whistling of the rattles.

"Beware! Beware! Beware!"

The man made a preliminary feint with his stick. Instantly the snake's heavy head and neck were bended back on the double curve and instantly the snake's body shot forward in a low, strait, hard spring. The man jumped with a convulsive chatter and swung his stick. The blind, sweeping blow fell upon the snake's head and hurled him so that steel-colored plates were for a moment uppermost. But he rallied swiftly, agilely, and again the head and neck bended back to the double curve, and the steaming, wide-open mouth made its desperate effort to reach its enemy. This attack, it could be seen, was despairing, but it was nevertheless impetuous, gallant, ferocious, of the same quality as the charge of the lone chief when the walls of white faces close upon him in the mountains. The stick swung unerringly again, and the snake, mutilated, torn, whirled himself into the last coil.

And now the man went <u>sheer raving mad</u> from the emotions of his forefathers and from his own. He came to close quarters. He gripped the stick with his two hands and made it speed like a flail. The snake, tumbling in the anguish of final despair, fought, bit, flung itself upon this stick which was taking his life.

At the end, the man clutched his stick and stood watching in silence. The dog came slowly and with infinite caution stretched his nose forward, sniffing. The hair upon his neck and back moved and ruffled as if a sharp wind was blowing, the last muscular quivers of the snake were causing the rattles to still sound their treble cry, the shrill, <u>ringing war chant and hymn</u> of the grave of the thing that faces foes at once countless, implacable, and superior.

"Well, Rover," said the man, turning to the dog with a grin of victory, "we'll carry Mr. Snake home to show the girls."

His hands still trembled from the strain of the encounter, but he pried with his stick under the body of the snake and hoisted the limp thing upon it. He resumed his march along the path, and the dog walked <u>tranquilly meditative</u>, at his master's heels.

Margin annotations:

???

Time moving very very slowly

Perspective seems distant—where is narrator? Who is seeing this? Who's telling us this story?

The lone chief loses.

Instinct makes you crazy—how can he feel the emotions of his forefathers?

It's the stick doing the killing, not the man—the man is only wielding the stick.

Like the Chinese-war thing; man is superior to the snake here but the snake is also hell and worse than fire?

Rover? C'mon!

"Mr. Snake" = condescending. Something cute to show the girls.

Why didn't the dog do anything? Just a battle between man and snake?

After annotating this story, already I can see some patterns. I can identify the tone and perhaps begin to make an argument about what this story is about on a deeper level. Based on the annotations above, I know I need to explore themes and ideas like the struggle between man and nature and what the snake represents about nature. There's definitely something here about instinct as well.

Try it for yourself:

- Read and annotate a story of your choice—try something short but challenging, like Kate Chopin's "Story of An Hour," or Karen Brennan's "Floating."

- Read and annotate whatever your instructor assigned you to read for the next class.

- Read and annotate something you were assigned to read for another course.

Why Annotate?

Once you've read through something for the first time and marked up the text with your notes, then you can go back and try to find patterns and think more about things that confused you. Student Brittney Martinez makes a very good point about the time-saving benefits of annotation:

> My suggestion for the Text-in-Context essay for future English 101 students is to read the primary text, which was a novel for my class, very carefully and put annotations in the margins of the book, so you won't have to read the whole novel over again to find a specific quote.

For more advice on reading arguments closely, see *Rules for Writers*, pages 371–79.

Instead of reading the whole book or story again, you just need to reread the parts you already pulled out, and your notes about those parts. Annotation makes thinking deeply about the text you're reading much easier: Maybe you realize that you circled a certain word more than once—what's up with that? Maybe something that confused you at the beginning makes more sense now that you've read the whole thing. Maybe you noticed certain kinds of images popping up more than once, or a certain feel to the text. Maybe you noticed that the addressee doesn't really seem to be listening to the speaker. Start asking yourself why these things you noticed might be happening. What effect do these things have on you as a reader?

Annotating a text is the first, and in many ways, most important step toward analyzing that text. If you are actively reading and processing the text as you go, writing down ideas as they pop up and marking things to go back to and ponder, you are already starting to take apart the text to see how it works, which is the basic definition of analysis. The things you underline or highlight may very well end up being the things you cite and quote in your textual analysis essay. The things that confused you may very well lead you to the meaning and significance of the text, which in turn may lead you to your argument about the text. Mortimer Adler and Charles van Doren wrote that "marking up a book is not an act of mutilation but of love. You shouldn't mark up a book which isn't yours." And you make a book you already own more yours by annotating it—you haven't made that book a part of your educational experience until you've thoroughly interacted with it through annotation. It might as well just continue sitting on the shelf, its spine un-cracked. And what's the point of spending time reading something if you can't incorporate it in some way into your own educational life and work?

Works Cited

Adler, Mortimer and Charles van Doren. *How to Read a Book.* New York: Simon and Schuster, 1972. Print.

Crane, Stephen. "The Snake." *The Literature Network.* Web. 16 March 2008.

3.3. Annotation and Genre

Once you can annotate one text, you have the skills necessary for annotating *any* text. If you remember that the purpose of annotating is to keep you engaged with your reading and to lead you to deeper ways of thinking about what you read, you can apply the skills you have practiced by annotating a short-story like Crane's "The Snake" just as effectively on a different kind of a text, like a poem, an essay, an article in a newspaper, a sacred text, a legal document, or even an advertisement. Having said that, we know that as a short story "The Snake" is different in many ways from other kinds of texts, or texts written in other genres. A genre is a type or form of expression. When we discuss written genre we often consider genres like the novel, the essay, the poem, the speech, the stage play, and the short story. You may have even come across genres that fit within a certain genre category. Poetry can be further broken down into categories like the sonnet, the haiku, the ballad, and the sestina, for example. Because different genres exhibit different traits, the way you annotate a text may take into account the text's genre.

This chapter includes three annotated texts, all of different genres. While there is definitely more to say about a text than how it fits or does not fit into the conventions of its genre, this can be a good place to start when making observations about a text. But before you can do that, you will need to come up with your own ideas about a genre and its conventions. Let's start with poetry, since you will be reading a poem in this section. When you think of poems, you might think of texts that are broken into *lines* and *stanzas*. Certainly not all poems fit this description, but again, noticing that a poem is (or is not) organized into lines and/or stanzas helps you to begin thinking about what might be happening in the poem. Other aspects of poetry that you might notice are the use of *rhyme* and *meter*. *Figurative language* and *metaphor* are fairly common in poetry, while writing techniques like using *dialogue* or citations are less common. In the genre of a short story, however, dialogue may be used much more frequently. Short stories are often organized into *paragraphs* and may use standard or nonstandard sentences to convey information. Because short stories are generally short, as their name suggests, the beginnings and endings are often especially important in the overall effect created by the text. The last genre included in this chapter is a speech, which is a unique genre. First, it is generally considered to be a **nonfiction** text. Second, a speech is delivered to a very specific audience at a specific moment. It is written to be delivered orally. If you think about these things while reading a speech you will notice genre conventions like spaces where a speaker might *pause*, perhaps to acknowledge or wait for applause. You will also notice figures like *repetition*, which can be especially effective for a listener. Can you think of genre conventions for these or other genres?

When you annotate a text, you comment on central ideas and questions about the text and your reading of it, but you may also comment on the way it is written and the relationship between the way a text is written and its genre. If you were reading a poem in which every line rhymed with the previous line until the last two lines, you might make an annotation about this break in form. Thinking about why this happens in the poem could lead to a very interesting writing topic. Similarly, if you read a newspaper article that has very long paragraphs you might make an annotation about that, since usually paragraphs in newspaper articles are quite short. You might consider the effect of the longer paragraphs on your reading experience. In the last section you saw how you might annotate a short story. In the example that follows you will see how annotation and other close reading strategies lead to a deeper involvement with a poem. As you read this section, think about how the annotations might be similar to or different from a reader's annotations on a text of another genre.

For more on genre see "Chapter 2: Academic Discourse as Writing for Specific Audiences and Purposes."

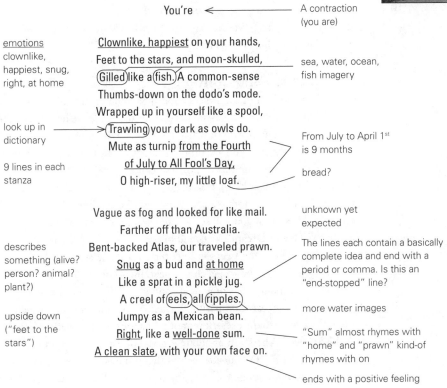

You're ← A contraction (you are)

emotions
clownlike,
happiest, snug,
right, at home

Clownlike, happiest on your hands,
Feet to the stars, and moon-skulled,
Gilled like a fish. A common-sense   sea, water, ocean,
Thumbs-down on the dodo's mode.   fish imagery
Wrapped up in yourself like a spool,

look up in
dictionary

Trawling your dark as owls do.
Mute as turnip from the Fourth   From July to April 1st
of July to All Fool's Day,   is 9 months

9 lines in each
stanza

O high-riser, my little loaf.   bread?

Vague as fog and looked for like mail.   unknown yet
Farther off than Australia.   expected

describes
something (alive?
person? animal?
plant?)

Bent-backed Atlas, our traveled prawn.   The lines each contain a basically
Snug as a bud and at home   complete idea and end with a
Like a sprat in a pickle jug.   period or comma. Is this an
A creel of eels, all ripples.   "end-stopped" line?

upside down
("feet to the
stars")

Jumpy as a Mexican bean.   more water images
Right, like a well-done sum.   "Sum" almost rhymes with
A clean slate, with your own face on.   "home" and "prawn" kind-of
                                            rhymes with on

                                            ends with a positive feeling

Based on the annotations shown above, ask yourself some questions:

• What does the reader seem to notice in this poem?

• The poem seems to be a chain of descriptions. What do you think the thing described could be?

• Can you categorize the descriptions (are they associated with nature, a certain place, sea creatures, kinds of emotions)?

• Don't forget to also consider what you might know about the author or how the very form of a poem can influence the reader.

• What other aspects of the poem do you notice as a reader?

As you can see from the annotations, the observations about the poem may seem random at this point; however, the reader's insights can be expressed in the idea-generating stage in the form of a journal entry, freewrite, or even a draft of an essay. On page 66 you will see an example of a journal entry made after annotating this poem and showing how that kind of informal writing to generate ideas can lead to a working thesis about the poem.

For more examples of annotating a reading, see *Rules for Writers*, pages 12 and 348–49.

Work Cited

Plath, Sylvia. "You're." 1960, 1965, 1971, 1981. *The Collected Poems of Sylvia Plath*. Harper Collins Publishers. Print.

3.4 Annotation and Context

You may have noticed in the first section that some of the questions to ask when reading a text deal with elements that occur *outside* the text. Whenever you consider the time period in which a text was written or the relationship of the author to the text, you are thinking about the text in a certain context. There are an infinite number of possible contexts for any text. You might find that you read a text in a social, historical, or political context, and when you closely read and annotate a text you might be thinking about a specific context. In this section you will see a reader's annotations on Martin Luther King, Jr.'s "I Have a Dream" speech. This speech is one of the most famous speeches delivered in the twentieth-century, yet many students have never read it closely. The way the speech has been incorporated into the ways we think and speak about issues of equality and inequality might influence your close reading of the text. Comparing the historic period when the speech was written (the 1960s) to the present is another factor that might affect how you read this speech. When you annotate a text, you can make comments that will help you identify the outside factors that influence the way you read it. Sometimes the annotations you make help you to realize that you have been reading the text in a certain context. You may not have realized this until you started commenting on these aspects of the text. While reading the annotated text of "I Have a Dream," try to identify some of the outside factors that seem to be a part of this reader's experience of the speech. Is this reader thinking about history? Race? The economy? The genre of a speech? The current political climate? What other outside factors affect your own reading of this text?

For more on context see "Chapter 9: Text-in-Context (Contextual Analysis)."

The I Have a Dream Speech
Delivered August 28, 1963, Martin Luther King, Jr.

King is addressing the audience—He sees the march as historically important. Did he know how important the speech would be in history?

Sounds like Gettysburg Address—four score and seven…

I am happy to join with you today in what will go down in history as the greatest demonstration for freedom in the history of our nation.

Five score years ago, a great American, in whose symbolic shadow we stand today, signed the Emancipation Proclamation. This momentous decree came as a great beacon light of hope to millions of Negro slaves who had been seared in the flames of withering injustice. It came as a joyous daybreak to end the long night of their captivity.

Time—one day vs. 100 yrs. in the next paragraph

But <u>one hundred years</u> later, the Negro still is not free. <u>One hundred years</u> later, the life of the Negro is still sadly crippled by the manacles of segregation and the chains of discrimination. <u>One hundred years</u> later, the Negro lives on a lonely island of poverty in the midst of a vast ocean of material prosperity. <u>One hundred years </u>later, the Negro is still languishing in the corners of American society and finds himself an exile in his own land. So we have come here today to dramatize a shameful condition.

Repetition: 100 years

In a sense we have come to our nation's capital to cash a check. When the architects of our republic wrote the magnificent words of the Constitution and the Declaration of Independence, they were signing a promissory note to which every American was to fall heir. This note was a promise that all men, yes, black men as well as white men, would be guaranteed the <u>unalienable rights of life, liberty, and the pursuit of happiness.</u>

This makes me think about today's economy.

Declaration of Independence

It is obvious today that America has defaulted on this promissory note insofar as her citizens of color are concerned. Instead of honoring this sacred obligation, America has given the Negro people a bad check, a check which has come back marked "insufficient funds." But we refuse to believe that the bank of justice is bankrupt. We refuse to believe that there are insufficient funds in the great vaults of opportunity of this nation. So we have come to cash this check—a check that will give us upon demand the riches of freedom and the security of justice. We have also come to this hallowed spot to remind America of the fierce urgency of now. This is no time to engage in the luxury of cooling off or to take the tranquilizing drug of gradualism. Now is the time to make real the promises of democracy. Now is the time to rise from the dark and desolate valley of segregation to the sunlit path of racial justice. Now is the time to lift our nation from the quick sands of racial injustice to the solid rock of brotherhood. Now is the time to make justice a reality for all of God's children.

He really builds this bad check/good check metaphor. Why are rights/justice compared to cash (the cash behind a check)? Is cash a sure thing? Was it in 1963?

It would be fatal for the nation to overlook the urgency of the moment. This sweltering <u>summer</u> of the Negro's legitimate discontent will not pass until there is an invigorating <u>autumn</u> of freedom and equality. Nineteen sixty-three is not an end, but a beginning. Those who hope that the Negro needed to blow off steam and will now be content will have a rude awakening if the nation returns to business as usual. There will be neither rest nor tranquility in America until the <u>Negro</u> is granted his citizenship rights. The whirlwinds of revolt will continue to shake the foundations of our nation until the bright day of justice emerges.

Time again—this time he uses seasons.

How has the use of the word "Negro" changed over time? Look this up!

Weather=another metaphor

55

But there is something that I must say to my people who stand on the warm threshold which leads into the palace of justice. In the process of gaining our rightful place we must not be guilty of wrongful deeds. Let us not seek to satisfy our thirst for freedom by drinking from the cup of bitterness and hatred.

We must forever conduct our struggle on the high plane of dignity and discipline. We must not allow our creative protest to degenerate into physical violence. Again and again we must rise to the majestic heights of meeting physical force with soul force. The marvelous new militancy which has engulfed the Negro community must not lead us to a distrust of all white people, for many of our white brothers, as evidenced by their presence here today, have come to realize that their destiny is tied up with our destiny. They have come to realize that their freedom is inextricably bound to our freedom. We cannot walk alone.

"Distrust of all white people" is an interesting phrase. I don't think a political speaker right now would use it. Or maybe he would. Hmm…

As we walk, we must make the pledge that we shall always march ahead. We cannot turn back. There are those who are asking the devotees of civil rights, "When will you be satisfied?" We can never be satisfied as long as the Negro is the victim of the unspeakable horrors of police brutality. We can never be satisfied, as long as our bodies, heavy with the fatigue of travel, cannot gain lodging in the motels of the highways and the hotels of the cities. We cannot be satisfied as long as the Negro's basic mobility is from a smaller ghetto to a larger one. We can never be satisfied as long as our children are stripped of their selfhood and robbed of their dignity by signs stating "For Whites Only." We cannot be satisfied as long as a Negro in Mississippi cannot vote and a Negro in New York believes he has nothing for which to vote. No, no, we are not satisfied, and we will not be satisfied until justice rolls down like waters and righteousness like a mighty stream.

The speech was delivered after an actual march but he's also talking about a metaphorical march!

This was before Rodney King.

Do we see voting as a privilege? A right?

Repetition: satisfied

I am not unmindful that some of you have come here out of great trials and tribulations. Some of you have come fresh from narrow jail cells. Some of you have come from areas where your quest for freedom left you battered by the storms of persecution and staggered by the winds of police brutality. You have been the veterans of creative suffering. Continue to work with the faith that unearned suffering is redemptive.

Go back to Mississippi, go back to Alabama, go back to South Carolina, go back to Georgia, go back to Louisiana, go back to the slums and ghettos of our northern cities, knowing that somehow this situation can and will be changed. Let us not wallow in the valley of despair.

The south

I say to you today, my friends, so even though we face the difficulties of today and tomorrow, I still have a dream. It is a dream deeply rooted in the American dream.

Time (present and future)

I have a dream that one day this nation will rise up and live out the true meaning of its creed: "We hold these truths to be self-evident: that all men are created equal."

Declaration of Independence: Refers to the historical document of a revolution: 1963 is a revolution!

I have a dream that one day on the red hills of Georgia the sons of former slaves and the sons of former slave owners will be able to sit down together at the table of brotherhood.

I have a dream that one day even the state of Mississippi, a state sweltering with the heat of injustice, sweltering with the heat of oppression, will be transformed into an oasis of freedom and justice.

I have a dream that my four little children will one day live in a nation where they will not be judged by the color of their skin but by the content of their character.

Brings in the personal: Family

I have a dream today.

I have a dream that one day, down in Alabama, with its vicious racists, with its governor having his lips dripping with the words of interposition and nullification; one day right there in Alabama, little black boys and black girls will be able to join hands with little white boys and white girls as sisters and brothers.

The speech actually goes on for a long time after the "I have a dream" part. Repetition: "I have a dream."

I have a dream today.

I have a dream that one day every valley shall be exalted, every hill and mountain shall be made low, the rough places will be made plain, and the crooked places will be made straight, and the glory of the Lord shall be revealed, and all flesh shall see it together.

Like the valley of despair above

This is our hope. This is the faith that I go back to the South with. With this faith we will be able to hew out of the mountain of despair a stone of hope. With this faith we will be able to transform the jangling discords of our nation into a beautiful symphony of brotherhood. With this faith we will be able to work together, to pray together, to struggle together, to go to jail together, to stand up for freedom together, knowing that we will be free one day.

King refers to faith and God a lot in this speech. Our politicians still do that.

This will be the day when all of God's children will be able to sing with a new meaning, "My country, 'tis of thee, sweet land of liberty, of thee I sing. Land

"America"

where my fathers died, land of the pilgrim's pride, from every mountainside, let freedom ring."

Repetition: "Let freedom ring"

And if America is to be a great nation this must become true. So let freedom ring from the prodigious hilltops of New Hampshire. Let freedom ring from the mighty mountains of New York. Let freedom ring from the heightening Alleghenies of Pennsylvania!

Difference in landscape/ geography is like difference between people.

Let freedom ring from the snowcapped Rockies of Colorado!

Let freedom ring from the curvaceous slopes of California!

But not only that; let freedom ring from Stone Mountain of Georgia!

Let freedom ring from Lookout Mountain of Tennessee!

Let freedom ring from every hill and molehill of Mississippi. From every mountainside, let freedom ring.

Interesting—this language still excludes a lot of people that make up today's U.S. but King seems to be using the list to include rather than exclude.

And when this happens, when we allow freedom to ring, when we let it ring from every village and every hamlet, from every state and every city, we will be able to speed up that day when all of God's children, <u>black men and white men, Jews and Gentiles, Protestants and Catholics</u>, will be able to join hands and sing in the words of the old Negro spiritual, "Free at last! free at last! thank God Almighty, we are free at last!"

You can listen to a recording of this speech online at <http://www. americanrhetoric. com/speeches/ mlkihaveadream.htm>.

In the next section, you will see some examples of how the reader has used these annotations to help solidify some ideas about this speech. Using the outlines and the summary paragraph included in the next section, the reader begins to make the transition from critical reader to critical writer. When you express the ideas that surfaced as reading notes or annotations in written phrases and sentences, you begin to think about a text as a writer does. While these are still preliminary steps, they help you to identify the ideas you will eventually explore in more depth when you begin to write about a text.

Works Cited

King, Martin Luther, Jr. "The I Have a Dream Speech." *USConstitution.net*. 2 October 2008. Web. 17 October 2008.

3.5 Putting It All Together: Reading to Write

Once you have read a text carefully, made annotations, and taken notes, you need to think of how you will use what you read in your writing. You can often read more effectively and save time by thinking as specifically as you can about how you are going to use the reading in your writing. For example, if you have annotated a text that will serve as your primary source, you will probably use the annotations in a way that will help you clarify what claim you are making about the text, identify the passages you think are most relevant to your argument, and define the main points that you will discuss and analyze in your essay. On the other hand, if you are reading an article that seems perfect for providing a background on a topic you're researching, but the ideas are difficult to grasp because the article is written for scholars and uses a complicated structure and technical vocabulary, then you'll probably want to first carefully look over the text and then make frequent annotations as you read to help you understand the author's main ideas. You should also keep in mind how the information in the source relates to the points in your essay: Does this text help define a concept your essay is exploring? Does it provide examples? Does it help you establish your credibility as a researcher by citing the opinions and findings of experts?

You can reconsider a text through your annotations. Each step in the process makes the text more your own, allowing you to better understand its structure and content. It can be helpful to read through a text a few times, adding annotations with each reading as your ideas become more focused. If you have annotated the text thoroughly, this process will be much simpler than it might appear. After annotating, you may want to employ at least one of the common techniques described in the following section.

Taking Inventory

After annotating your text, consider taking an inventory. The annotation process involves putting down your thoughts as you read. When you take inventory you actually begin to sift through that information. Make a list of important items and group them into categories. In an inventory of your reading, you look for patterns in your responses to see what they add up to and review the text itself to strengthen your overall impression. More specifically, you may:

- Scrutinize the text for patterns and repetitions of words, images, phrases, argument structure, examples, and writing strategies.

- Categorize these patterns.

- Decide how these patterns affect the meaning of the text.

- Consider how these patterns are similar to or different from those you have noticed in other texts on the same topic, and thus, how the text you are examining is unique or worth discussing.

In Stephen Crane's story, for example, you might notice that he begins by describing the landscape and the day, alludes to the Bible, repeats terms such as *instinct* and *war*, and uses assonance, or repeated vowel sounds. In Sylvia Plath's poem, your annotation might highlight the ways in which she addresses the reader, or you might remark upon the relationship between the form of the poem and its subject matter. You might also look at repetition, types of images, or word choices in order to help you define an argument or claim about your reading of the poem. Remember that taking inventory should help you clarify some way to analyze the text and make a claim about it. In Martin Luther King, Jr.'s speech, you might think about how techniques like repetition and metaphor work within the genre of an orally delivered speech. Or you might emphasize which aspects of the speech are indicative of the time it was written and which seem equally relevant now. The process of noticing these details and categorizing them helps you see which details were important to the author and should help you make decisions about your own writing on the topic.

Outlining and Summarizing

Outlining will help you map the development of the text so you can see where it's going and how it gets there. For example, if you're writing an analysis of a journal article and your entire paper depends on your understanding of it, you'll want to create a very thorough outline that highlights the author's main points, as well as highlighting the ways in which those points are supported and analyzed. This would also be important when reading a short story or novel because understanding narrative structure is a crucial step to writing about literature. You might want to make an informal, formal, or descriptive outline (such as a web).

An **informal outline** can be as simple as a short description of each paragraph. The main advantage of an informal outline is that it's quick to construct, especially if you've already annotated the text. When creating an informal outline, you should accurately describe the main ideas of the text. An accurate description is not always easy. Although this type of outline can help you identify the larger themes and patterns in the text, it won't always help you focus on specific textual elements such as style, repetition, forms of argumentation, and types of evidence that you'll need to focus on if you're doing a close reading or rhetorical analysis. For example, in King's speech, an informal outline might look like this:

Paragraphs 1–3:   Begins in the style of the Gettysburg address, and establishes the problem the speech addresses: inequality.

Paragraphs 4–5:   Introduces the metaphor of the insufficient funds check. People of color have been promised equality but instead received a "bad check" from America.

Paragraphs 6–7:   States that this is a time for revolt but revolt must not be based in "wrongful deeds."

Paragraphs 8–9:   Compares the revolution to a walk that will not end until equality is achieved.

Paragraphs 10–11:   Addresses the audience directly, acknowledges their hardships.

Paragraphs 12–20:   Lists the components/examples of King's "dream."

Paragraphs 21–22:   Compares the dream to the "hope." The hope is to "let freedom ring…with new meaning."

Paragraphs 23–29:   Uses "let freedom ring" to express the vast inclusiveness of the America of King's dream.

Paragraph 30:   Concludes with the idea that when this dream is universally achieved the country will be "free at last!"

As this example illustrates, an informal outline focuses on the key idea of each paragraph or section rather than going into details of imagery and language use. Depending on your purpose for using the outline, such details may or may not be necessary.

A **formal outline** is probably familiar to most readers. This type of outline will take longer to create as it requires a more thorough understanding of the text. What you get out of this process might be crucial to your success in writing many kinds of papers because this type of outline focuses more on structure and detail. The emphasis of this type of outline could be on the language of the text, the content, or both. Two of the challenges of creating a formal outline are (1) distinguishing between main ideas and supporting points and (2) succinctly illustrating those points. If you go into too much detail (as is easy to do), you've missed the point of creating an outline. An outline should not be as long as the original text. On the other hand, an outline of a twenty-page paper should be long enough to encompass all the main points. In most cases this will take a few pages.

A formal outline for the first five paragraphs of King's speech might look like this:

I.   This is a historic moment

   A. The demonstration is historic

   B. The speech follows other historic moments/texts in American history

     1. Emancipation Proclamation

     2. Constitution

     3. Declaration of Independence

   C. People of color are still not free

II. Situation is like an insufficient funds check

   A. Racial injustice exists but justice is possible

   B. It is time to take action against injustice

For advice on outlining, see *Rules for Writers*, pages 350–51.

Outlining the speech in this way shows you its most important points and the details that support them.

In some cases, you may prefer to summarize a text rather than outline it. One advantage of writing a **summary** is that you get to restate the main ideas of a text in fully developed sentences. Depending on the complexity of the paper you are writing and the text you are analyzing, you may even be able to include your summary of the text in your paper. Here is a very short summary of King's speech. It contains the aspects of the speech that the reader considered most important:

> In his 1963 speech "I Have a Dream," Martin Luther King, Jr. uses the well-known language of the Gettysburg address, the Declaration of Independence, "America" ("My Country, 'Tis of Thee"), and the Negro spiritual, "Free at last," to create two images. The first is of the unfair and racist society of his time. The second is his "dream," a world of freedom and equality. Using metaphors of time, the weather, geography, and the insufficient funds check, King shows the strong contrast between these two images of society and encourages nonviolent revolution to achieve a peaceful and more equal America.

Different readers have found other effective metaphors and strategies in this speech. What devices do you think are the most powerful? Why?

If you look back to the annotations on this speech you will see that the ideas selected for inclusion in the summary were marked with annotations. Annotating the text helped this reader to pick out the key elements of this speech. Those elements are condensed into just four sentences here. Your own summary of King's speech might include some different elements of speech but would probably also share many of the ideas included here. Summary can be a very useful tool at the start of the analytical writing process.

For more information on summarizing, please see "Chapter 6: Working with Sources: Summary, Paraphrase, and Quotation" and *Rules for Writers*, pages 417–18 and 424.

Mapping the Idea Structure

While the various forms of outlines work very well for many people, some writers prefer a more visual approach such as mapping out the ideas of a text. **Mapping**, also called **webbing** or **clustering**, allows you to represent visually how the ideas in a text are related to both the main point(s) and each other. For some people, this may work better than the more rigid structure of a formal outline. A formal outline emphasizes linear structure, while an idea map emphasizes the interconnectedness of ideas. Indeed, mapping would work better than a formal outline for texts that are less linear. As demonstrated by the partial map of Crane's story below, an idea map can reveal very different information than an outline. Notice that the map shows how different parts of the speech relate to each other—something you can't see in an outline.

Idea Map of Stephen Crane's "The Snake"

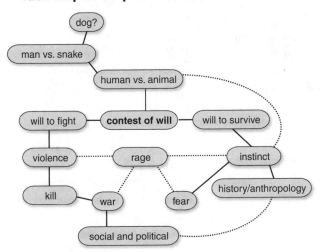

You can use the web or cluster as the starting point in creating a linear outline or journal. This can be done by following various paths represented in the map. Based on the diagram above, for example, you could create an outline or an exploratory paragraph by filling in the connections between the circled ideas. The words that are highlighted in the following paragraph are the same words that are circled in the cluster above, showing one way you might incorporate these ideas into a more linear prose format:

For more tips on close reading and organizing your ideas, see *Rules for Writers*, pages 11–16.

Crane's story is about a **contest of will.** Crane examines the **will to fight** and the **will to survive**. The story shows how the contest of will is motivated or complicated by **instinct** and emotions like **rage** and **fear**, and how this contest of will is tied to human history. It also has more social or political connections like war. There is clearly a contest between **humans and animals** in the story, but where does the dog fit in? Rover seems more aligned with the man than the snake. What does this say about **history** and evolution? Crane brings everything together in an act of **violence**, when the man kills the snake.

Pushing the Limits of Close Reading

This chapter is primarily concerned with close reading a written text, a necessary process for many textual analysis assignments. However, as you will see in other chapters, not all texts are written texts, and not all close reading processes will follow the same pattern. In this chapter you work specifically with a short story, a poem, and a speech, but you can also close read a sculpture, a painting, a building, a street corner, an advertisement, a film, a sound recording or any other *text* that you choose to analyze. Sometimes the texts that provide us with the most helpful information about how society operates are the most mundane texts, texts out of everyday life. Although you cannot exactly annotate a street corner (or a film or a statue), you'll probably find that the way you must observe these non-written texts bears many similarities to what the readers do with "The Snake," "You're," and "I Have a Dream" in this chapter. Close reading *any* text requires you to pay close attention to it, to look at its minute details, to examine how it is constructed, to find its idiosyncrasies. Close reading demands that you find a way to engage with the text, to read actively. With a short story, this might mean you are annotating and idea-mapping. With a street corner, the process might involve walking around, standing in different locations, and looking under and behind shaded areas. Regardless of your text or your method, you will pause when you find something interesting and you will probe that interesting aspect of the text. You will write about it and, ultimately, make an argument about it.

In the *Guide* you'll find several in-depth discussions of other types of texts and other types of analysis. Chapter 8, for instance, explores visual and spatial analysis and film analysis. Chapter 10 will be useful as you practice different methods of rhetorical analysis. In Chapter 12, you'll find a discussion of how you analyze a literacy experience. It can also be helpful to think about the ways written texts are related to non-written texts. For example, "I Have a Dream" was delivered orally as a speech at the march on Washington in August of 1963. When you close read this speech on the page, you will notice certain characteristics. If you watch a video of the speech or listened to a recording you will probably notice something different. When reading the speech, you might

Visual mapping can help you articulate what you see a text doing, saying, and interrogating overall. When drafting a textual analysis essay, you would want to explore in more detail the "how" and "why" claims and questions articulated in such an inventory, using and discussing specific examples from the text to make your own statements about how the text works.

In the next section, Elizabeth Larakers demonstrates another writing tool that combines close reading and analysis, the writing journal. You may be asked to write journals about the texts that you read in your English classes. As you will see in the next section, these journals can be the perfect place to work out a potential thesis or argument about a text.

See "Chapter 8: Analysis" for more on writing a textual analysis essay. As shown in "Chapter 4: Writing as a Process," outlining and mapping are also useful techniques when drafting or revising your own essays.

not know that it ran more than fifteen minutes in length due to sustained applause throughout the delivery. Knowledge like this can complicate any understanding of a text by bringing new ideas for interpretation to the language of the text itself. Thinking about the performance of a text is just one way that you can push the limits of close reading beyond the words you see on the page.

Another way to push the limits of close reading is to experiment with the ways in which you interact with texts. This chapter provides several different close reading practices and strategies, but you may already have some practices that work well for you. Or you might try to develop your own blend or hybrid mix of close reading practices, but most importantly, don't be afraid to read a text in a new way. Trying out a new method to interact with the text can help you to stay engaged and focused throughout your active reading process.

You may want to try one of the following as a journal entry:

Close read a painting:

- What is depicted on the canvas?
- How are the figures arranged?
- What colors or shapes are used?
- What is the feeling or mood of the painting?
- What details in the painting help to create this mood?
- Does the painting suggest or infer anything?
- What details in the painting contribute to this suggestion or inference?

Or

Close read a sound recording:

- What types of sounds are included in this recording? (speech, music, noises, etc.)
- What is loud and what is quiet?
- Do you notice the speed or rhythm of the sounds?
- Are pauses or moments of silence part of the recording?
- Does the recording have a message? What is it?
- What details in the recording contribute to this message?

3.6 Journal Entry and Working Thesis on Sylvia Plath's Poem "You're"

By Elizabeth Larakers

Here's a sample journal entry and consequent working thesis that I wrote based on the annotations of Sylvia Plath's poem "You're," shown earlier in the chapter.

> When I first read this poem, it was really confusing. I didn't know what she was talking about or even what all her descriptions meant. The poem seemed to have a happy tone though, and I thought I could start to put together some of the lines to figure it all out. Each line was a description of something, and the title of the poem, "You're" made me think that maybe each line was like a clue to what the "you" was. The "you" was clownlike, upside-down ("feet to the stars"), mute, expected with anticipation ("looked for like mail"), far away, snug where it was, jumpy like a bunch of eels or a Mexican jumping bean, right and clean. Some of these things seemed to describe something human, some of them definitely not ("gilled like a fish"), some of them seemed to describe a place ("farther off than Australia"), and some of them seemed to maybe describe something abstract, like a feeling or emotion. I tried to think of what sort of thing would match or fulfill all of these descriptions without much success until I really started thinking about the line "oh high riser, my little loaf." I close read this to mean maybe that the thing (whatever it was) was growing, and could be likened to a loaf of bread that rises because of the yeast in it. And then I thought of the old saying "she's got a bun in the oven"—this saying usually means that a woman is pregnant.

The first paragraph really just strings together observations that I had while annotating the text. Remember that the annotations indicate how I noticed certain kinds of descriptions in the poem (images of sea creatures like fish, prawns, and eels, for instance, or kinds of emotions portrayed, like expectation). Just by trying to make logical sense of how these images could work together to mean something, I was able to come up with a tentative conclusion: that all the images could possibly describe a baby.

After coming up with this idea, I had to go back and test it against every line of the poem in order to make sure that my idea would be supportable in an essay. Notice that I am never totally sure about the interpretation, but I try to make it work; this feeling of uncertainty is productive because it forces me to look for proof of my interpretation in the text.

Certainly, babies make people happy, which could mean they're clownlike, they're upside-down in the mother's womb, they're wrapped up in themselves literally (in the fetal position), they're mute, and they're mute for nine months (from July 4th to April 1st). They're expected with great anticipation because everyone asks the mother when she's due, but they also seem really far away; they're jumpy, and they kick in the womb like eels or jumping beans, and finally, babies are new and clean and haven't made any mistakes yet, which means they have a clean slate on life.

Working Thesis: In "You're," Sylvia Plath describes a baby using a lot of nature symbols. She may use a lot of symbols that we wouldn't necessarily connect with babies, such as eels and gilled fishes, but the tone and word choice of the poem make it clear that her baby is a source of life just like all the other life on the planet is, and each source of life is portrayed as also a source of new hope for humanity.

Journal Entry vs. Working Thesis

The basic difference between the journal entry and the working thesis is that while the journal entry comes up with an interpretation of what the poem is *about*, the working thesis comes up with an argument about what the poem *means*. In the journal, I logically piece the poem together to discover its subject material, but in the working thesis, I came up with an idea about that subject material. By analyzing the word choice and tone that is used to describe the baby, I am able to make an argument that could be explored and proven in a paper. My central claim would be that the baby is a source of life and hope for the speaker of the poem, and the parts of the text highlighted in the annotations and discussed in the journal entry would provide the textual evidence for that claim.

For more on writing a working, or tentative, thesis, see *Rules for Writers*, pages 16–17.

4

Writing as a Process

4.1 Exploring the Possibilities of the Writing Situation

Writing can be a wonderfully (and sometimes painfully) messy process. Sometimes you feel in control and know what you want to say and how to put it down on paper. Other times you might feel as if your essay has somehow gotten away from you and you don't know how to get it back. More often than not, the writing process is a combination of both of these feelings. Student Alexander Chavez describes the challenge of getting started:

> When I write a lab report, I have all the data right in front of me. But when I write a draft for English, all the information is in my head and throughout the text, so it's a lot harder just to put it down on paper.

If you break down the writing process into stages, you can avoid feeling overwhelmed, as can happen when you try to think about everything from developing ideas to spelling words correctly at the same time. Additionally, if you divide the process up, you can hone your writing skills in a more focused way and improve the effectiveness of what you write. If you spend some time familiarizing yourself with the writing process, you will be better able to improve your writing and leave your composition courses feeling more confident in your ability to compose different types of assignments, regardless of whether these are analysis papers, lab reports, timed exams for history class, or letters to potential employers.

This chapter guides you through the process of composing an essay, showing you different ways to approach assignments. Keep in mind that everyone writes differently; some people quickly write a whole first draft and then begin revising, while others revise after writing each sentence or phrase. It could be that some strategies are more effective than others. You have to discover what works best for you, which will become the basis for your own writing process. Krystal Carillo explains how she discovered a new way of writing in her university writing classes:

> One of the many things you will learn in your English composition classes this year is not to be afraid to think outside of the box. I know when I first came here, I had this preset notion that essays had to be written a very particular way. I quickly found out that this wasn't true. Forget the strict guidelines you were taught in high school. Five paragraph essays are a rarity in college. Don't begin a paper thinking about what your teacher will want to hear.

> Also, be willing to talk to your teacher and classmates about your paper. I never thought workshopping a classmate's paper could be beneficial, but it allows you to see different writing styles and ideas, which could help you improve your writing. Although you will probably have to write a paper longer than four pages, numbers really aren't an issue. My class has been told that quality is better than quantity, something I've found to be very true. As long as you take an interest in what you're writing about and you have sufficient information to back it up, worrying about length shouldn't matter. I hope some of what I've said makes sense to you or at least calms some fears. The last piece of advice I have to give is to just go in with an open mind. The experiences you have are up to you.

For more information on considering your audience, refer to page 203.

As you gain more and more experience writing in varied areas of study, at work, and for public audiences, you'll realize how critical it is to carefully evaluate your specific **writing situation**. Considering your writing situation means that you ask yourself these questions: What **topic** do I want to share with my readers? Who will be my **readers** and **why**? What do they already **know** or **believe** about the topic, and what do I want them to understand about the topic? **How** am I going to **organize** and **develop** my ideas to make them convincing to these readers? Every time you write, you should consider your **rhetorical situation**, which includes the purpose, topic, audience, situation, and context for which you are writing. The rhetorical situation will affect the language, evidence, and tone that you develop, increasing the effectiveness of your writing because you can tailor it to each particular situation. In fact, you already consider differences in rhetorical situations when

Keyword:
rhetorical situation

you communicate with varied audiences on a daily basis. For example, if you were explaining why you need to work extra shifts, you might tell your supervisor about how expensive college is, and you might tell your friends about how you'd have extra money to do things with them. In communicating with different audiences on the same topic, we all try to develop lines of argument with the evidence that will be most convincing to each audience. As you move through the writing process, you will often make differing **rhetorical choices** based on your audience and your purpose. After you leave your writing class, you will be writing for varied purposes and audiences. To help you transfer what you learn in your writing classes to these writing situations, you should consider how different rhetorical situations affect how and what you write. Reflecting upon how your assumptions differ from your readers' can also help you reflect upon your own views and assumptions, analyze and critique others' views, and learn to communicate with others—no matter what you end up doing when you're out of school. Improving these skills will help you handle various academic tasks in your undergraduate studies and write more confidently and effectively in your future career or work in the community.

For more ideas on how to assess your writing/rhetorical situation, see *Rules for Writers*, pages 2–11 and "Chapter 10: Rhetorical Analysis."

Defining Your Purpose for Writing

Discovering your purpose for writing is essential because it largely determines other decisions you make in your writing process: what to include, how to include it, and what not to include. For example, for a persuasive essay, you might choose to argue that medical doctors should become more open-minded about treating the common cold using alternative medicines, like herbs (Echinacea), vitamins (Vitamin C), and minerals (zinc lozenges). If you decide your purpose is to influence Western doctors, you might write your essay as an editorial to doctors in *The New England Journal of Medicine*, structuring your argument in a way that a medical audience would find most convincing and using scientific studies and medical language. On the other hand, your purpose may be to refute an opinion cited in a *New York Times* article that criticized the "guru" of alternative medicine, Dr. Andrew Weil, and his treatments of the common cold. In this case, you might choose other persuasive strategies to make your point, perhaps telling a personal story of how Weil's treatments helped you. Each of these purposes dictates that you emphasize different aspects of the issue—each suggests a particular focus, audience, language, tone, organization, and persuasive strategies.

For more ideas about how to define your purposes for writing, see *Rules for Writers*, pages 6–8.

Audience and purpose play complex roles in the writing process. You might think that writing for your English class is a simple matter of telling your teacher what you think she or he wants to hear. However, you may find that writing effectively requires you to begin your writing for only yourself so that you can establish a personal stake in what you are writing. In writing classes, you will be collaborating with others on your writing, and you should find that these discussions of drafts give you a much more concrete sense of writing for real readers. Student Julie Espy's thoughts below reveal how her awareness of multiple audiences has changed since high school:

> Over the past year, I've stopped just writing what I think my teacher wants to see in my paper like I usually did in high school. I concentrate more on what I really want to say, how I want to say it, and doing it in a way that gets my point across. Keeping an open mind, and coming up with new ideas has allowed me to write some great papers. Having lots of other people read your paper is one of the best things you can do. It gives you different perspectives on your work, many of which you may not have thought of. You can incorporate other people's strengths to make your paper better, and strengthen your own writing skills in the process. This also allows you to see how your paper really does affect the audience you are presenting it to, not just how you think it will affect them.

Identifying Your Audience

For more ideas on how to think about audience, see *Rules for Writers*, pages 8–10 and 360–61.

Just as you need to have listeners to make a discussion into a conversation rather than a monologue, you need to have readers when you write. It is critical to *try* to know your audience and to be aware of their assumptions and expectations. Unless you can convince your audience that your ideas are worthwhile, your essay will not be effective. Unlike a conversation where you come face to face with your audience, you can't see your audience when you are writing. Therefore, in order to communicate effectively through writing, you have to imagine your audience. Try to see your readers (your audience) in your mind's eye:

- Who are they?

- How old are they?

- What are their sociopolitical and economic backgrounds?

- What position might they take on the issue you're addressing?

- What will they want to know from you?

- How can you best persuade them?

Then, keeping these questions in mind, try to address your readers as best as you can. UA student Angela Moore provides her thoughts on the importance of defining your audience:

> When you write, one of the most important steps is to consider your audience. If you don't consider your audience, you will end up with a paper that only you understand. To consider your audience is to know their needs and expectations so that you will include information they want to learn in a language they can understand.

As Angela's comments suggest, you need to consider your audience, purpose, and situation at various points in the writing process. For example, when you come to what seems like a dead end and you feel blocked, you may want to stop writing and take a minute to imagine that you were talking to your readers. What would you tell them? What would they find most interesting or unclear in your topic, and how would you make the topic clearer or more interesting? Imagining your reader's response is one strategy that you can use in the writing process.

For more information about the writing process, see *Rules for Writers*, pages 1–39.

Choosing Your Subject Matter

Every writing situation will limit the possibilities for what you may write. Read assignment sheets and talk to your instructor to get an idea of acceptable subject areas and then try to find something of interest to you and narrow the topic down to an issue you can address within the length of the assigned paper. One strategy for a textual analysis assignment, for example, is to choose a text you reacted to strongly, whether your reaction was positive or negative. If you had questions about a text, that text might be a good choice for a paper in which you can work out the answers to some of those questions. For a research project, one useful way to find ideas is to look into what others have written and said about a subject area that you are already interested in, such as alternative healthcare. Topics arise from personal experience, discussions with others, emotional response, and an awareness of the sites of conflict, debate, and discussion in the world. Explore the differences in how people are discussing a topic. Watch the news. Go to the library and look at the editorials or letters in a journal, or skim the tables of contents of books. Another option would be to make an appointment with a professional related to your field of inquiry. Ask him or her about issues that are currently being debated in his or her field. Your instructor might ask you to integrate primarily scholarly journals into a research paper, but you can still go on the Internet to various sites to investigate the many conversations surrounding your topic before you do more focused research.

For more discussion on choosing a topic for a research paper, see "Chapter 7: Research as Part of the Writing Process."

For more ideas on how to choose and explore your subject, see *Rules for Writers*, 11–16.

For more on choosing and exploring subjects for a research essay, see pages 382–85 in *Rules for Writers*.

In this chapter we break down the writing process into phases that will allow you to separate writing a paper into specific tasks that you can address in turn, without feeling overwhelmed by trying to do everything at once. The phases presented in this chapter—invention, imagination, focusing, drafting, and revision—can be approached as a step-by-step, linear process or as tools that can be used on an individual basis, as needed in your writing process.

4.2 Discovering Your Writing Process

Writers go through various stages as they move through the writing process: **inventing**, **focusing**, **drafting**, and **revising**. Writing would be much easier if the writing process were a simple matter of moving through these stages in a step-by-step way. Sometimes it is. Sometimes you may think up a topic and generate ideas for it. Then you draft and organize those ideas in an essay form, adjusting content as you revise. Finally, you read the essay over, add or delete a few sentences, and correct some spelling errors. You might have thought that all writers move through these stages sequentially, completing one and moving on to the next without looking back. However, writing is often more messy and less orderly. The writing process is **recursive**, meaning we move forward by looking backward at what we have already written to re-evaluate what we have said, make changes, and often think of new ideas as we look back at what we wrote. Thus, not all your ideas will come to you in the invention stage. Even experienced writers do not arrive at all their ideas before they write. David Rosenwasser and Jill Stephen describe this situation:

Keyword: recursive

> The common observation "I know what I want to say; I'm just having trouble getting it down on paper" is a half-truth at best. Getting words on paper almost always alters your ideas and leads you to discover thoughts you didn't know you had. If you expect to have all the answers before you begin to write, you are more likely to settle for relatively superficial ideas. And when you try to conduct all of your thinking in your head, you may arrive at an idea but not be able to explain how you got there (6).

Writers often read or write to brainstorm, then they read some more, talk to other people, begin drafting, decide to re-focus the essay, read some more, freewrite, write a new thesis statement, throw out huge sections of a paper and import new material, revise the new draft heavily, and finally proofread and edit. Consider how you wrote your last paper for a moment. Did you move in a step-by-step manner, or did you write in a more disorderly manner? Many of us write in a back and forth, recursive progression, but it is easy to feel lost or helpless when writing does not follow a neat, linear process. Just as you walk around with ever-changing, complex thoughts in your head, those thoughts will shift and remain complex and at times disorderly when you put them on paper. UA student Bob Pagek emphasizes the back-and-forth process of writing:

> The best advice I can think of is just to start writing. When you get an idea (even if you have no thesis developed), just sit down and write. Don't worry about anything like grammar, etc. Eventually you will have a few pages to read through and see what your ideas are pointing to. Write a conclusion and then turn it into an introduction and thesis. Then go back and cut and paste everything into a logical order. Then correct your grammar, etc. Now you almost have a completed paper. Read it a few times, add more to it, and ask others what they think. Make changes. Then, finally, you're done.

If you accept that the writing process is often messy and unclear, you may be able to be open to new ideas as you write and revise. Also, continue to keep in mind that writing is a multifaceted process that doesn't just magically happen when you sit down in front of your computer. It can start when you're walking across campus or shopping in the UA bookstore. You might see something outside or engage in a conversation with an acquaintance that leads to an idea about what you're writing about. You go home and write this down, but then later, as you're riding the CatTran or walking down 4th Avenue, you rethink what you wrote and decide to revise it again. Writing is a layered process and, as mentioned before, can be messy. Just don't get overwhelmed at the mess—relish it and continue to play with and revise your ideas as they come. Above all, don't think your ideas have to be perfectly worked out during the drafting stages. Writers who make the mistake of expecting a "perfect" draft often have trouble writing down any of their thoughts, and may end up forgetting many early insights that could have proved valuable. Remember: A draft can be incomplete and will often seem to be lacking a great deal, but that's to be expected.

In addition, different writers have distinct writing habits that also dictate how they write. Lisa Ede, a scholar in composition studies, has identified four basic trends among writers:

Heavy Planners. These writers "generally consider their ideas and plan their writing so carefully in their heads that their first drafts are often more like other writers' second or third drafts. As a consequence they often revise less intensively and frequently than other [writers]. Many [heavy planners] have disciplined themselves so that they can think about their writing in all sorts of places—on the subway, at work, in the garden pulling weeds, or in the car driving to and from school" (32).

Heavy Revisers. These writers "need to find out what they want to say through the act of writing itself. [. . .] Heavy revisers often state that writing their ideas out in a sustained spurt of activity reassures them that they have something to say and helps them avoid frustration. These writers may not seem to plan because they begin drafting so early. Actually, however, their planning occurs as they draft and especially as they revise. Heavy revisers typically spend a great deal of their writing time revising their initial drafts. To do so effectively, they must be able to read their work critically and be able [. . .] to discard substantial portions of the first draft" (32–33).

Sequential Composers. These writers "devote roughly equal amounts of time to planning, drafting, and revising. [. . .] [S]equential composers typically rely on written notes and plans to give shape and force to their ideas. And unlike heavy revisers, sequential composers need to have greater control over form and subject matter as they draft" (33). These writers often slowly squeeze out paragraph after paragraph, rereading and revising as they draft, working from outlines, planning ahead.

Procrastinators. Although we all occasionally procrastinate, the group Ede labels as "procrastinators" are people who habitually delay writing anything until they can only write a final draft. They might wait until the night before the paper is due to begin; therefore, they only have time to scribble out one draft and maybe, if they are lucky, to proofread it before handing it in (36). Procrastinators may justify their process by claiming that they work well under a deadline, but they have rarely explored alternative approaches. If you are a procrastinator, you might be surprised at how much your writing improves through multiple drafts.

Does any of this sound familiar? You might find that you exhibit a combination of the above approaches or even undergo a different process depending on whether you're writing an essay for a history class or a summary of a lab experiment. The important thing here is not to pinpoint exactly what kind of writer you are but to recognize your general tendencies and consider the advantages and disadvantages of your approach. When might other writing processes be more helpful? You'll benefit from knowing your own writing habits. For example, if you know you're mostly a heavy planner or a heavy reviser, you can look more carefully at the specific writing strategies suggested in those areas to expand your ways of planning or revising. In addition, you can deliberately work to develop new writing strategies. That way, if your usual method ever fails you, you'll have another option for how to proceed.

- What type of writer do you consider yourself to be?

- Does your writing process include several of the above approaches? If so, which ones?

- Does your writing process seem to be successful? What are your strengths and weaknesses?

- Do you think it might be beneficial for you to try a different approach? What might you do?

Works Cited

Ede, Lisa. *Work in Progress: A Guide to Writing and Revising*. New York: St. Martin's Press, 1992. Print.

Rosenwasser, David, and Jill Stephen. *Writing Analytically*. Fort Worth, TX: Harcourt Brace College Publishers, 1997. Print.

4.3 Invention Strategies

The process of writing begins even before writing begins. Perhaps you have heard the term "**prewriting**." This is the stage that generally involves thinking about your writing situation, exploring possible topics to write about, choosing a topic, generating ideas about the topic, researching the topic, and outlining the essay. Depending on the type of essay you are assigned to write, or depending on the kind of writer you are, one or more of these steps might not be part of your prewriting process. For example, if your instructor gives you a topic to write about, you don't need to choose the topic, or if you're writing a personal, reflective essay, you probably won't need to do research. Invention can happen anywhere—not just when you're at your desk and in the mindset to write. A lot of this might go on in your head, so pay attention to your ongoing thoughts about your topic so that you can remember them later on when you are drafting. Neil Galassi, a student at the University of Arizona, reflects upon how important the choice of topic is to the writing process:

Keyword: prewriting

> Out of all the essays I composed, the ones that yielded better grades were those that dealt with topics I could develop genuine interest in. The more I liked a topic, the more willing I was to do necessary research and revision for my paper. Also, the more interesting my topic was, the more helpful were the comments I would receive from others. The bottom line is that it was my paper so that it should be a topic of my own choice. This made the whole process much easier.

Generating Ideas about Your Topic

After a preliminary assessment of your rhetorical situation, you need to start generating ideas for your topic and testing your assumptions or preconceived notions about your topic, purpose, audience, and organization. Here are some of the strategies many experienced writers use to generate ideas.

Learning journals are also known as writers' notebooks because they are the notebooks that writers use to jot down ideas at any time. Your instructor might assign specific journal entries to help you find a topic or a focus for an essay. You might also use your journal for other purposes. For example, you could use it to record your responses to the assigned readings. For that purpose you would pick passages from the readings that spark your interest, quote them, and discuss why they struck you as important. You could also use your journal to write down memories, observations, and passing thoughts that are relevant to your writing assignments. Many writers find that jotting down their random thoughts on a topic helps them get through the most intimidating phase of the writing process: sitting down and beginning to write when your mind is as blank as the page in front of you. If you write your thoughts in your journal throughout the semester, you can leaf through it as you search for a point of entry into an analysis of a text or use it to help you define the issues you find compelling enough to explore further in an essay.

For a sample journal entry, please see "Chapter 3: Close Reading and Interacting with the Text," page 66.

Freewriting is designed to trick your unconscious into shaking loose some ideas by turning off the critical editor in your head that often causes writer's block. It works like this: Set yourself an amount of time—say five or fifteen minutes—and write nonstop for that period. Don't go back and fix your spelling or grammar. Don't pause—barely lift your pen from the paper or your fingers from the keyboard. If you don't know what to write, then just write, "I don't know what to write" until another idea comes into your head. Don't reread until you have finished. If you keep freewriting, you might stumble into some interesting territory. Try freewriting not only at the beginning of the brainstorming process but any time you can't figure out what comes next as you write your first draft or anytime you need to clarify an explanation or illustration you're having trouble getting just right. If this is the case, try freewriting on a separate piece of paper or on a new screen so that you won't feel like you need to keep what you've written. You'll find new words and new ideas, and you'll likely be refreshed. Freewriting can be very helpful for many students, as Holly Coleman found out:

> During this course, we get to write a lot of freewriting. This is helpful because you can say whatever you want. Doing a lot of freewriting makes writing itself less terrifying. And even though I listen to others' journal entries and feel stupid compared to their brilliance, I feel more confident. For journal

entries we don't have to worry about spelling or grammar, which allows me to focus solely on my thoughts and ideas and to build courage without having to harp on my ignorance.

Looping is a variation of freewriting: You review what you've produced in a freewriting exercise, circle some phrases or words that interest you, and use them as the starting point for another round of freewriting. You can continue looping until you've focused on an idea you want to pursue.

Brainstorming is where you list any idea that comes to mind. As with freewriting and looping, you need to find a way to turn off your critical voice as you create a list of possible topics. The main rule here is not to criticize your ideas while you construct your list. Rather, push yourself to write as many ideas as possible. As you get closer to writing, you may find that ideas you had previously discarded seem more interesting or doable, or you may find a way to combine aspects of two or more ideas.

Talking is a very useful invention strategy. It is especially effective in helping you deal with a blank screen. Often you think of an idea in your head over and over again, but you just don't know how to put it on paper. When this happens, you might want to talk about it with imagined readers or your instructor, classmates, or any friend who is willing to listen. Jessica Burger, a current student, attests to the usefulness of talking as a prewriting strategy:

> Talking over my ideas is a very useful strategy for me. In the beginning of the semester, I went to my English teacher to tell him a very broad topic I had for the personal narrative essay. After hearing me with care, he showed me the many themes of my story and helped me focus on and develop one of them for my essay. Our subsequent conversations helped my paper stay focused and well structured.

Clustering is also called **mapping** or **webbing**. It is a more visual invention technique in which you place a significant word at the center of a piece of paper. Then you brainstorm by adding words or phrases that relate to the original word. Draw lines among them and circle these. As you draw visual links among related ideas, consider what idea or fact links those ideas, and write down terms or details that form those links. Continue attaching words and phrases to any of the circles on the diagram. When you're done, your page will look like a web filled with bubbles. Your webbing will represent a mapping of the concepts and relations that are important in your topic. This conceptual mapping can be very useful if you are a visual learner who sometimes gets lost in trying to find the right word for an idea. Think about the links between the bubbles as important sites for writing to take place.

For more on clustering, please see "Chapter 3: Close Reading and Interacting with the Text," page 63.

You have some important ideas written down in words; now your job is to articulate the connections between those ideas.

Web that Explores Cloning

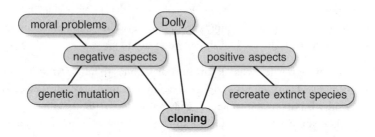

Student LeAnne Alcorn likes webbing for the following reasons:

My favorite brainstorming activity is webbing because of its complete simplicity. I begin with my main idea, and in a mad rush, I scribble down all kinds of thoughts that describe that idea. I then start to expand on those thoughts and continue this same process until I can no longer think. I end up with some very useful ideas and a wonderful web that shows all of my ideas are related.

Asking key questions is a common technique that a reporter might use when investigating a story. These questions include the five W's that enable a journalist to get the crucial details for a story: *who, what, where, when,* and *why*. A reporter may then ask a sixth question to deepen his or her sense of what happened: *how* did the event occur? Using these questions will help you consider a topic from various angles. For example, consider how the following basic questions might apply to a novel such as *Harry Potter*:

1. Who is the author? Who are the main characters? Who are the primary and secondary audiences? Who might have influenced J.K. Rowling's writing of this novel?

2. What are the important plot points? What happens to the main character? What happened to the author before, during, and after writing the novel?

3. Where does the novel take place and what do we learn by comparing and contrasting the different settings?

4. When did Rowling write the novel? When does it take place? Are there contemporary connections with events and themes in today's world?

5. Why does Harry take such risks against his powerful enemies? Why do some people identify with his character while others find him annoying?

6. How did Rowling come up with these characters and this storyline? How does the novel reflect the cultural characteristics of the time in which it was written? How does the novel invite us to reflect on social issues such as inequalities of race, class, and gender?

As you can see, these questions move from description to analysis, allowing you to consider multiple aspects of a text or topic. You could use the same technique with topics such as stem-cell research or restrictions on street-lights in Tucson. After being assigned an essay, what steps will you take to begin generating some idea of what you will write about? You may want to try several approaches in order to determine which will be most successful. Consider which techniques you want to try first.

For more examples of prewriting strate-gies, see *Rules for Writers*, pages 11–16.

4.4 Invention and the Imagination

By Ben Ristow

Writing is an act of the imagination and perhaps one of the best ways for us humans to interact with real and invented worlds. The act of writing always begins in nowhere, in the void of the blank page, and arrives (hopefully) at somewhere, and what is made visible on the page becomes a small testament to our experience as creatures of a special gift. You have heard about various techniques in evaluating your rhetorical situation, invention strategies, and sage advice from fellow students about coming to speak on the page, but the imagination is valued ground we have yet to speak of, and perhaps one of the most indispensable gifts you must cultivate as writers.

Do you remember how when you were five years old and you told your parents there was a black bear in the front yard who was flinging herself about on your favorite tire swing? It was a June morning, and your parents had not yet had their coffee, and inevitably, they told you to quit being so silly and finish your Cheerios. If you were luckier though, one of your parents asked you how big this particular bear was, where it strolled in from, or if you really wanted to ask the bear to dance with you after breakfast. Bears are dangerous, and presumably characters for youngsters to avoid, but what is more hazardous is to stifle the engine of the imagination once it starts to hum. We might think that the imagination is what leaks out of our ears as we age or that it is the particular mental turf of one kind of writer or another. Is it only the poets who imagine? Only fourth graders in Miss Duncan's class? The imagination, if I may speak candidly on its behalf, does not always like to be told what-how-where-when-why to do something, but it also must be a crucial faculty to nourish (or itch) as your writing process develops.

During the process of invention and drafting, my students often get stopped before they begin. The classic student question goes something like "How do we know what to write about?" The question is honest to be sure, but it assumes the teacher has something for you to write about that will please them, and whether your instructor gives you less or more room to come up with a writing topic, you will find it better and more gratifying to generate your own imaginative questions. What has begun to interest you as a Planetary Sciences major? How do Martin Luther King Jr. and Malcolm X's rhetoric differ? Why would Shakespeare include all those fools in his plays? Imagining questions that seem irresistible to you and your imagination will give you the momentum to write further and with greater devotion.

As you begin writing and drafting, it is often instinctual to write once through and leave that essay well enough alone, but if you keep the imagination on board, you know that the introductory paragraph (for instance) can always be re-imagined with different detail, voice, audience, or purpose. Allowing the imagination to function fully is to realize that it is not often satisfied with the first or second way of saying something. More often the imagination likes to move fluidly through your essay, and by focusing your imagination on particular tasks, such as honing a new introductory paragraph or finding a better voice to reach your audience, you will avoid the sporadic or superficial cosmetic revisions that tend to bog down the early stages of the writing process.

Rewriting and rearranging your words around the new ideas your imagination discovers in the process of writing requires the mental flexibility and fluidity of an ocean fish. It is easy to keep the first word or the first sentence as it darts through your mind, but it often helps to pause to entertain the larger movements and sheen of larger fish as they jet across your brain or try to hover toward the bottom and just out of sight. Pausing to hunt can become procrastination, so it is important to swim while you look for words and concepts you wish to communicate. Writing creates imagination in the process of production and revision, and it acts as the stimulation that triggers the waterfall of words or the prickle that forms on your neck when you see a profound work of art. Imagination requires no particular training, it can be flexed like a muscle, it can be hummed like a poem, or it can be bent like a tool to your latest writing task.

4.5 Focusing

Outlining is another strategy many writers use when writing an essay—*after* generating ideas but *before* writing a first draft. An outline does not have to be divided up into elaborate divisions to be a useful writing tool at those points when you have many ideas that can go in multiple directions or if you're having a hard time focusing on one aspect of a single issue. An outline will help you organize all your relevant thoughts. This will allow you to reconsider some of your points or examples and get rid of irrelevant or insignificant points before you present the essay as a rough draft to your instructor. Traditionally, an outline looks like the table of contents of a book and includes brief points representing different parts of an essay. The main parts of an outline are generally the same, but the contents will change depending on the type of essay you're writing. Below, you'll find a sample outline for a text-in-context essay, but this is only one way to outline an essay. Depending on the assignment your instructor requires, you might need to change its structure and content.

For more information about outlining, see *Rules for Writers*, pages 17–20.

ESSAY OUTLINE TEMPLATE

Note that this simply shows how an outline may be constructed: An actual outline will include information that specifies the content of the text you are breaking down.

Introduction
- Draw readers into the essay, using a hook.
- Introduce the text—**summarize** and explain its significance.
- Introduce the context.
- Present your focus—include a **thesis statement** that encapsulates your argument about the text and how it reflects the context you're focusing on.

Body
- **Point 1** → Give your first argument about how the text informs a certain context.
  - **Illustration** → Give examples from the text that show how you reached your point.
  - **Explanation** → Give examples from outside sources that show the accuracy of the point you made; support your illustrations with research.
  - **Connection** → Reiterate the connection between the text and the context you're focusing on, clarifying the connection between your thesis and the point.
- **Point 2 (same order as Point 1).**
- **Point 3 (same order as Point 1).**
- **Point 4 (same order as Point 1).**

Conclusion
- Paraphrase your thesis, emphasizing the text-and-context connection; make a connection to the larger world.

A variation on outlining, especially if you're a "heavy reviser" and need to write to discover your ideas, is to try writing an outline *after* you've written a draft. Experiment with both forms of outlining and see which method works best for you.

For more strategies on outlining, please see "Chapter 3: Close Reading and Interacting with the Text."

Keep in mind that, as mentioned above, the points you have in the outline, the organizational structure of your essay, and the content of the paper depend on the expectations of each type of essay and your instructor. Writing teachers might have different perspectives on how you should approach the writing assignment, and might emphasize different elements of an essay such as content, organization, and voice. Therefore, be sure to find out what your teacher expects you to do with the assignment.

4.6 Drafting

Once you've generated some ideas for your topic and perhaps prepared an outline, you begin writing the first draft. How you draft depends very much on your preferred writing style. "Heavy Planners" and "Sequential Composers" might take time to outline their essays before they begin drafting. "Heavy Revisers," on the other hand, might blast through the introduction quickly, knowing that they will return to it later. Their goal is to get words on the page—any words at all—and to follow their thinking as fast as possible to see where they are going. They leave blank spaces or notes to themselves if they cannot think of a proper word. They might even skip the introduction altogether and begin the essay in the middle.

Similarly, some writers might view their first paragraphs differently early in the writing process. "Heavy Planners" and "Sequential Composers" might spend a great deal of time on the introductory paragraph before moving on. They might see the introduction as the final stage in their planning process: as they compose that opening paragraph, they figure out what they wish to say and set out a potential order for the rest of the essay. Therefore, they spend time evaluating their words, determining if they agree with what they have said, and deciding if they want to pursue the ideas that the introduction suggests.

Some writers might feel daunted by the blank page or screen and experience writer's block, even if they have a detailed outline. Beginning is often the toughest part. In that case, just start writing your opinion or idea, keeping in mind that you can always go back and revise to meet the needs of your readers. This approach is like freewriting. Don't worry about getting it right! Once you've begun, your ideas might come faster. Then go back and get rid of the first few sentences, revising toward a better introduction. Technology makes the writing process much easier—you can always hit delete, so don't worry if you're not completely satisfied with the words on the page while you're drafting. You can also save multiple drafts of your essay, trying out different organizational patterns, key points, or tones. Some writers find it helpful to print out a draft and read it on paper to see what works best. You may even decide to integrate a few of your drafts to complete your final essay. Also, if you need some direction about where to go with your essay, don't forget that your instructor welcomes you in office hours.

Regardless of your writing habits, remain flexible as you write. Be wary of locking yourself into a set outline—unless you're short on time. Instead, give yourself permission to go back and rework earlier sections if, halfway through your writing, you discover a new angle or a better approach.

For more information about drafting your essay, see *Rules for Writers*, pages 20–27.

Drafting a Thesis Statement

The thesis statement is the "writer's declaration of what the paper is about" (Fulwiler and Hayakawa 108) and reveals the focus of the paper. The writer presents readers with the basic argument through the thesis, which generally appears in the introductory paragraph and is usually one or two sentences.

For more ideas on how to draft a thesis statement, see *Rules for Writers*, pages 21–24 and 411–12.

Although a thesis statement usually occurs in the introduction, it's not always written, at least not clearly, in the first draft of the introduction. Some writers need to start drafting with a clear argument, or thesis, in mind. Others might have a vague notion of their argument and should just start writing. They may end up writing the thesis after they have completed a draft and then they will use the thesis to help them focus paragraphs on points that are related to their thesis. Regardless, by the time you've reached the end of your first or second or maybe third draft, you'll likely have a much clearer idea of what your essay is trying to accomplish. Instructors often find the best-expressed thesis statements hidden in conclusions. The key is to be aware of this part of the writing process and to be ready to rewrite what you thought was your thesis. Then make sure your thesis matches the body of the essay. It can be easy to get distracted by writing a beautifully declared, clear thesis statement. Just make sure it matches what you actually argue in the body of your essay.

Two students, Vanessa Lopez and Bethany Bell, share how they approach the development of a thesis in different ways. Vanessa feels that "When writing a first draft of a paper, it's easier for me to start the body and then develop a thesis at the end," but Bethany says, "For me, it is much easier to develop a good thesis and essay by writing the intro first. There I jot down my thesis and some main ideas I want to cover." Be open to the idea that as you write and revise, you might change your mind about an issue. You might need to narrow your thesis because you have too much information to include in one short essay, or you might change your focus altogether. Modifying your thesis is a normal part of writing, but you might need to discuss the change with your instructor, depending on how close you are to the final deadline. Keep in mind that if you cannot identify the main idea of your essay, your readers will have the same difficulty, and they will conclude that you needed to think through your thesis more carefully.

It is important to remember, however, that thesis statements vary depending on the type of essay you're writing. For example, in a researched essay intended to persuade an academic audience, you generally need an argumentative thesis that clearly states your point of view on the issue. For a reflective essay, on the other hand, you might not need such an explicit kind of thesis; you might develop your ideas so that they work toward a unified theme throughout your essay, or you might choose to state your thesis in a less explicit way until you have laid out your evidence. The reason for this may be because you believe that your readers will not accept your viewpoint until you have provided evidence for it since they have a different perspective on the issue. However, remember that readers may misunderstand your point unless you state your thesis statement clearly. Your instructor will clarify what to expect in each writing situation. But for many academic essays, readers expect a clear, direct thesis statement by the end of the introduction to help guide them through your essay.

To check the effectiveness of your thesis statement, Fulwiler and Hayakawa suggest that you think about the following questions:

- **Is it interesting?** An informational thesis should answer a question that is worth asking; for example, *What tricks do advertisers use to mislead the public?* or *In Amy Tan's short story "Mother Tongue," what does the relationship between the narrator and her mother reveal about those characters' society and environment?* An argumentative thesis should take a position on a debatable issue and should include a proposal for change: *Mountain bikes should be allowed on wilderness trails.* The thesis for a reflective essay might provide an especially thoughtful way of approaching a topic without stating a definite conclusion on the issue; for example, *I have never understood why my parents got divorced, but I have come to understand that it was not my fault.*

- **Is it precise and specific about what is at issue?** You can sharpen your understanding of the thesis by stating what the issue is as exactly as you see it. For instance, consider how much more effective it might be to argue that mountain bikes should have more access to specific wilderness trails rather than to argue that they should have more access to the wilderness in general. Often you can make a thesis more specific by introducing qualifications that acknowledge your readers' concerns: *Nobody wants to be run down by a wilderness bike on a narrow trail, but if mountain bikers were given access to designated trails, hikers would know when to look out for mountain bikers.*

- **Is it manageable?** You may have collected more information than you can actually write about. If necessary, take this opportunity to narrow both the thesis and the paper you expect to write, often by making it more precise or by adding qualifiers that specify what sorts of cases you are considering.

- **Does it adequately reflect my research and the expected shape of my paper?** Your thesis should explain all of the examples and evidence that you researched. Instead of ignoring facts or examples that complicates your claim, you should revise it to better explain that information.

Read the following thesis statements. Indicate which ones seem to be the strongest and weakest and why. Try reworking the samples below to better match the criteria outlined above.

1. Hemingway's story "A Clean, Well-Lighted Place" serves as a metaphor for loneliness and old age.

2. Television news presents an exaggerated view of violence in today's society.

3. "The Yellow Wallpaper" by Charlotte Perkins Gilman challenges patriarchy.

4. Many advertisements for alcoholic beverages employ images that are degrading toward women.

5. Colleges and universities should eliminate letter grades and instead evaluate each student on a pass/fail basis.

Paragraph Development

Paragraph breaks are important because they signal to readers where one idea ends and another begins. A single body paragraph should have a single main idea. You have likely been taught that each body paragraph needs a *topic sentence*—that is, one sentence that states the main point of the paragraph, but keep in mind that the topic sentence does not necessarily need to be the first sentence, since you might need a transition or introductory sentence to move into your point. Every other sentence in the paragraph should be related to that single main idea developing, illustrating, or defining the point.

For more information on developing effective paragraphs, see *Rules for Writers*, pages 39–57.

PIE is a mnemonic device to help writers remember how to develop a paragraph successfully. It is an *acronym*, a word made up of the first letters of other words, such as NOW for the National Organization for Women. PIE stands for Point, Illustration, and Explanation. PIE is a helpful way to think about paragraph development, especially for analysis essays and persuasive arguments. However, PIE is not the only way to develop a paragraph. Other methods of paragraph organization include examples and illustrations, narration, description, comparison and contrast, analogy, cause and effect, classification and division, and definition.

The following section created by Dr. Anne-Marie Hall, a professor in the UA English department, discusses the important features of a PIE paragraph.

PIE (Point, Illustration, Explanation) Structure

PIE refers to the structure of well-written paragraphs that provide full coverage of the single topic each individual paragraph should address. In academic writing, in particular, each paragraph should address *one* point.

Readers should be able to identify the separate points that you are making, but they should also realize that the points are cohesive—they cannot be teased apart or else the whole purpose of the paper is weakened. That is, readers should be able to notice the **point**, the **illustration**, and the **explanation** for themselves, but they should also be able to understand what it all means by seeing how each works together to make and express a single, coherent idea.

Point

This is the topic sentence of the paragraph. It is one of the claims you've identified as supporting your essay's primary argument, or thesis. Your essay should consist of a number of such supporting claims. Each topic sentence should be one of the first two or three sentences in any paragraph. It should cover the whole paragraph—everything the paragraph does will relate to this point. Any information that doesn't go under this point belongs in a different paragraph. Remember: one paragraph = one point!

Illustration

This is the best textual evidence you have to support your paragraph's point. It's the part of the PIE that consists of needed evidence such as another author's ideas and language, your own personal experiences and ideas, or a combination of the two. You can provide such evidence in the form of direct quotations, paraphrases, summaries, personal narratives, or a combination of these. You need to give your readers as much textual or personal evidence as appropriate to *show* your point. Remember the saying, "Don't merely *tell* me, *show* me what you mean." Also, remember to be consistent; stick to making *one* point.

Explanation

This is *your* reasoning of the connection between the point and the illustration(s), and it is how you connect your purpose in the paragraph to the goal of the paper as a whole. Without it, your point can easily be misunderstood or be ambiguous. Therefore, make sure you take ample time to give readers your detailed insight into the text you are dealing with by explaining the point and illustration(s) you make. Don't leave your reader guessing what you might mean. You must convince readers that you understand your own point, how your illustration(s) support it, and how both relate to your essay's thesis.

Part of creating a PIE paragraph is integrating sources correctly. If you use PIE, your paragraph is more likely to contain the following elements, as illustrated in the boxed example below, written by English 102 student J.T. Sand:

Another tactic that Michael Moore uses is interviewing people who have been affected by American health insurance companies. First, he talks to people who have been hurt by the system. *For example, he interviews a woman who was denied payment for being "too young to have cervical cancer" at age twenty-two (Moore).* By connecting the viewers to the people who have been through the harsh realities of flawed healthcare, Moore captures the emotions of the viewers and campaigns for a change in this corrupt system.

◄— Point

◄— Illustration

◄— Explanation

Remember, for MLA in-text citation, you normally need, in parentheses, the *author's last name* and the *page number* the cited material came from—unless you mention the author in your signal phrase. **You *must* use in-text citation for direct quotations, paraphrases, and summaries.** Basically, if you're using information that isn't your own original idea and isn't general, well-known public information, you must cite it both in the text and in your works cited. In the previous example, because the writer is referencing a film, no page number is given, but using the PIE structure tells the reader where the information came from and helps to maintain the flow of the writing.

For more information about paraphrasing, summarizing, quoting, and integrating and documenting sources, see *Rules for Writers*, pages 415–63.

Once you have mastered the PIE paragraph, which is an excellent paragraph model in any academic argument, your instructor may encourage you to experiment with other types of paragraphs.

Work Cited

Fulwiler, Toby and Alan R. Hayakawa. *The Blair Handbook*. Upper Saddle River, NJ: Prentice Hall, 1997. Print.

4.7 Revision

Revising is the last stage in the process that we'll cover in this chapter. It's not last because it is the least important phase in writing but because you have to have something written to revise. In fact, it's so important that we devote an entire chapter to discussing revision, so we'll be brief here and just introduce this stage in the process. Revisions can be divided into **global** changes in the overall organization and development and **local** revisions such as editing a particular sentence. We'll discuss this distinction in the following chapter, but you need to understand that revision is about more than just "fixing" your paper after it's written—it goes much further than such local revisions as correcting spelling mistakes or comma errors. Revising is something that you'll want to do throughout the writing process—you can revise your ideas, your focus and your writing again and again. As student Greta Bauer learned, multiple revisions of a particular essay can be particularly helpful:

For more information about revising your essay, see *Rules for Writers*, pages 27–39.

> The Writing Center guided me through my first semester. I went there for every paper, more than once, which is the key. When you think your paper is perfect go again, because there is always going to be something that you missed. Correcting your paper as many times as possible is the golden key to getting the grade that you want.

Revision means to "see again," to re-envision, your work-in-progress in order to assess how well it conveys your purpose for your audience. Revision is probably the most critical, but most underrated part of the writing process. To revise your essay is to ask yourself questions like these: "What is my essay really saying?", "What do my readers really need to understand to accept my thesis?", "Have I supported my points with enough details?", "Are there any sections where I have lost my focus on the thesis? If so, do I need to freewrite more or conduct more research to link those paragraphs to my thesis?" A crucial step in revising is to establish enough distance from your work to enable you to distinguish what you intended to say from what you actually wrote. This ability is basic to being able to re-envision your essay, and it's a difficult skill even for experienced writers. One technique is to read your essay out loud to yourself, rather than just reading silently on the computer screen or the printed page. Another technique is to put the essay aside for a period of time—a few days or at least several hours—so you can return to it with fresh eyes. Unfortunately, however, given the time constraints in most college classes, finding this kind of time is difficult. Fortunately, you can rely on people other than yourself and your instructor—your peers. The next chapter about using feedback will give you guidelines for how to give feedback to peers and how to use the feedback you receive. In addition to peer feedback, you should also strengthen your own ability to re-envision your writing. We continue this discussion about revision in the next chapter.

5
Re-Visioning Your Work

5.1 Feedback, Peer Review, and Revision: An Overview

Feedback and assessment from your peers and instructor will help you to identify areas that could be improved by revisions. You might consider the revision process in terms of large and small revisions, or **global** and **local** revisions. Let's start with what local revision means. When you read carefully back over your work to check for grammar mistakes, misplaced punctuation marks, or awkward sentences, you are revising your paper locally. Another way to think about this basic type of revision is to see it as revising the *surface* of your paper. If you haven't read your persuasive essay in a few weeks and then pick it up again, you'll probably see it through fresh eyes and find sentences to rearrange, vague adjectives to enliven, weak verbs to strengthen, grammar mistakes to address, and so forth. At the very least, you should perform multiple surface revisions of any paper you turn in for a grade, as even small errors can reflect the overall presentation of your work. Such local changes are necessary, but they are still just a form of editing.

Your instructor will require you to go beyond local revisions to reexamine your ideas and your expression on a more *global* level. This is when others' feedback really comes into play—your peers and instructor can assess your writing to offer a fresh perspective on how your paper works overall. Think about global-level revisions as whole-document revisions, where you might even rewrite large parts of your paper. In global revising, the writer reconsiders the ideas put forth in her thesis, as well as how these ideas are articulated

Keywords:
local and global revision

For more advice about and examples of global and local revision, see *Rules for Writers*, pages 27–39.

and arranged throughout the essay. Some paragraphs might need more developments, others might need to be entirely rewritten, and others need to be removed altogether. When you revise your paper globally, it will end up looking quite different from when you started. An example of global revision would be to reorganize your paragraphs to bring related points together to build a stronger line of argument. Global revision means to re-envision your essay to consider its organizational pattern, tone, depth of analysis, and use of examples, and how these components contribute to the overall success of your essay. Also known as *deep* revision, this level of revision may mean that you completely *rewrite* your paper based on the exploration of your ideas in the first draft. You may discover that you create a point and thesis at the end of the paper and need to start there, deleting all of the previous work. Don't get hung up on the terminology of different levels of revision. Rather, try to understand the difference between *minor* editing for sentence-level mistakes such as comma splices and *more significant* revisions, such as writing a completely new introduction to better appeal to your target audience. You'll learn about these differences in class and will have ample time to practice different types of revision.

It is helpful to always keep in mind that your first draft won't be your final draft. Neither will your second or "final" drafts be truly final. Throughout the revision process, the feedback you receive from teachers and peers will help you develop your ideas, improve your evaluation of the writing situation, and organize your texts to fit your purpose and audience. You will not only get feedback in various ways from your instructor, peers, tutors, and other readers, but you'll also *give* feedback to your classmates. This is important for many reasons. First, the feedback that you give and receive can offer a fresh perspective to a draft, which is essential because oftentimes writers are too close to their own work and already understand what they are trying to say. Respondents will be able to tell the writer what does and does not make sense to them. Furthermore, the process of giving and getting feedback is also the process of assessment. As a writer, you will develop your skills in assessing effective writing through the process of looking at your own drafts and your peers' drafts. You will also develop the assessment skills necessary to evaluate the peer feedback that you received, making critical choices about what you need to incorporate in order to best serve the purpose of your essay. Finally, this process of reconsidering, assessing, and revising will aid you in the recursive practices of writing, from making decisive choices early in the process to understanding audience responses and needs.

You will encounter many perspectives during your revision process (peer, instructor, writing center responders, tutors, and so on), and there is no "perfect" process. Part of the challenge of this class is finding a revision process that works for you. Small group work will assist in the revision process—peer feedback is an excellent way to get a new look at your paper. You will also receive feedback from your instructor, either in the form of written comments or in face-to-face group or individual conferences. It's important to remember that revision does not first take place after you've finished your essay. Rather, revision is an *ongoing* process. Never be afraid to rewrite complete paragraphs, revising so much that you might not even recognize the new paragraph as stemming from the old one. Sometimes you may need to delete and rewrite whole sections of your paper if you find that you are not actually saying what you intended to say. It's tempting to want to leave the draft as is because you've done the work and want to be finished, but your success in first-year writing as well as in future writing will depend, in part, on your willingness to revisit your essays multiple times and consider angles that need to be rewritten to get your point across to your readers.

There are many ways to provide feedback—some of them described below—and your instructor will have his or her variation on these activities. The different ways you'll likely receive feedback are written or oral comments from your instructor, small-group **peer review**, conferences with peers and your instructor, and whole-class reviewing or **workshopping**. We also strongly encourage you to seek additional feedback from the Writing Center, the Writing Skills Improvement Program, and the University Tutoring Center. Below, we have included experiential advice from former first-year writing students:

You can find the contact information for the Writing Center, WSIP, and other resources in Appendix A.

- **On time management:** I think the main reason I was successful in English 101 was that I always finished drafting my papers a few days before they were due. This helped lift all the stress off my heart. Then, I would re-read my papers over and over again. Every time I reread my paper, I made changes in the text. I was not a great writer by any means, but being ahead of time helped me succeed. —*Nick Vaughn, student*

- **On the benefits of reading aloud to revise:** I find it very useful to read each draft of my essay out loud before turning in the final draft. That way I can listen to certain phrases that might not make sense and paragraphs that don't flow. —*Bethany Bell, student*

- **On the writing process:** I always thought writing draft after draft of a paper, and the whole revising process, was a huge waste of my time. I have a good foundation in composition, and I thought my first draft would be just as good as a final draft. I never wrote first drafts, second drafts, or final drafts. It was always just a one-time thing. I would sit down at a computer and write. Whatever came out, that would be what I would turn in. This year, I was forced to go through the whole drafting process. We were required to not only turn in our first draft, second draft, and final draft; we had to do assignments that showed the research we were doing and what we thought of it. To an experienced procrastinator such as myself, this was hell. This class forced me to go through the entire process, which my teachers have been trying to get me to follow for years. What resulted from this process really impressed me. All the papers I have ever written could have been so much better. This shows that revising and rewriting are not pointless efforts of teachers to make their students work hard to no end. They actually help. That is probably the most valuable lesson I have learned about writing this year. —*Katherine Byrnes, student*

- **On writer responsibility:** Peer review is an excellent tool for improving essays. However, if an adequate rough draft is not presented to reviewers, then useful feedback cannot be expected. —*Britt Burridge, student*

- **On your responsibility as a peer reviewer:** When doing a peer response, be honest. The student won't benefit from your opinion if it's glossed over with fluffy language. And don't ditch the peer response. It is very helpful to have someone else's opinions and/or ideas during the revising stage, especially if you are all writing on the same topic but their argument opposes yours. —*Christina Stephens, student*

When writing peer edits, really dig deep into their paper. Don't just look for the obvious, because they are writing a peer edit for you as well. Think what would be useful for you. —*Rebecca Peterson, student*

- **On student/teacher conferences:** It is very important when you go into your conference with your teacher that you have a strong thesis and a good sense of direction for your paper. It helped me very much to receive advice from my teacher because I had a good start and knew what I wanted to do, thus my teacher was able to give me good advice to refine my ideas. I know that you can fall into the trap of knowing that it's still a couple of weeks from being due, so why start it early? It really makes a difference in getting strong feedback. —*Richard Karasch, student*

This chapter will ask you to consider different writing and revision strategies while also giving you a sample of concrete revision techniques. We do not include all of the writing and revision strategies in this chapter alone. This chapter is intended to provide a foundation; then in "Part III: Assignments," you can find additional writing and revision strategies that address the following:

- **Analytical Thesis Statements** in Chapter 8: Analysis

- **Tips on Writing Introductions for Essays** in Chapter 9: Text-in-Context (Contextual Analysis)

- **Revising for Transitions** in Chapter 10: Rhetorical Analysis

- **Tips for Writing Conclusions** in Chapter 11: Exploring a Controversy Analysis and Writing a Public Argument

- **Vivid Description** in Chapter 12: Personal and Reflective Writing

These are broken out into shaded boxes so that you can find them easily.

5.2 Re-Envisioning Your Writing Situation

Assessment is not only something that your teacher does when he or she grades a final draft. Rather, assessment is part of the process—an on-going practice that enables you to think through your ideas, choose directions, and provide critical feedback to yourself and your peers. As part of the process, you will integrate new approaches that will convey your points more clearly and effectively to your particular audience, and you will learn strategies that you can use in your later writing as well. This section, then, will discuss different ways to assess your writing situation, including your role as a writer, your audience, your topic, and the assignment. Then you will assess how to improve specific aspects of your paper: content, organization, expression, mechanics, and style. As you read through this section, consider the complexities of the various components and the ways they interact in a given piece of writing.

For more information on your writing situation, see *Rules for Writers*, pages 2–11.

Looking at the Writing Situation

You as Writer. The writing voice you develop through your attitude and tone causes your audience to form an impression of you as a writer. The impression of yourself that you create through your writing is like a role you adopt. It's also called a **persona**. Your instructor will evaluate whether you have presented the writing persona that best appeals to your audience. In addition, because you are a representative of the academic community, your

Keyword: persona

instructor might evaluate how well your writing persona conveys the conventions of that community. You may think about the following questions:

- How will your reader see you? As a friend? An authority? A skeptical investigator? An ally in a cause?

- What kind of language should you use to achieve your desired persona?

- What in your experience might you draw from to establish your persona?

- Regardless of your writer persona, is your own voice still coming through in your writing?

Your Audience. You and your instructor will discuss the most appropriate audience for a topic or the best way to approach a topic for a specific audience. For example, you could write about using natural medicines for the subscribers of *Ethnopharmacology*, a journal that explores alternative treatments to illnesses (for instance, arguing that certain herbs, vitamins, and minerals should be used to treat the common cold). In all probability, you will be trying to persuade an audience that already knows a lot about this issue. Therefore, you will need to make writing choices that are based on shared knowledge. You can get right to the specifics of your evidence without providing a general justification for using alternative treatments. A different audience for your essay, such as medical doctors who practice traditional or allopathic medicine and may have reservations about homeopathic treatments, would require a substantially different approach in the writing choices that you make. One way to reach this audience would be to write a letter to the editor of *The New England Journal of Medicine*.

Here are some questions that can help you assess how well you have addressed your readers' needs:

- How much did you assume your readers knew about the issue?

- Did you insult them by explaining things they already know, or did you confuse them by leaving out crucial facts they would not know?

- Did you appeal to their beliefs, values, and assumptions?

- Did you draw on their prior experience to develop your points?

- Did you anticipate their potential responses to your claims and respond to them appropriately?

- If your readers will be from a cultural background different from your own, did you consider how their different world perspective might influence how they receive your argument?

These questions can also help you to write in your other courses. For example, in an introductory astronomy class, your instructor already knows the intro-level information, but that instructor will expect you to demonstrate your grasp of intro-level knowledge in your work.

Topic. To evaluate your choice of topic, your instructor will consider how it intersects with the other elements of the writing situation. You may want to consider the following questions:

- Will this topic interest your readers?

- Have you done enough research to convince your readers that you understand it thoroughly?

- Do you have the evidence you need to support your points, and do you reason clearly?

Your instructor will also evaluate whether you have taken on a topic that is too broad or too narrow to effectively discuss in an essay of the assigned length.

The Assignment. Your instructor will determine whether the rhetorical situation you've constructed is suitable for the assignment. For example, suppose you need to analyze the symbolism in a poem for an audience who has read the work. If you spend most of your essay summarizing the poem, your essay will not meet the challenges posed by the assignment. Your readers do not need a summary because they have already read the poem. They need an analysis of the poem.

While you often have a lot of flexibility in terms of how you write to a particular assignment, keeping in mind the assignment's major goals and specific requirements will help to make your paper more effective for the given writing situation. Consider the following questions:

- If the assignment sheet specifies certain formatting requirements, have you adjusted your document accordingly?

- Read over the assignment or discuss it again briefly with a classmate or the instructor. What is the "big picture" goal of the paper? What writing or analytical skill are you being asked to exercise? Does your paper demonstrate that you can apply this skill to your writing?

- How does the assignment sheet implicitly or explicitly indicate what your persona, topic, and audience should be? What tells you this?

For more information on understanding an assignment, see *Rules for Writers*, page 7.

5.3 Practicing Global and Local Revision

It is a good idea to start with your **global** revisions when you begin revising a draft. Remember that global revisions are the larger changes that will have a greater impact on your essay as a whole. **Local** revisions, on the other hand, are smaller changes. When you perform local revisions, you are generally making changes to the language of the essay, but not the structure, organization, or argument. Since global revisions may require you to move paragraphs around, eliminate sections of writing, or change the focus or audience, it will reduce your overall workload if you do these revisions before starting the local revisions. Otherwise you might change the tense or sentence structure of an entire paragraph only to realize you will not even be using that paragraph in the final section of the essay!

Suggestions for Global Revisions

As you learned in Chapter 4, writing is a process. It is something that is ongoing, and revision is one of the ways that you transform an exploratory draft into a more developed essay. Keeping this in mind will help you to see every draft and every revision as an important part of the writing process. In the early drafting stages, you might not feel very confident about your ideas. This is completely normal. In fact, you may not even know what you think about a text or a topic until you start writing. When you plan to write multiple drafts and make use of revision in your writing process, you will see drafting and revising as important parts of developing a successful essay. Don't let yourself feel discouraged; instead just keep writing.

Why Are You Writing? Revising for Purpose, Argument, and Thesis: When you write an academic essay, you write with a specific purpose in mind. Once you have written a draft, you are ready to assess your purpose. The following questions will be helpful when you do this.

- What do I hope to achieve with this essay?

- What are the requirements of the assignment?

- Am I making an argument? If so, what is the argument? How do I support the argument?

- Does my essay have a thesis? How does the thesis relate to my purpose?

- In what ways does my essay achieve my purpose? In what ways does it fail to achieve my purpose?

You can use your answers to these questions to help you with your first set of global revisions. For example, if you were writing a textual analysis about Charlotte Perkins Gilman's story "The Yellow Wallpaper" and your assignment required you to make an argument for an interpretation of the story, your purpose might be to convince your readers that the narrator's madness is a metaphor for the crazy way nineteenth-century American society restricted the activity of women. The assignment could require you to state your argument in your thesis. While reading through your draft, you might see that although your purpose is to convince readers of the validity of your interpretation, you have not actually written a thesis statement. In fact, you might see that your first draft does not do much analysis or interpretation and contains more summary than necessary. In this case your first global revision might be to rewrite your essay as an analytical argument with a thesis statement.

For more on thesis statements, see "Chapter 4: Writing as a Process" and "Analytical Thesis Statements" in "Chapter 8: Analysis."

How Does It Work? Revising for Organization:

In an academic essay, organization is very important. The way your paper is put together will help you to achieve your purpose, which you have identified and worked on in the last section. When you evaluate the organization of your essay, you may want to consider the following questions:

- How is my essay organized?

- Do I state my purpose in the essay? If so, where do I do this? If not, should I do this? (These answers will vary greatly depending on the type of essay you are writing.)

- Do my paragraphs have topic sentences?

- How does each paragraph relate to the purpose of the essay?

- Why have I put these paragraphs in this order? Does the order make sense? Is it effective? Persuasive? Interesting?

- Does each paragraph follow logically from the paragraph that comes ahead of it?

- Within my paragraphs, do the sentences follow a logical and easily understandable progression?

- Do I transition smoothly between ideas? Do I make connections?

When asking yourself these questions you might realize that you have written about each idea in the order in which it occurred to you. However, after reading for organization, you may realize that your first and third paragraphs are closely related because they both deal with establishing the context for the primary text you are analyzing, while your second paragraph is a close-reading analysis of that text. You might decide that it makes much more sense to switch the locations of your second and third paragraphs within the essay. When you do this, however, you will need to adjust the progression of ideas so you maintain the logical flow of ideas. In contrast, if you are writing a persuasive essay, you may want to move your strongest supporting claim to the end of your essay to allow the essay to *build*. After reorganizing your essay, make sure that each paragraph clearly relates to your purpose and that the organization helps you achieve that purpose rather than getting in the way of the purpose.

Who is the Reader? Revising for Audience:

Sometimes students confidently assert, "I write for myself," and, of course, it is always good to write for yourself. At the same time, whenever you find yourself writing an assignment in college, you must write not only for yourself, but also for the academic community. When you write in college you are writing as a scholar *for other scholars*. Your audience is important because your writing is designed to reach and affect your audience. So when you perform global revisions, remember to consider the important function of your audience. You might consider the following questions when revising for audience:

For more on academic communities, see "Chapter 2: Academic Discourse as Writing for Specific Audiences and Purposes."

• Who is going to be reading this essay? (My teacher, my classmates, members of my academic community, members of the local community, etc.)

• Is there more than one intended audience?

• What biases might my readers have? What are their expectations?

• What strategies might be particularly effective or non-effective with these readers?

• How much information do I need to give my audience?

• What tone should I use with my audience? Do I use this tone consistently throughout my draft?

As you examine the role of audience in your essay, you might realize that you need to define certain terms, because if you don't, your audience will not understand the point you are trying to make. On the other hand, you may realize that you have provided *too much* explanation of ideas that your audience will already understand. You can remove anything that might bore or insult your audience. You may see that the first half of your essay uses a fairly formal academic tone that is appropriate for your academic audience, but the second half becomes very informal, which is not appropriate for your academic audience. Being aware of your readers and trying to anticipate their critiques can make your academic writing much more effective.

Suggestions for Local Revisions

After you have globally revised your essay, you are ready to start local revisions. Revising at the local level allows you to demonstrate the general proficiency of your writing. Start by correcting any errors. Run a spell-check, check for grammar, and make sure that your paper is formatted according to your instructor's specifications, but local revisions are not just about correcting mistakes. In fact, this can be a fun part of your revising experience, because you can work to perfect your *style*. Once you have created a strong essay and checked it for mistakes, you can fine-tune the way you express your ideas. The following are a list of stylistic elements you might consider when performing local revisions:

Wordiness: Too many words take all the energy out of a sentence. Practice expressing your ideas concisely. See how many unnecessary words you can eliminate from your writing.

Example: Instead of "In light of recent discoveries in English Composition Studies, it has come to be known that students have trouble connecting ideas in texts they read to historical events in the time the texts were written," which is both unclear and uninteresting, you can simply write, "Students have trouble making connections between the texts they read and their historical contexts."

Active and Passive Voice: Do you fall into the habit of overusing the passive voice? This too can get boring. Try to rewrite some of your passive sentences as active sentences. When possible use strong (active) verbs like *perform*, *interrogate*, *organize*, and *persuade* rather than "to be" verbs like *am*, *is*, *are*, *was*, and *were*.

Example: Instead of "The idea was considered by Mrs. Mallard," you could write, "Mrs. Mallard embraced the idea," which is more interesting and easier to understand.

For more on academic verbs, see "Chapter 2: Academic Discourse as Writing for Specific Audiences and Purposes."

Remember that using academic verbs like "maintain," "constitute," "decrease," and "suggest" can help your writing sound more scholarly and professional.

Tense Usage: Be consistent with your tenses. While you do not need to write your entire essay in a single tense, make sure that if you do change between the present and the past or future tense, that there is a logical reason to do so.

Pronoun Usage: Pay attention to the pronouns (I, you, we, he, she, they) you use in your essay. Pronouns are little words, but they carry a lot of power. For example, Jamaica Kincaid's use of the pronoun "you" in *A Small Place* often makes readers feel as if they are under attack. What effect do your pronouns have?

Variety: One of the best marks of good writing is variety. By varying the types of sentence structures, paragraph structures, vocabulary, and punctuation that you use, you can help your reader to stay focused and engaged. Look for repeated sentence structures, words, punctuation, and phrases, and experiment until you have included more variety and fluidity in your writing.

5.4 Tips for Successful Workshopping

By Laura Gronewold

The most important thing to bring to your workshop is an open mind. As a former editor at a book publishing company, I can tell you that *everyone* needs an editor! Even the very best writer sends her/his writing through at least four different drafts, and along the way the writer collaborates with other editors and writers so that a number of people contribute to the final, polished product. (That is the reason authors thank so many people in the acknowledgments at the beginning of books!) So think of your peer group as a group of editors working together to produce the best essay possible—a clear, coherent argument; a focused thesis statement; supporting examples; and careful textual analysis. Only after several pairs of eyes have seen your work will it truly be finished.

To achieve the most success in your workshops, you can do a few things ahead of time. **First**, get to know your classmates. You are more likely to give *and* receive valuable feedback if you know your workshop partners' names and feel comfortable with them. **Second**, pay attention in class when your instructor talks about writing. Although your instructor will likely give lectures on writing technique and style, some of the best "aha!" moments happen in class discussions about your assigned texts. **Third**, carefully read the texts assigned for your class and think about how you can emulate an author's style, tone, or argumentation. If you like the way a particular author uses personal experience or builds credibility through her/his writing voice, then strive in your own writing to model your argumentation or tone after the original author's work. When you get to workshop, you can also refer to the texts you've read for class. For example, in your feedback on another student's paper, you might suggest that she/he write her/his introduction in imitation of an introduction written by an author such as Malcolm Gladwell (who wrote *The Tipping Point*). **Finally**, begin drafting early! This will allow you to participate in your workshop with a *full* draft. (Believe me, published authors do *not* begin their writing at the last minute!) Your understanding of the assignment will allow you to read your workshop partners' work thoroughly so that you can give them detailed feedback to improve their essay.

Advice for the Writer

Come to the workshop prepared to receive a critique of your work. Even if you feel that your draft is well-written with a clear argument, remember that your classmates will give you constructive criticism that will help make it even better. Remember to bring an attitude of open-mindedness to your workshops so that you can *really* listen to what ideas your classmates offer to improve your essay.

- Listen to the criticism you receive with a non-judgmental attitude.

- Listen quietly to the discussion of your work when it is happening.

- Take notes! You should have a page of *specific* notes that you can refer to when you revise your paper.

- Ask questions throughout the process so that you are clear on the feedback being offered by your classmates. At the end of the discussion, voice any additional concerns or questions about your essay.

After workshop, you will have a number of drafts with comments from your classmates, as well as your notes from the class period during which your essay was critiqued. Once you have that feedback, take a day off. This will give you some distance from your writing and will help you consider the comments from your workshop partners from a more objective angle. Getting some distance from your writing *and* from the critiques offered by your peers will allow you to begin your revisions with a fresh start, after having some time off. As you revise, think about the different comments from your readers. Do they all say that you need a more focused thesis statement? Then you should be mindful of the consistency of the comments. However, if only one student comments about your paragraph breaks, then you will need to assess whether or not you want to change that. Remember this is your essay, so you will need to consider your intentions and the effect you want to achieve, and how you will incorporate your readers' comments to help sharpen your argument and tone in your paper.

Advice for the Reader

Your job as a reader is to carefully assess your classmates' drafts so that you can give them detailed feedback about their essay. You should be able to tell the writers **what** needs to be fixed in their essays, but you should also provide advice about **why** the writers need to rewrite their essays, as well as suggestions for **how** the writers can improve their essays. Giving written (and verbal) feedback is another genre within which you will work in this class, and it requires practice and skill, just like any other form of written or verbal communication. Even if you feel like you are not the best writer in class, your feedback during workshop is very important! If you are not clear about why a paragraph is in another student's essay, it is not because you don't "get it." It is because the paragraph does not have smooth enough transitions or a clear link to the thesis statement. Sometimes the most powerful feedback points out the thing we might think is "obvious."

As you read through your peers' drafts, consider the following:

- Read the writing as closely and carefully as possible.

- Consider the writer's intentions and provide *specific* feedback.

- *Read the essay at least twice*.

- Write specific suggestions for revision on each page as you are reading (see below).

- At the end of the essay, give your overall reflections about the argument, the organization, the tone, and the style.

Giving Written Feedback

Your goal when you critique your workshop partners' drafts should be to write specific comments and questions that the writer can understand later, even if you are not there to explain them. Marginal comments such as "good!" or "???" are vague and will not help when the writer revises. Instead, strive for comments such as "Your close reading and analysis of this quote helps explain your argument," or "This sentence is confusing. How does it relate to the rest of your paragraph?" Make sure you give your classmates feedback about the argument and *not only* the grammar and style—after all, it is much easier to correct a poorly phrased sentence than it is to fix a flawed argument. Your workshop partners need your help, and you need theirs. Learning to give and receive useful feedback on your drafts is one of the most productive things that you will learn in your writing class. When you can lean on each other, you will benefit from both the writing *and* reading process of the workshop.

Questions to Consider When Giving Feedback

- Does the introductory paragraph establish the **theme or idea** of the essay? If the introduction jumps around or is not specific, then it will confuse your reader. If the introduction does not give the basic facts about the topic (summary of a text, overview of a political issue), then the reader will be confused. As the reader, your job is to make suggestions for how the writer can make her/his introductory paragraph specific and interesting.

- Does the author have a precise **thesis statement** (or central claim) that includes a **specific opinion** that the reader can agree or disagree with? If you cannot agree or disagree with the thesis statement, then it is not a strong argument. Your job is to provide suggestions to the writer so that she/he can make her/his topic more focused and include an opinion. Oftentimes, the opinion can come from answering a question, such as, "What do we conclude or learn as a result of looking more closely at these particular aspects of the novel/issue/essay?"

- Does the author have too much summary of the text's plot, or too much vague information about a research topic? How can the writer add quotations from the text? How can the writer incorporate her/his own opinion, and not just offer a summary of experts' opinions? Your job is to make suggestions for places in the essay where the writer can add analysis. Mark places where the writer can do more close reading of a quotation by underlining words or phrases, or mark the margins where the writer could offer her/his own opinionated analysis of a research topic.

- Does the writer use **direct quotes or statistics** from the primary texts to introduce points and support her/his argument? Does the writer then explain *why* the quotations are important? Are the quotations introduced with a signal phrase? Your job is to make suggestions for how the writer can introduce her/his quotations clearly with signal phrases.

- Does the writer integrate her/his secondary sources appropriately in the essay? Does the writer make it clear to the reader when another text is being quoted? Do you ever have any questions about the original source for a quotation or an idea (especially if it is an idea that is paraphrased)? Your job is to help the writer establish credibility and ensure that all of her/his sources are utilized effectively.

- Does the organization of the essay make sense? Should any paragraphs be moved around?

- Does the author have smooth transition phrases between her/his paragraphs and sentences?

- Does the conclusion leave you with one new thing to consider? Does it do more than simply restate what has already been argued?

Getting the Most Out of Your Workshop Experience

In order to really benefit from a writing workshop, you will need to do several things. First, come to the workshop prepared. This means that you need to submit the very best draft you can write to your peers for their feedback, and you also want to spend plenty of time reading your peers' papers in order to give them quality feedback. Second, come to the workshop with an open mind. Instead of trying to defend your essay, listen carefully and thoughtfully to your peers when they give you feedback. Ask questions about their suggestions. Take some time to think through your options. Remember, you don't have to make all the changes your peers or instructor suggest, but you do want to give careful consideration to their feedback. Third, give helpful, specific, constructive feedback to your peers. Although it is nice to tell your peers what you like about their essays, this is only helpful if you explain your opinion in detail and let them know why you like it. Here you will see some examples of *not very helpful*, *somewhat helpful*, and *very helpful* workshop comments.

Not Very Helpful	"I really like this paper!" This is friendly, but provides no concrete suggestions for the writer.	"Well, I'm just not that into poetry, so I couldn't get into your paper." This comment is about the reader, not the paper itself. It does not provide any suggestions for revision.	"You use way too many commas." While this writer may indeed have a problem with comma over-usage, at the drafting and peer review stage, it is often much more productive to work on global suggestions, rather than local suggestions. This comment is much too general to be useful as a revision suggestion.

Discussing Your Peer's Essay During the In-Class Workshop

When you come to class, you will need to be ready to discuss your class-mates' writing. Think about the ways you have talked as a class about the essays, fiction, poetry, and/or film texts you have read. When you talk as a class, you are not making judgments about the *writer*, but you are mak-ing assessments of the *writing*. The same goes for workshop. You want to keep your comments constructive and *always specific to the writing*, so that the author of the essay will have concrete suggestions for improving and re-organizing her/his draft.

Somewhat Helpful	"I really like your first body paragraph, but after that you kind of lose me." This comment identifies strong and weak areas but does not tell the writer what makes them strong or weak.	"You assume that I already know what this poem is about and that I think it's a great poem. Since I don't know anything about the poem, I feel alienated when I read this paper." This is an honest reaction that identifies the assumptions made in the draft. If the assignment requires the writer to assume that the reader is not familiar with the poem, then this comment identifies a great opportunity for global revision.	"In this sentence, the com-mas actually make it harder to understand. Maybe you should take them out." While this is still a local editing sug-gestion, it might be very appropriate at a later stage of workshopping. It effectively identifies a problem sentence, it connects the idea (or the content) to the form, and it provides a specific suggestion.
Very Helpful	"I really like the first body paragraph because you choose an interesting example from the text to support it, and also because in the last sentence you show how this paragraph supports the thesis. In the oth-er paragraphs, you don't always use examples from the text, and you don't come right out and tell me how the ideas relate to the thesis." This comment identifies what makes the paragraph strong and gives the writer specific suggestions for im-proving the weaker paragraphs.	"You assume that I already know what this poem is about and that I think it's a great poem. Since I don't know anything about the poem, I feel alienated when I read this paper. If you gave a little bit of summary and back-ground at the beginning of the paper, it would really help. You could also connect the argument you are making about racism in this poem to something that has happened locally and recently. Then you could help people who don't know much about poetry to be more interested in the overall argument about the poem." This comment expands the Some-what Helpful comment, by providing specific suggestions for revision.	"In this sentence, the commas actually make it harder to un-derstand. You could take them out. In the next sentence, you have an unnecessary comma again, but you also have a run-on. Here you could insert a conjunction or simply break this into two separate sen-tences. That makes it easier to understand and gives the para-graph more variety." Again, this is a local revision sug-gestion, but it identifies specific problems, provides specific sugges-tions, and addresses both clarity and style.

During your workshop, your instructor will be in the classroom, listening and participating with the group. Your instructor will help guide the workshop with questions, comments, and ideas to help you focus on giving constructive criticism to your classmates, but the heart of any workshop's success is you and your classmates. Remember: the goal of the workshop is not just to give your classmates feedback, but to train yourself to make these same assessments of your own writing in the future.

5.5 Receiving and Making Sense of Comments

You may already know that your peers can be a valuable source of comments and suggestions for your writing. Another valuable source is, of course, your instructor. Because teachers are very familiar with the conventions and expectations of academic audiences, your instructor's response is critical to the success of your revision. Writing instructors are also experienced academic writers themselves. Therefore, they're able to help you see more accurately the strengths and weaknesses in your essay. However, don't underestimate your peers' commentary; they are in the process of writing an essay just as you are and, therefore, will have valuable insights and questions for you that might push you in a clearer direction.

Throughout the course, your instructor will play various roles. He or she will support you as you plan, draft, and revise your essay. In this role, your instructor will ask questions to help you understand the rhetorical situation of each writing assignment, teach you ways to interact with your audience, and offer pointers about how better to reach that audience. Your instructor will also be the judge of the essay and will evaluate it by assigning a grade to your final draft. In particular, he or she will evaluate how well your stance (as the writer), your audience, and your topic work together to achieve the purpose of your essay.

Many instructors respond to your work by noting areas that are strong or interesting while, at the same time, noting areas that could use more attention. Additionally, instructors often use questions as a way to converse with you, show their interest in your work, or give suggestions for future revisions. If you are ever confused by your instructor's comments, then you should ask your instructor to clarify the comments. This is the perfect time to utilize your instructor's office hours.

Once you receive written and oral comments from your peers and instructor, how do you decide what to use? What do you pay attention to first? What if there's too much for you to take in all at once? This can sometimes happen if you're doing a whole-class workshop. Here's some advice:

- Read through all the comments from all the reviewers before making revisions, whether it is from two people or twenty-four.

- Look for large-scale issues such as content, focus, and organization that need attention before you attend to sentence-level problems such as grammar and word choice. You will waste your time if you fix sentences that you decide to delete later on because they were tangential.

- Always keep an open mind as you read comments. Try to see it from the reviewer's point of view. Did you leave out important information or explanation that would solve the problem?

- If you really think a comment is questionable, ask other readers what they think. Sometimes you will decide not to take action on a suggestion or comment.

- Think critically about all comments, and then do what you think is best. You are the writer and make the final decisions. Just try to make well-informed decisions.

5.6 Feedback Leads to Revision

By Jen Heckler and Kristen Haven

In the following sample rough draft, a student explores her interpretation of Raymond Carver's "So Much Water So Close to Home." As conscientious writers, we try to provide students with the feedback we'd like to receive. Notice the global (development and organization) and local (grammar and mechanics) suggestions we make on the draft. Reflect on these comments— Can you break them down into local and global? How would you rewrite your paper based on these responses? (Remember that it makes sense to consider global feedback first.) Which comments would you take into consideration?

A Draft in Process...

Give your paper an original title as you continue revising.

Author name?

You have a fairly broad introduction, which successfully eases readers into your discussion; however, there are a few places where being more specific will help readers understand your purpose. For example, what is "over done violence"?; "suspicious behavior"?; "scary"?; "dangerous and unfortunate situations"?; "shady"? These are interesting descriptive words, but they are broad and general; consequently, readers will not know what you are talking about. How does all of this relate to the story?

This sentence sounds like it contradicts itself. First you mention that she is "aware of his actions" (what actions? Fishing?), and then I hear mention of murder. What's the connection?

Use first or third person instead of second.

Use stronger vocabulary here—how is it bad?

Redundant—"situation" used twice within same sentence. This seems rather broad for a topic sentence. Perhaps letting readers know what you are trying to prove will help guide readers. Your thesis seems to say that her husband (What is his name?) killed someone. Is that what you are trying to show in this paragraph?

Run-on—needs punctuation
I thought you said he killed the girl in your thesis...

---------------- Draft of essay one

"So Much Water so Close to Home"

Suspicious behavior and over done violence are all scary tell tale signs of a criminal. People that are often involved in dangerous and unfortunate situations usually have obvious characteristics that seem to comply with their behavior. In the short story, "So Much Water So Close to Home" a housewife Claire is terrified of her shady husband. Claire hears about a murdered girl close by to the place her husband and his friends were fishing and camping. Claire is immediately very aware of his actions and is investing him and facts about the murder for fear that it was in fact of her husband. Whether or not Claire's husband is really guilty, he gives many signs that could cause someone to believe, in this situation Claire, that he did murder the young girl.

Many people would expect that when something traumatic and mysterious happens to you on a trip, one of the first things you would do when you got home was to tell your family about it so that would understand the severity of the situation and be sure their family members had nothing to do with such a bad situation. The exact opposite happens to Claire and her husband. Claire's husband sees a girl dead in the water when he is camping, but he and his friends decide to just leave her there over night and deal with it in the morning. Claire's husband comes home and goes to *sleep and doesn't say anything to Claire about it until later the next day. "Why didn't you tell me last night?' I asked. 'I just...didn't. What do you mean?' he said". (280) Rightly so Claire found it wierd that she woke up to hear her husband screaming (cusses) in to a telephone and then he saying to her "I have to tell you something" (280). The situation is awkward, one would think that if you dragged a body to police in the morning and were wanted for murder you might want to first tell your wife about it. This is one of the many odd behaviors that Claire's husband displayed.*

Another sign that there might be a problem is a person's violence and overall behavioral tone. Throughout the short story, Claire's husband is increasingly moody and violent. At different points, Claire's husband snaps out at her and even acts in a violent manner. "Suit yourself then. I could give a fuck less what you do" (285).

Great quotation, but it's dropped into the text without integration. Introduce it, and explain how it illustrates your point.

Per MLA, should be text, close quotation mark, citation, period. Remember, the citation should be included in the sentence by the period.

Sp. weird. Actually, "strange" or "startling" might work better here.

Slang—"curses" or "obscenities" would be better.

Comma splice.

Stay in present tense.

Is this your topic sentence? (What are you trying to prove in this paragraph?) It seems like all of your topic sentences are at the end of paragraphs. Perhaps you should move them to the beginning, so that readers will know what you are trying to prove. Check for this throughout.

This is really general for a topic sentence. Try to make your topic sentence specific to the text you are analyzing

Not sure what you mean by this phrase. Clarify.

Dropped quotation. Integrate into your writing.

Stuart, Claire's husband, starts to really scare Claire with his overzealous behavior and temper. Claire does not understand why Stuart needs to really act like this, and this causes her to question his behavior and the murder situation. If Stuart had been normal and not lashed out at her in specific situations, she would less likely want to question, but since he acted in such a harsh way it caused her to question his motives.

He was harsh, so she suspected him of murder? I think this is making a huge leap here. What else made Claire suspect Stuart? Was it his reaction to the subject of the discussion?

How does this paragraph relate to your thesis? It seems like it is contradicting what you are trying to prove.

Just a few questions: 1. Are you trying to illustrate that Stuart is capable of killing someone or are you trying to prove that there is a "problem?" Or are you trying to prove something else that I missed? I'm not exactly sure. Your thesis sounds like you are trying to prove that Stuart's behavior indicates that he has the potential to kill someone, but that is not what your topic sentence says here... Perhaps you should mention Stuart's name before this paragraph. 2. Does Claire suspect Stuart of murdering the girl? 3. What is the overzealous behavior like?

Wordy. I would suggest simply "is." "Common" already tells us says the same thing as "can often be."

A common characteristic of a criminal can often be substance abuse. Many criminals have problems that root from an alcohol addiction or other drug problem. Yet because one decides to partake in these activities does not necessarily mean they are out to kill someone. In the short story, Stuart is constantly drinking and smoking, even around his child. When Claire mentions she wants to go to the store, alcohol is the first thing Stuart asks to get. When Stuart seems upset or wanting to do something, smoking or alcohol is seemingly the first thing he turns to.

Again, a general topic sentence. Think about making a claim about the text here.

Use a quotation from the story to back up these claims.

Throughout the short story, "So Much Water So Close to Home" Claire is afraid that her husband is involved in the murder of a young girl. Stuart's actions start to become very mysterious and shady to Claire, and she is struggling with believing her husband. There are many different things Stuart does that would make many people believe he is guilty. The point is that whether or not he is guilty his actions prove otherwise. A person's actions can have a great impact on the people around them and cause them to be more and more questionable.

"struggles" would read more smoothly

Okay, I'm hearing that it doesn't matter if he's guilty or not guilty; his actions prove he is guilty. Doesn't this seem rather repetitive? This is also a rather general final sentence. Keep the story in mind.

Revisions in Action

The student then reworked her draft to include her instructor's feedback. Compare the two versions. Would you have integrated the instructor's feedback in ways other than this student did? What additional changes would you have made? Do you see more local or global revisions at work here?

A Criminal Mind in Carver's "So Much Water So Close to Home"

Suspicious behavior and violence are all seemingly obvious telltale signs of a criminal. People that are often involved in dangerous situations usually have obvious characteristics that seem to comply with their behavior. What things do many consider traits of a criminal? Does one have to be shady or over violent? What about if a person is just displaying suspicious behavior or acting in a dangerous manner? In Raymond Carver's short story, "So Much Water So Close to Home" a housewife Claire becomes terrified of her shady husband, Stuart. Claire hears about a murdered girl close by to the place her husband and his friends were fishing and camping. Claire begins to become more and more nervous that her husband was involved with the death of the girl, and starts to analyze her husband Stuart's actions. Whether or not Stuart is really guilty, he gives many signs that would cause any person to believe that he is guilty. A person's actions are key in determining a crime situation and Stuart does not seem to be innocent.

Carver's portrait of guilty behavior hinges on Stuart's lack of communication with Claire surrounding the discovery of the dead girl. Truth and honesty, two devices that hold a relationship together, are two devices that Stuart fails to uphold. His initial silence regarding the discovery of the dead girl in the water near a campsite he is vacationing at with friends, and his ensuing reticence and verbal abuse lead the reader (and Claire) to suspect his capacity for serious, even murderous, violence.

One of the actions that causes Claire to question her husband is his late mentioning of the dead body he encountered on the trip. Many people would expect that when something traumatic and mysterious happens to them on a trip, one of the first things they would do when they got home was tell their family about it so they would understand the severity of the situation and be sure their family members had nothing to do with such an awful situation. The exact opposite happens to Claire and her husband. Claire's husband sees the body in the water, but he and his friends decide to just leave her there over night and deal with it in the morning. Claire's husband comes home and goes to sleep and doesn't say anything to Claire about it until later the next day. Claire is deeply troubled by this lack of communication. "Why didn't you tell me last night? I asked. "I just...didn't. What do you mean? he said" (280).

Rightly so Claire finds it unsettling that she wakes up to hear her husband screaming obscenities into a telephone and *then* saying to her "I have to tell you something" (280). Claire questions her husband because she finds it odd that he would not tell her when he got home that he saw a dead body on his camping trip. If Stuart helped get the body to authorities in the morning he would have to know the police are going to call and question him about it. What did he think his wife would feel if we were getting police calls? It doesn't make sense that he did not tell her quickly that there had been some problems on his fishing trip. The situation is awkward; one would think that if you dragged a body to police in the morning and were wanted for murder you might want to first tell your wife about it. This is one of the many odd behaviors that Claire's husband displayed.

Stuart's violence and overall behavioral tone are indicative of his dangerous potential. Throughout the short story, Claire's husband is increasingly moody and violent. At different points Claire's husband verbally lashes out at her and eventually abuses her physically. When Claire tells him she wants to spend the night alone, he snaps, "Suit yourself then. I could give a fuck less what you do" (285). Stuart starts to really scare Claire with his overzealous behavior and temper, and particularly with the way he responds to her confusion and questions with sexual advances rather than answers. Claire does not understand why Stuart acts like this; the effect is only to alienate her further from him. I think this makes Claire more likely to believe that Stuart was involved in the assault and murder of the girl. If Stuart had been normal and not lashed out at her in specific situations, she would less likely want to question, but since he spoke so violently and rash it caused her to question his motives.

A common characteristic of a criminal can often be substance abuse, and Stuart fits this description. Many criminals have problems that root from an alcohol addiction or other drug problem. In the short story, Stuart is constantly drinking and smoking, even around his child. When Claire mentions she wants to go to the store, alcohol is the first thing Stuart asks her to get. When Stuart seems upset or wanting to do something, smoking or alcohol is seemingly the first thing he turns to.

Throughout "So Much Water So Close to Home" Claire is afraid that her husband has been involved in the murder of a young girl. Stuart's actions become increasingly confounding and distancing to Claire and she struggles with believing him and eventually with even being near him. Indeed, Stuart's behavior would make many people believe he is guilty. Carver convey's the way that a person's actions in the face of trauma can have a great impact on the people around them, and in Claire and Stuart's situation, can expose and widen the fractures already present in a relationship.

Work Cited

Carver, Raymond. "So Much Water So Close to Home." *Writing as Revision*. Boston, MA: Pearson Custom Publishing, 2003. Print.

Discussion Questions:

1. Which instructor comments address local concerns? Which instructor comments address global concerns?

2. How does the student define the writing situation? How can you tell?

3. Considering that this is still a rough draft, how would you revise this paper again both globally and locally? List three suggestions for each.

6
Working with Sources:
Summary, Paraphrase, and Quotation

6.1 Working with Sources: An Overview

This chapter explains how to write using sources. Specifically, it will help you:

- Name the text's author and appropriate pages that were consulted (in-text citation);

- List the text's author, title, and other relevant publication information in a bibliography at the end of your text;

- Demonstrate clear distinctions between your own ideas and the ideas of the sources that you are using;

- Represent the ideas of your sources fairly and accurately by using effective summary, paraphrase, and quotation; and

- Incorporate peer and instructor feedback about your use of sources into the final version of your text.

Whether you are writing a poem, an engineering report, a grant, or a paper for a biology class, you will often draw upon the ideas of other writers and integrate them into your own writing. There are occasions when writers do *not* borrow from others, but most of us don't even realize the extent to which we are influenced by what we read. Especially in the context of college writing, skilled writers are also skilled readers, and the quality of their work demonstrates the depth of their knowledge. Writers make good use of the energy and ideas that they encounter in texts. In fact, it's a good bet that the coursework in your first-year writing class began with the close reading and analysis of another person's work: a story, a poem, a film, or some other text. You may have been focusing more on your own close reading or analysis of the text itself, rather than "how to use the text" to support your own analysis. Eventually, though, you have to work on incorporating the ideas of others in your own work, especially when writing for academic audiences.

Writing documented essays would be simpler if all writers cited their sources in exactly the same way. However, as you can imagine, different writing situations call for specific rules about how to incorporate other people's work into your own. Let's begin by reviewing the different definitions of summary, paraphrase, and quotation. A **summary** is an abbreviated version of a longer text—your statement of what you see to be the major points of a text, *using your own words*. A summary can be one sentence long, one paragraph long, or one page long, depending on the length of the text and your purposes as a writer. A **paraphrase** is often confused with summary, but in a paraphrase you work much more closely with the original source. To paraphrase is to rephrase part of a source in your own language, often just a sentence or even a phrase, while retaining the general meaning of the original source. Your paraphrase may be shorter (or even slightly longer) than the original, but it must always change the language, sentence structure, and word order so that it is recognizably distinct from the original. The final way that you can work with the words of others is through the use of **quotation**—using the exact words from a writer's original source, with no changes in language or punctuation (some words may be omitted, which will be explained below). Whether you are summarizing, paraphrasing, or quoting, one rule remains constant: Always cite the source that you are using so that your readers know where the material is coming from. This chapter explains how to cite sources when writing for academic audiences and how to use the work of others effectively and properly.

Keyword: summary

Keyword: paraphrase

Keyword: quotation

For more information on MLA in-text citation, please refer to *Rules for Writers*, pages 415–26.

For more information on creating a list of works cited, please refer to *Rules for Writers*, pages 426–63.

6.2 Summary: Main Ideas

Whether you are reading a journal article, a chapter in a book, or a story, writing a summary can help you to put the writer's most important ideas into your own words, which in turn will help you develop a deeper understanding of the text. This process also helps you to remember the subject matter, which is particularly important when gathering research material. By condensing the most important ideas of a text, you make it easier to use the ideas later. This process also helps you to understand which aspects of a text are most interesting to you, and this is important to consider when you begin to make an argument about a text. Along with quoting and paraphrasing, summary is one of the main ways you will integrate other writers' ideas into your own writing. However, summary can be more complex than it seems because it requires you to figure out ideas and arguments that may be quite difficult.

A **summary** is a concise statement of a text's main ideas written in the reader's own words. The length of a summary varies depending on the length of the text to be summarized and your own purposes for summarizing. In other words, the amount of information or details you choose to include in your summary depends on how you wish to use that information later. For instance, you may wish to set the context for an analysis of part of the text or another text. A summary can be as short as one or two sentences. For example, if you were to summarize Stephen Crane's "The Snake" (in "Chapter 3: Close Reading and Interacting with the Text") for the purpose of defining its relationship to your other sources, your summary might focus only on the text's overarching ideas instead of all of Crane's points. Your summary might look something like this:

> In "The Snake" Stephen Crane describes a man who encounters a rattle-snake while walking with his dog. As the man and the snake face each other, both are filled with a rage and desire to kill the other that is likened to instinctual violence and the experience of war.

On the other hand, if you were surveying many of the important texts related to the ecology movement, you might write a longer and more detailed summary of Crane's poem, capturing connections between all of this text's main ideas and the claims made by authors of other ecology texts, instead of simply identifying the main ideas. In this way, you could then compare the points he makes to ideas developed by other authors writing on the same subject and in the same time period.

A good summary has to make sense to someone who hasn't read the original text. Therefore, you should introduce the author before or early in the summary, as illustrated in the brief example above. In addition, your summary should be smoothly integrated into your writing, and you should clearly distinguish your own opinions from those of your source. Summaries don't usually evaluate a source. If your instructor gives you the assignment of summarizing a text, you may be asked to limit yourself to presenting the author, the context, and the ideas in a rather descriptive manner. However, when you incorporate a summary in an essay or other academic writing, don't hesitate to blend summaries with your own judgments and analysis of the various texts you are working with. Look at the sample student essays included at the back of this book to study how writers use brief summaries (often in the introductions of their essays) to orient their readers, introduce a quotation, or initiate a discussion.

A good way to begin a summary is to create an **informal outline** of the text, like the one found in "Chapter 3: Close Reading and Interacting with the Text." This provides a sense of the sequence of ideas before writing the summary. However, merely stringing together the main ideas in each paragraph does not make a good summary; you also need to fill in the logical connections between the author's main ideas and maybe even reorganize them so they make more sense to someone who isn't familiar with your source. As you summarize, focus on the main claim and the most important supporting evidence so that you can capture the logic of the analysis.

For more information on summaries, please refer to *Rules for Writers*, pages 417–18 & 424.

For example, if you wanted to provide advice to another writer on constructing summaries, how would you summarize the previous paragraph in no more than one sentence? Take a moment, reread the paragraph, think about its main points, and then reduce them to a single sentence. Now take another minute and review the paragraphs in this section. If you take a moment to summarize them in a couple of sentences, you will find that you have a clearer sense of what you just read and how to use it. You will also be able to remember it more clearly and use it more readily in your own writing. Annotating while you read and stopping at important points in your reading to summarize will help make your studying more efficient; these are crucial skills that will help you write about what you are reading.

6.3 Paraphrase: Specific Ideas

Learning to paraphrase the works of others is an essential writing skill, especially when doing research-based writing. Writers paraphrase when they need to include specific information and ideas from other writers in their own work. As a responsible writer, you should acknowledge the original intent of other writers and then discuss your ideas in relation to their ideas.

When you paraphrase, you borrow from the writings of others, but you must use language that is different from the original source. Paraphrasing is not just summary, but instead follows a single idea in the original text quite closely. To avoid plagiarism, keep these rules in mind:

• Change the language so that it no longer follows the original.

• Change the word order and sentence structure so that it no longer resembles the original.

• Cite the source using in-text citation so that readers know where the original material comes from.

Summaries should also make these changes, but a summary's purpose is to abbreviate and capture main ideas; paraphrases are used to communicate the meaning of specific passages or parts of a text. Read the following passage from Edward Said's *Culture and Imperialism* and before reading further, try to put the passage into your own words while keeping to the spirit of the text's meaning.

> Appeals to the past are among the commonest strategies in interpretations of the present. What animates such appeals is not only disagreement about what happened in the past and what the past was, but uncertainty about whether the past really is past, over and concluded, or whether it continues, albeit in different forms, perhaps. This problem animates all sorts of discussions—about influence, about blame and judgment, about present actualities and future priorities. (3)

A one-sentence, quick summary of the above paragraph (as you might write if taking notes while reading or preparing for research-based writing) might read as follows: "Fights over the past are not just about 'what happened' but where the past ends and the present begins." This sentence functions as a decent summary of Said's paragraph because it captures the main idea of the paragraph. But it isn't exactly a paraphrase because it loses important details and context: Nothing is mentioned about "interpretation" or "blame and judgment," for example.

Read the following attempt at paraphrase. Does it effectively paraphrase the passage without plagiarizing the language?

> References to the past are some of the most typical strategies used to interpret the present. These appeals are animated not just by disagreements about things that happened in the past, but also about whether the past is really over or just continuing on in a different form. This problem gives life to discussions about blame and judgment and about present realities and future priorities.

The above example has serious problems, enough that the writer could be accused of plagiarizing the passage from Said. Why? Although some words are changed and some of the word order appears to be different, too much of the original passage's language and sentence structure remains intact—these are the hallmarks of an incorrect paraphrase. Also, notice that the passage is not cited, giving no indication that the material actually comes from a source.

Here is a more effective paraphrase:

> A standard tactic used to make sense of the present is to refer to the past. As Said notes in his book, discussions of the past are often marked by disagreements over what happened and what it means. However, another important consideration concerns whether the past has actually ended or whether what has happened before is still taking place, but carrying on in a new way. Disputes over where the past ends and the present begins lead to problems about responsibility, material realities, and what the future should look like. (Said 3)

Notice that the second attempt at paraphrasing features very different sentence structures and word choices. The writer also cites the author by name at the beginning of the paraphrase and at the end includes an in-text citation to show readers the original source of the ideas. While a paraphrase does not have to retain all of the content from the original, it should capture most of its substance. Above all, the meaning and intent of the original passage should not be changed. Paraphrasing is especially useful when there is no compelling reason to use the exact words of your source in order to further the discussion. However, when the author's language seems especially effective or unique, or you want to analyze it in more depth, you should choose the last method of working with sources: quotation.

For more information on paraphrasing, please refer to *Rules for Writers*, pages 417–18 & 424.

Work Cited

Said, Edward. *Culture and Imperialism*. Vintage: New York, 1993. Print.

6.4 Quotation: The Source's Words

Writers use quotations for a variety of reasons. Quotations can help to demonstrate a key point using the source's exact words, to set up the writer's analysis of a source, and sometimes to begin or conclude an essay with a provocative, exact statement from an author—as is seen so often in literary criticism and popular forms of writing. Whatever your motives for using quotations, bear in mind that quotations will be most effective when you use them with paraphrasing.

Paraphrasing can help you set up quotations so that readers understand the context of the quotation. When a writer begins or ends a paragraph with a direct quotation and never again refers directly to the quotation, readers may wonder why it was included and how it figures into the discussion. Consider this example of how to use paraphrasing to lead into a quotation:

Said concludes his argument by criticizing how the dominant legacy of imperialism has been to convince people of their differences from one another. He writes,

> No one today is purely *one* thing. Labels like Indian, or woman, or Muslim, or American are not more than starting-points [...]. Imperialism consolidated the mixture of cultures and identities on a global scale. But its worst and most paradoxical gift was to allow people to believe that they were only, mainly, exclusively, white, or Black, or Western, or Oriental. (336)

Notice how the writer introduces the quotation from Said with a paraphrase of his text, followed by the full quotation. While readers may have an idea what is meant by "to convince people of their differences from one another," the full quotation from the original source gives us a much clearer picture of the type of "differences" involved in this discussion, including race, national identity, civilization, and gender. For the writing to be even more effective, we would expect this writer to then "unpack" Said's words and explain, for example, the paradox he is talking about, and how his ideas are relevant to the writer's own topic. Below is another example of quotation, this time with a sentence before and after to introduce and then follow the quoted material with discussion, again using Said:

> Another legacy of imperialism, especially among Western powers, continues to be the drive to dominate other cultures by categorizing them or understanding them only by comparisons that serve no meaningful purpose. To undo this legacy, Said argues for "not trying to rule others, not trying to classify them or put them in hierarchies, above all, not constantly reiterating how 'our' culture or country is number one (or *not* number one, for that matter). For the intellectual there is quite enough of value to do without *that*" (336). Judging by the global events of recent years, in particular the U.S. adventures in Iraq and the triumphant media coverage of the early days of the war in 2003, it appears that his call continues to be little more than a cry in the darkness.

The writer has supplied important contextual information before the quotation. Without this contextual information, a reader might not understand that the quotation relates to Said's discussion of imperialism. After the quotation, the writer has provided an example to connect Said's point to his own argument. In this way, the source has been integrated into the paper, and readers know how Said contributes to the larger discussion.

For more information on using and integrating quotations, please refer to *Rules for Writers*, pages 415–26.

The next section provides some additional rules to follow when using quotations in your writing.

Work Cited

Said, Edward. *Culture and Imperialism.* Vintage: New York, 1993. Print.

6.5 Integrating Sources: Using Quotations

The following is a practical guide for integrating quotations correctly, which will help you produce writing that is more persuasive and logical. (Some portions of this guide have been adapted from *The St. Martin's Guide to Writing,* 6th ed., Boston: Bedford/St. Martin's, 2001.)

When to Quote

• When the wording of the source is especially effective or unique or expresses a point so well that you cannot restate it without altering the meaning or effect;

• When the words of reliable and respected authorities, scholars, or authors support your point;

• When you wish to emphasize an author's opinion;

• When you wish to cite an author whose opinions challenge or vary greatly from those of other experts; or when you wish to disagree with a particular author;

• When you are going to discuss the author's choice of words (this is close reading!)

The biggest challenge when using quotations is to include them in a way that does not break up the fluidity of your writing. The writing styles of the individuals you quote will probably differ from your own style. To avoid a jarring experience for your reader, try to integrate quotations smoothly. Here are some different ways to introduce quotations.

Integrating In-Text Quotations

Use the in-text format for quotations of three or fewer lines of poetry, or four or fewer lines of prose. Name the author in the signal phrase. Place the quotation:

• At the beginning

"When Gregor Samsa woke up one morning from unsettling dreams he found himself changed in his bed into a monstrous vermin," begins Franz Kafka's famous story of transformation and realization, *The Metamorphosis* (3).

- In the middle

Stevenson shows that Mr. Hyde's acquaintances describe him very differently, but they all perceive his "haunting sense of unexpressed deformity," which suggests that Hyde possesses an abstract yet observable abnormality (64).

- At the end

In *Borderlands/La Frontera*, Gloria Anazaldúa describes the experiences that lead one to develop *la facultad*, or "the capacity to see in surface phenomena the meaning of deeper realities" (60).

- Divided by your own words

"Enlightenment's program," Horkheimer and Adorno write, "was the disenchantment of the world" (1).

Punctuation

Using punctuation effectively will also add to the fluidity of your writing.

- Introducing a statement with a colon—a colon follows an independent clause.

In this space, Anzaldúa suggests we have the potential to undo dualisms and end oppression: "A massive uprooting of dualistic thinking in the individual and collective consciousness is the beginning of a long struggle, but one that could, in our best hopes, bring us to the end of rape, of violence, of war" (102).

Or if the author is not named in the signal phrase, your citation will look like this:

In this space, we have the potential to undo dualisms and end oppression: "A massive uprooting of dualistic thinking in the individual and collective consciousness is the beginning of a long struggle, but one that could, in our best hopes, bring us to the end of rape, of violence, of war" (Anzaldúa 102).

- Introducing a statement with a comma—a comma usually follows an introduction that incorporates the quotation into its sentence structure. You will generally capitalize the first word of the quotation.

For example, Louise Newman begins a review of *Woman Suffrage and Women's Rights*, "Since 1975, Ellen Carol DuBois has helped shape the field of women's history, making it her mission to emphasize what is explicitly political in the history of feminism" (1).

- Introducing a statement using "that"—no punctuation is generally needed with that, and no capital letter is used to begin the quotation.

    Noting this failure, Adorno asserts that "he calls himself nobody because Polyphemus is not a self" (53).

Punctuation Review

- In-text citation: Quotation + End Quotation Mark + Parenthetical Documentation + Period

    "Quotation sentence" (Author 35).

- You don't need to name the author if the author is named in the signal phrase:

    Signal Phrase with author "Quotation sentence" (35).

- Quotation in block form: Quotation + Period + Parenthetical Documentation (no quotation marks)

    End of long quote in block form. (Author 35)

- You don't need to name the author if the author is named in the signal phrase:

    End of long quote in block form with a signal phrase. (35)

Changing the Quotation

- If the quotation has an error, copy it as is and add the notation *sic* in brackets.

    According to a recent newspaper article, "Inner dating [sic] is a problem among instructors as well as students" (Blaze 62).

- When you omit words, use ellipsis marks in place of the missing words (three dots for an omission within a sentence, four dots for an omission that is a full sentence or more).

    Rackin observes the "liberatory potential of Shakespeare's...cross-dressed heroines" (74).

- To insert your own material into a quotation, use brackets.

    "[This group] is a quasi-historical community" (Sartre 145).

Miscellaneous Reminders

- Source quoted in another source: use (qtd. in)

    According to Kung-fu Tze, "All wisdom is rooted in learning to call things by the right name" (qtd. in Hamill 548).

- For poems, use line numbers for your citation—the first time, use the word "line" or "lines"—after that just use the line number(s).

- For plays, give act, scene, and line number(s).

- For prose, use page numbers. There is no need to use the word "page" or "pg."

- When you use more than one text by the same author in your essay, your citation should use a short version of the title, following the author's name, when it is not named in the signal phrase.

(Lamberton, "Sacred" 37)

- Use block form (the quotation should be indented one inch) for long quotations—more than three lines of poetry or more than four lines of prose.

Works Cited

Anazaldúa, Gloria. *Borderlands/La Frontera: The New Mestiza.* 2nd ed. San Francisco: Aunt Lute, 1999. Print.

Hamill, Sam. "The Necessity to Speak." *Writing as Revision.* Ed. Beth Alvarado, Barbara Cully, and Michael Robinson. Boston: Pearson Custom Publishing, 2003. 546–53. Print.

Horkheimer, Max and Theodor W. Adorno. *Dialectic of Enlightenment: Philosophical Fragments.* Trans. Edmund Jephcott. Stanford: Stanford UP, 2002. Print.

Kafka, Franz. *The Metamorphosis.* New York: Bantam, 2004. Print.

Lamberton, Ken. "Sacred Regrets." *Wilderness and Razor Wire.* San Francisco: Mercury House, 2000. 33–44. Print.

Newman, Louise M. "*Book Review: Women Suffrage and Women's Rights.*" *The Journal of American History.* 88.1 (2001): 215-16. *JSTOR.* 9 May 2009.

Rackin, Phyllis. *Shakespeare and Women.* Oxford: Oxford UP, 2005. Print.

Sartre, Jean-Paul. *Anti-Semite and Jew.* New York: Schocken Books, 1995. Print.

Stevenson, Robert Louis. *Dr. Jekyll and Mr. Hyde.* New York: Signet, 2003. Print.

6.6 Using Sources in the Writing Process

You might find that taking notes on your sources can be a productive form of discovering exactly what you want to write about. The task of pulling out the main ideas (summary) and putting key passages into your own words (paraphrase) will push you to consider more closely what effect(s) the text had on you. Summarizing or paraphrasing is not in and of itself an analysis. However, in an analysis or research essay, good notes will help you to create a working knowledge of your text in order to support your interpretation. You should focus on pulling out the main ideas and stating them clearly, being sure to set off your own opinions from your summaries and paraphrases. If you focus on summarizing or paraphrasing the source clearly before responding with your own opinion, you may be able to understand the source more fully. Then you can examine your notes from different perspectives to choose a point of inquiry and eventually a thesis statement for your paper.

For more information on taking notes while you read, please refer to "Chapter 3: Close Reading and Interacting with the Text."

When you are writing a research paper, it will save you time if you summarize as you read. If you read six articles and then sit down to write, you may forget some of the main points that stood out to you when you were reading. However, if you summarize in the margins of the text or on a separate document as you read, you'll be able to go back and make connections between the articles. Before you know it, you'll have several different perspectives on an issue summarized in front of you, and you will be better able to consider the direction your essay will take. Also, using summary as a research practice will enable you to see gaps that need to be filled. For example, if you're researching the discourse surrounding anti-immigration legislation, you may find that your sources all speak out *against* this issue. By examining your summaries, you will realize that you must augment your research by reading about other sides of the issue. This will enable you to become better informed about the different perspectives surrounding this controversial subject.

Whatever type of paper you're writing, you will have to summarize in order to clearly demonstrate your point to your readers. Summarizing specific selections from an essay or short story helps to bolster your argument because you are illustrating to your readers exactly why you came to the interpretation that you did. If you're writing an analysis essay, for example, and are trying to illustrate that the author uses strong, abrasive language to get her point across, you will want to give an example of that language in the form of correctly cited quotations.

When you write a research essay, you deal with multiple outside sources. You will have to summarize them—perhaps by paraphrasing—in order to show your reader the focus of your argument. Additionally, a clear, concise summary will help your reader to see the connections between the various arguments surrounding the issue. You have choices when summarizing—you can pull out those parts of the text that best assist you in supporting your stance on an issue.

Beyond that, you will want to create a context for the summaries, paraphrases, and quotations that you use. Your writing will not be effective if you just list a bunch of quotations from the text—you need to show *how* the author uses the material by setting up your summary to demonstrate the context of the language you quote. For example, if you are in the middle of a paragraph and decide to list three examples of the author's racy language in order to illustrate your point, you will have to set this up by explaining *what* she is talking about when she uses this language. If you do not do this, your use of the source will be confusing to readers—even if they have read the text. Why? Because you are trying to do something specific with that quotation— you are illustrating your point. Therefore, it is up to you to explain *how* that particular quotation supports your point.

Summarizing, paraphrasing, and quoting texts may seem like trivial academic skills. However, don't forget that college writers must live up to higher expectations. There are ethical issues in the way you use texts that your instructors expect you to understand. For example, when you paraphrase an author or quotation directly from the text, you want to make sure that you are representing the context accurately, without twisting the text's words for the sake of your own argument. That is, if you take quotations out of context, you could make it seem that the author expresses an idea that is not actually present in that text. Yes, readers will interpret texts in different ways, so two people might come to a different understanding of what an author means. But there is a significant difference between reading a text in a unique way and changing its meaning altogether. Make sure that you work to give an honest representation of the text itself and the context surrounding the author's words. The guidelines in this chapter will help you cite sources honestly and enable you to work with texts in ways that are appropriate for academic audiences.

7
Research as Part
of the Writing Process

7.1 Research: An Overview

Most of you probably wrote a research paper at least once in your high school career, and it may seem at first that the research you do at the university will simply be more of the same kind of work. However, just as expectations for writing at the university level frequently differ from how you were taught to write in high school, research at the university is more complicated than simply collecting and reporting information. This chapter will provide a basic introduction to how research is situated as an integral part of the Writing Program at the University of Arizona. The online Research Lab, which you are taking as a companion course to your first-year writing course, will also teach you basic research and information skills. In addition, each instructor will also help you learn how to conduct research tailored specifically to his or her particular course, assignment, and subject. You can also learn a great deal by going to the University Main Library and asking for help at the Information Commons/Reference Desk. The librarians are an invaluable resource because they are specially trained to find and evaluate information. You can get general reference assistance and also consult with one of dozens of subject specialists who will be glad to help you with any of your projects throughout your college career.

Visit the UA Library in person and visit it online at <http://www.library.arizona.edu>.

You may think of research and writing as two separate activities: First you go to the library or search online to find sources and take notes, and then you write your paper. However, as you become a more experienced writer, you will be asked to integrate research into your own writing in a more sophisticated manner. Instead of thinking of research as an isolated activity to complete *before* you write your paper, consider it part of the writing process. The processes of research and writing enrich each other, and the insights and knowledge gained from researching an idea can strengthen our own arguments. As you learn more about your chosen field or paper topic, your professors will expect you to do more than simply report on your findings: you will also be required to formulate your own opinions and present and support those opinions in carefully thought out papers. This chapter, and the *Guide* as a whole, will ask you to think of the process of researching in several related ways:

- Research as entering into a conversation or dialogue rather than as simply collecting and reporting information;

- Research as a way of becoming aware of the range of viewpoints on a given topic or in a particular discipline;

- Research as a way of helping formulate and refine your own points of view.

Research as entering into a conversation: In your first-year writing courses, you may be asked to write a researched paper that also attempts to persuade your audience to accept your point of view on your chosen topic. As you begin to research for this essay, you will need to refine your thesis and find credible sources to support your argument, as well as those that present alternative positions or counterarguments. Your research will generally uncover a wide range of opinions, and instead of simply accepting them all at face value, you will be asked to evaluate and assess their relative merits. Expressing your opinion about the sources will therefore be a vital part of the research and writing processes.

For more information on reading critically and evaluating sources, please see "Chapter 3: Close Reading and Interacting with the Text."

Research as a way of becoming aware of a range of viewpoints: You may think before you have researched your topic in depth that there are only two sides to an issue, a "pro" and a "con," and believe that you will be required to choose one of these two positions. However, more complex arguments allow for multiple shades of gray, and academic discourse generally requires that you consider the finer shadings of an issue and qualify your arguments in order to formulate reasoned appeals to your audience(s). You will find in evaluating sources that some are more extreme than others, and you may want to discuss their suitability with your teachers before deciding whether they will be appropriate for your particular project.

Research as a way to discover your own opinion: Even if you begin your research with a firm opinion on your chosen topic, you may find that your reading will help clarify your point of view. For instance, in reading the extreme "pro" and "con," you may realize that you prefer to situate your argument in between the two ends of the spectrum; other times you may identify more strongly with one side of the issue and find that arguing against the other side will help you explain why you hold a certain position. You may even find after researching an issue that your initial viewpoint has changed.

It is important to realize, however, that even for experienced writers and researchers, conducting research can often lead to confusion about how to incorporate the ideas of others into their own writing. Sometimes students become confused about where their own ideas start (and where the ideas of others begin) and feel discouraged because another writer has already expressed a similar opinion. Learning how to choose the appropriate sources, how to interact with them and how to properly incorporate them into a paper will help to alleviate those concerns. Research is a way of learning how to ask the right questions for your particular writing situation. With your teacher's help and the assistance of the librarians, you can learn how to conduct research that will support your own ideas rather than overpowering them, which will help you to become a more confident academic writer and thinker.

For more information on conducting research please see *Rules for Writers*, pages 381–404.

Along with your first-year composition courses you may be enrolled in the online course, English 197R. This course is a set of online tutorials that will help you work in more detail with the research skills described in this chapter. You should think of English 197R as a complement to the information provided in the *Guide* and the resources of the library.

7.2 Choosing a Research Topic

Sometimes the hardest parts of writing a researched paper are discovering what you want to write about and finding an appropriate focus. Some students are accustomed to working with assigned topics and may find it difficult to choose one that they find sufficiently interesting to research. Others are interested in so many ideas that they find it hard to choose the "right" topic. Whether you fall into either of these groups of students or somewhere in between, you will have to be very careful in choosing your research topic for a given assignment. A researched essay is generally one that you will spend a great deal of time thinking, reading, talking, and writing about, so be sure that the topic of that essay is one you are committed to exploring. Your teacher will generally help you decide if your topic is appropriate to the assignment, but you should first think of several possible ideas to start the discussion. In addition, most first-year writing classes will include assignments that ask you to find a "debatable" topic; this means that you will be researching an issue that other researchers have investigated and written about, so that you will be able to locate sufficient resources that will inform your understanding of the topic.

A good place to begin exploring topics is to reflect on the discussions and readings in your classes, both in your first-year writing courses and your other courses. If you are in a history class, for example, you might explore a historical event for which there are different interpretations and decide which one seems most compelling to you, based on your research and prior knowledge. Or you may simply want to explore a subject that is discussed in a class more fully because you find it intriguing or problematic. In addition, many first-year writing courses are organized around particular themes that will allow you to take a position on a debatable issue or idea within that theme.

Another effective way to decide on a topic for research and writing is to explore issues in your chosen major or in a particular field you find interesting. Each academic discipline contains its own set of hot topics or controversial issues, and if you are interested in this field as a possible career, you may find it helpful to discover what topics are currently debated in that discipline. For instance, pharmacy students may want to debate the merits of current laws that require medications containing pseudoephedrine to be dispensed only from behind the counter because of the use of that substance in manufacturing methamphetamine, while future teachers may choose to explore the efficacy of current testing standards in evaluating student and teacher performances.

For more on generating ideas for the researched essay, see "Chapter 4: Writing as a Process" and "Chapter 11: Exploring a Controversy and Writing a Public Argument." For more on posing a research question that leads to a debatable topic, see *Rules for Writers*, pages 383–85.

Some of your first-year writing teachers may ask you to identify your non-academic interests as a way of discovering issues of interest that you may be able to write about. For example, students who are passionate sports advocates might look into the regulations governing university athletics and suggest different approaches, while people who follow current events or environmental issues could take a position on the economy or on the debate around global warming.

No matter what approach you take when choosing a topic, however, it is important that you maintain your "authorial" voice and your own point of view. Your instructor wants to learn about your opinion, so try not to lose it in the voices of your sources. One way to be sure that your voice is prominent in your researched paper is to choose a topic based on your own interests, experience, knowledge, and prior opinions. The research you do can then *support* your point of view, not overtake it. It is often a tricky balancing act, but keep in mind that the research should achieve several goals: It should show that you are informed about the history of your topic, that you are aware of the complexities of the debate on which you are choosing a position, and that you have explored the various controversies, as well as the definitions and assumptions that are important in the arguments you have researched. It is extremely important to communicate with your instructor as you are considering research topics, however. Some instructors set limits on topics that have been overly debated or those that tend to be difficult to write about, such as capital punishment, euthanasia, legalization of marijuana, or abortion. Other instructors may allow students to write about these "hot button" issues, depending on the student's individual approach to the topic.

In choosing a **topic**, you should also keep in mind an important distinction: a topic is *not* an argument. A topic is a general area of inquiry, the overall subject of your essay. Using the examples discussed above, a topic might be "federal laws regulating pseudoephedrine," "educational testing standards," "plans to stimulate the economy," or "global warming." Once you have identified a topic, you will have to refine its focus in order to generate an **argument** and a thesis. A thesis is a debatable statement that takes a position or expresses an opinion about your topic: you might argue that the laws regulating pseudoephedrine are either beneficial or harmful to the public or to professional pharmacists, for instance, or you might present a position that acknowledges some of the benefits as well as drawbacks to these regulations. Or you might want to argue that the federal government should implement certain specific measures to address the problem of global warming. In each case, there is probably someone in your audience who will disagree with all or part of your argument, and you will want to consider that reader's position when you express your own.

Keyword: topic

Keyword: argument

For more on writing an effective thesis for an argument, see *Rules for Writers*, pages 23–24 and 360–62 and "Chapter 4: Writing as a Process."

Think of yourself as a participant in a debate. You must argue for a position, whatever it happens to be. Finding a paper topic that interests you will help you approach the process of researching with an open mind and a willingness to learn more. Remember, though, that you are not a passive reader; you should read a wide variety of sources, evaluate their credibility and effectiveness within the context of your assignment, and attempt to present a well-balanced argument.

7.3 Finding Sources

Once you have settled on a topic for research, the next step is to decide where to go for more information. The first and most appropriate place is the University of Arizona libraries. You may think of the library as one place or building, but in reality, the University maintains many different collections in various locations and an extensive online library. In addition to the Main Library, sometimes you will want to visit the Science and Engineering Library, the Fine Arts Collection, or Special Collections.

Since you are likely to be conducting much of your research online, you will want to familiarize yourself with the many resources available to you. One good way to do this is to use the English Composition subject guide. This guide provides links to the online catalog, many appropriate article databases, and other resources that you will need to successfully complete your research. This is just one of many subject guides; there are guides for every discipline taught on campus. It is wise to also plan on going to the library in person, however, and this section will provide a brief discussion of using both online and print sources.

To begin your online research, use the research guide for English Composition: <http://www.library. arizona.edu/ search/subjects/ englishcomp/>.

Conducting Research Online: One of the joys of research in the 21st century is that you can start at home or anywhere that you have access to the internet. Information is available 24 hours a day. However, simply being comfortable surfing the internet does not necessarily turn someone into a discerning reader or researcher. Many students come into the classroom with a great deal of confidence in their research skills, only to find out how much there is left to learn about the process. Although your teacher may allow you to use search engines like *Yahoo* or *Google*, you will also need to explore the databases to which the University libraries subscribe. These databases are collections of a wide variety of resources, such as newspapers, magazines, and scholarly journals that have been compiled online and are searchable by keyword, author, title, subject, and more. Some are available "full-text" online, which means that the entire article is readable online, while others provide an abstract or summary, which will allow you to decide whether you want to find and read the hard copy of the entire article. The journal articles are generally written with an academic audience in mind and will differ from newspaper and magazine articles in language, presentation, and depth or detail of coverage. Be sure to consult with the librarians and talk to your teachers about which sources are most suitable for your purposes; more information about online sources is found in Section 7.4, "Evaluating Sources" and at the library's website.

You can access the library's databases by title and subject, from the library's web site. Please go to <http://www .library.arizona.edu/ search/articles/>.

Using Print Sources: Although online researching is becoming increasingly convenient, sometimes you also need to go to the library. Not all journals are online yet; some are still available only in hard copy, and sometimes you'll want to use a chapter in a book that is on the shelves. Visiting the library can be helpful in the research process as well. Experienced students and professors know that when they find a book they think will be useful to their projects, another strategy for finding sources is to scan the shelves around that book for others that contain related information. For instance, if you located a book that analyzes Shakespeare's "Hamlet" by using the library's online catalog, you might see a book near it on the shelf that looks at the relationships between "Hamlet" and Shakespeare's other dramas, one that you had not found in the online catalog. Another way to use your resources is to scan the bibliographies and works cited of books and articles you have already found for more possible sources.

To use the library's online catalog, please go to <http://sabio. library.arizona.edu/ search/X>.

Sometimes the book you want is not available at the library, but can be requested via "ILL," or Interlibrary Loan. Libraries maintain lending policies with each other that allow you to take advantage of more than your local collections, but you need to plan ahead if you wish to use ILL. You can also request articles and book chapters via Interlibrary Loan which will deliver sources in electronic format to your UA email in just a couple of days.

Information about getting help in the library is found on the library's web site at <http://www.library. arizona.edu/help/ask/ index.html>.

As mentioned in Section 7.1, you should also take advantage of the librarians' specialized training in finding and evaluating information. Go to the reference desks or contact the subject specialists via email and ask for tips on where to find the kinds of resources you need.

7.4 Evaluating Sources

Every day you encounter information from multiple sources: books, teachers, friends, the internet, television, magazines, and more. When researching an essay or project, your job as a student and a critical thinker is to sift through the many conflicting claims and competing opinions and decide which are the most credible and reliable. Evaluating sources is as important a part of the research process as finding them, and there are general guidelines for both print and internet resources.

First, you will want to consider the question of "**credibility**." How believable is the information? In order to answer this question, you will need to be aware of a few basic academic rules of thumb. One distinction that is important in academic research is that made between "**scholarly**" and "**popular**" sources. A scholarly text is written for an audience with specialized knowledge and is considered part of an ongoing debate or discussion, and this is clear from the author's citation of related work that has been published on the same or related subjects. Depending on the field, the author's citations may consist of literature reviews, quotations, paraphrases, summaries, footnotes, endnotes, bibliographies, works cited, or some combination of these elements. Scholars are expected to make original contributions to their chosen fields of study, but they rely on the authority and knowledge of their

Keyword: credibility

Keyword: scholarly source

For more on credibility, see "Chapter 10: Rhetorical Analysis." For advice on determining if a source is scholarly, see *Rules for Writers*, page 401.

predecessors. An article in a scholarly text is generally longer and more detailed than one in a popular source.

Another important element of a scholarly text is where it is published. A scholarly article will not usually be available via free search engines, such as *Google*. Instead, it will be published in a journal that utilizes a process called "peer review," which means that before being accepted for publication, the article is read by experts in the field who assess its reliability and the quality of its research and writing. Only after extensive review and revision is a scholarly text published, which means that readers can consider its arguments seriously; if they disagree with an author's assertions, they must marshal their own evidence and counterarguments in an effective and thoughtful rebuttal. This give-and-take and exchange of researched opinions is an accepted part of academic discourse and is a model for what first-year writing students will begin to learn how to produce.

Keyword:
popular source

By contrast, non-academic, or "**popular**" sources rely much less on the research done by other authors. Articles in popular sources, such as newspaper or magazine articles, may quote experts, but the author does not need to provide information on how to access those expert opinions beyond naming them and perhaps providing the titles of any books or articles they have written. Even a magazine that seems to rely on factual information, such as *Newsweek* or *Scientific American*, is not considered a scholarly source, although it may work well as a starting point or even be an acceptable resource depending on your teacher's requirements. An article in a popular source is written for a general audience, so the author may not assume that the readers of such a text have any specialized knowledge. A popular article is generally shorter than an article written for a scholarly journal.

For more information on evaluating print sources, please see *Rules for Writers*, pages 387–391.

Tutorials & Guides created for English writing students, which includes a quick lesson on the differences between scholarly and popular sources, can be found on the English Composition research guide at <http://www.library.arizona.edu/search/subjects/english-comp/>.

These general guidelines apply to both print and online sources, but in evaluating online sources, there is more specific information to be considered.

Reading and Analyzing Internet Sources

One of the first discussions about research in your first-year writing courses will probably center around the differences between using a search engine such as *Yahoo* or *Google* and using a library database such as *Academic Search Complete* or *Lexis-Nexis Academic Universe*. Anyone can use a public search engine simply by going online, but the use of library databases is restricted to those with permission to do so: the students, staff, and instructors at the university. Part of your university tuition is used to pay for the information available at the library, so be sure to take advantage of this resource while you are able to do so. Never pay for an article that you find on the web. If you are ever asked to pay for an article, write down the citation information and get in touch with a librarian at the Information Commons/Reference help desk. He or she will be able to help you find it for free. More information about evaluating the credibility of various sources such as journal and newspaper articles is found above, but it is also important to think critically about other information accessible on the internet.

Some instructors will allow their students to use non-scholarly internet sources as part of their researched essay documentation, and it is especially important to evaluate these sources critically. Webpages, though frequently written by knowledgeable individuals, are not subject to the review process of a peer-reviewed scholarly source or even that of a respected popular source such as the *New York Times* or *Time* magazine. Anyone with the technical skills and access to the internet can publish a webpage on any topic even without expertise in the subject. For instance, an angry consumer can publish a webpage denouncing a certain product even if the consumer's dissatisfaction arises out of misuse rather than any defect of the product itself. If student researchers rely only on that consumer's webpage, the research and any conclusions drawn by the researchers would be limited at best and perhaps seriously incorrect. Therefore, it is important to employ the skills of rhetorical analysis when evaluating internet sources. Looking critically at the audience and purpose can shed light on the credibility of the source.

For more on rhetorical analysis, see "Chapter 10: Rhetorical Analysis."

A commonly cited internet resource is the online encyclopedia, which can range from *Encyclopedia Britannica*, which is available through the university library, to *Wikipedia*, which is a free online resource that can be edited by its users. Your instructor may or may not allow you to use encyclopedias, but if you research using these sources, you should be aware of the distinctions between them; although *Wikipedia* may well be authoritative, its quality is not monitored in the same way as an encyclopedia such as the *Encyclopedia Britannica*.

Even when a webpage looks and sounds official, you should be careful to verify that it is valid and credible. Although a web site hosted by a university with the ".edu" designation may appear to have impeccable credentials, individuals employed by universities can often post their personal opinions using a university server, and these personal opinions are not always reliable for research purposes. Other problems with information on the internet include outdated information, cursory or neglected proofreading, and frequent commercial use. Because of the array of information available on the internet, we have provided a list of questions that should prove helpful in evaluating online information. These are by no means the only questions possible, but they do serve as a starting point.

- What is the URL? Does it end with .com, .edu, .org, .gov, .biz, .name, .info, .net? What does each of these domain names imply?

- Can you identify an author for the information? Can you verify the author's expertise?

- Does the webpage provide information about when it was last updated? Is there any way of determining whether the material is out-of-date? What sorts of links are on the page? Where do these links lead you? Are the links still working?

- Is there any information on how to cite the source? Web sites catering to academic audiences are more likely to include this information than those geared for more general audiences. When citing an online article from a library index or database, the name of the database is part of the citation.

- What is the intention of the text? Is its purpose to inform, entertain, amuse, or engage the reader's interest? Or is the purpose to promote a commercial product, an idea, philosophy, or way of seeing something?

- Are there graphics? If so, what do they illustrate and why?

- Is the source biased, one-sided, incomplete, or erroneous? Who profits if viewers of the website believe its information to be true? Can you verify the information with other online or print sources?

- Does the source suggest avenues for further inquiry such as possible readings, research, or links? Does it cite reputable sources or note the extent to which claims in the text are connected to recognized authorities in the field?

For more information and additional examples of how to evaluate and use Internet sources, please refer to *Rules for Writers,* pages 397–404.

Evaluating websites carefully is an essential part of your research process, since the reliability of your own argument in an academic context will depend in large part upon the credibility of your citations and sources. Whenever you are in doubt about the suitability of a certain source, consult your teacher and the librarians.

7.5 Engaging with and Keeping Track of Sources

As you research your topic, make a conscious effort to keep track of the sources you find. Keeping track of sources is about more than organization, although staying organized while you do research will save you a lot of time in the long run. In addition to keeping track of basic information about your sources, you can begin the actual writing process as you collect your sources by taking notes in which you interact with the source. This section will address both aspects of tracking sources.

Recording Crucial Information

When you use the online and physical library to search for books and journal articles, and as you copy or print articles, it is easy to forget to keep track of all the bibliographic material you will need to compile your Works Cited page at the end of your essay. It is annoying and frustrating to retrace your steps later to find a publisher's name, a page number, or the database for an online article. Here are a few tips:

- Keep track of your research in a research log—to do this, record the databases and indexes you search and the keywords that you use in each database. Keep this log with the notes you take. This will help you keep track of where you have looked and what sources were good for your topic.

- Copy materials you cannot check out of the library for an extended period (such as journals). Print or download articles or texts that you find online. Do not assume that you will be able to find such sources again later; they may be in use or in the process of being re-shelved when you look for them again. In the case of online materials, don't assume that you can find the article again easily. It will save you time to print or download the article at the time you find it.

- Another option for compiling resources is a software product called RefWorks that formats and organizes your citations and bibliographies as you work. A librarian can help you learn to use this resource.

  Use RefWorks to keep track of your resources.

- Whenever you copy or print materials out of a book, journal, or online database, immediately write down any information that you will need for either your in-text citation or your Works Cited page. Make it a habit to write this information on the first page of anything you copy or print and record it in your research log. A complete listing of the information commonly required for citation follows.

  You can find RefWorks on the English Composition page.

For books:
- Author(s) and/or editor(s).

- Title of book.

- Edition of book (if multiple editions have been printed).

- Date book was published.

- Name of publisher.

- Place of publication.

- Page number for direct quotations, paraphrases, and/or summaries.

- When citing chapters of edited books, you also need the authors of the chapter, the title of the chapter and the page numbers of the chapter, along with the above information.

For journals—both print and online:

- Author(s) of article.

- Title of article.

- Title of journal.

- Volume number of journal.

- Issue number of journal.

- Page numbers of article.

- Date of publication.

- Date of viewing (in case of web-based materials).

- Name of index or database, if you get article online.

- URL of publication (in case of web-based materials).

- Page number for direct quotations, paraphrases, and/or summaries.

For more information on keeping track of sources, see *Rules for Writers*, pages 405–10. For citation models in MLA style, see updated *Rules for Writers* pamphlet about MLA citations.

An example of a citation in MLA Style for an article found online from the index *Academic Search Complete* is below. If you end up using this source in the final version of your paper, you could simply copy the citation from your notes or research log, thus saving time and work.

Antoniou, Maria, and Jessica Moriarty, "What Can Academic Writers Learn from Creative Writers? Developing Guidance and Support for Lecturers in Higher Education." *Teaching in Higher Education* 13.2 (Apr. 2008): 157–167. Academic Search Complete. Web. 15 Apr. 2009.

For more information on paraphrase, summary, and quotation see *Rules for Writers*, pages 408–10 and 415–26. Also see "Chapter 6: Working With Sources: Summary, Paraphrase, and Quotation."

Compile an Annotated Bibliography, in which you include all the bibliographic information (in the required format for your paper) and a brief description of each text. This will help you keep track of who said what. You can easily flip through it to remind yourself of each author's main points. See the discussion of Annotated Bibliographies in Chapter 11.

- As you are drafting your paper, write the author and page number in the margins next to any quotation or paraphrase you use. If you are typing your paper, insert this bibliographic information right after the material from the source. That way you will be certain to cite all your references, and when you revise you won't have to look through all your materials to find the correct citation again.

- When you begin compiling your Works Cited list, refer to "MLA Documentation" in *Rules for Writers*, starting on page 424. There is also an MLA tutorial with examples of how to cite print and online sources at <http://www.library.arizona.edu/help/tutorials/citation/mla/>.

Engaging with Your Sources

Note-taking is an essential and potentially very productive part of both the research and the writing processes. Think about taking notes as having a conversation with a source and asking questions you might eventually address in your paper. "Chapter 3: Close Reading and Interacting with the Text," illustrates how to annotate a primary text as you close read. When you take research notes, you can follow a similar process, only you are responding to each source and considering it under a particular light, as opposed to just trying to understand what it means. If you write or type substantial notes while you study your sources, you will find it much easier to integrate ideas about those sources into your essay. Looking back over your notes, you will probably find that you have already recorded ideas, made points, and interacted with evidence that can fit nicely into your working draft.

When reading through your sources, you should not just highlight large sections of the text. This is because when you look at such highlighted text later, you will either not remember why you highlighted that section, or you could be overwhelmed by the amount of text, leading you either to quote too much of the source in your essay or to skip that section of the source altogether because it isn't manageable. Asking questions and making comments while you read your sources helps you to do the work and to think critically through the issues as you go along during the research process. Note-taking can also help you see patterns among sources, which may help you identify where your voice comes into the conversation. You may realize that you have only found one-sided sources, thereby giving you a direction for further research while you still have plenty of time left to write.

The first step to saving time and note-taking work for you is to record the citation of the source you are working with, as described above. You can copy this citation directly from your research log. Let's say you are writing about problems in the elementary education of minority children, particularly in relation to reading and their being able to relate to the characters in the books they read. You find and read the article by Nancy Tolson listed below. At the top of the page you would write the bibliographic information. Below this, you would begin to take notes. One effective approach is to begin by dividing your page into two columns. On the left side, write the page number and a quotation or paraphrase from the source you are working with that you find particularly interesting, relevant, well-stated, or even confusing. Writing the quotation will help you to consider it more fully than if you just looked at it on the page and recorded the page number. Now, on the right, interact with this passage you have referenced. Ask questions and discuss how relevant the particular piece of information from the source might be for your proposed topic. If an expert's name is mentioned, you might want to make a note to look further into that person's work on the subject. You can be informal when conversing with texts; taking notes is like talking back to your sources. Being casual can demystify the process, making it more comfortable and generative, and you can always dress up your language in your actual draft. See the student-written example below provided by UA librarian Vicki Mills:

Tolson, Nancy. "Making Books Available: The Role of Early Libraries, Librarians, and Booksellers in the Promotion of African American Children's Literature." *African American Review*. 32.1 (1998): 9–16. *Academic Search Complete*. Web. 1 Oct. 2008.

Source Material	Notes, Questions, etc.
"African American children's books are in existence today because of the determination and dedication of African Americans who decided more than sixty years ago to remove negative depictions of servile, impoverished African Americans from library shelves. These people were able to establish criteria, petition publishers, and creatively write stories for African American children that reflected positive images at a time when few of these books could get published." (15)	This seems to be Tolson's thesis, and I agree with it. The focus is pretty historical throughout the article though. My question would be, what is happening with the depiction of minorities in children's books now? Surely they are still problematic at times. So I need to look for more contemporary articles on this. I also wonder what these negative depictions did to children's desire to read and to their own identity. I need to reread this article more carefully and then look for other articles that relate the lack of books with positive minority role models to the reading ability of minority children.

| "Bontemps, being both an educator and the father of six children, knew the importance of writing books that would reflect positive African American images; this meant, among other things, freeing his African American characters from the heavy dialect that most other authors had imposed upon them." (10) | The part of the article brings up two issues for me. One is that Bontemps was a father and realized the importance of reading to children. So this is one way I might go with this paper—the importance of parents reading to children and the problem of minority parents finding enough appropriate books to read. Also, I like the way Tolson says that the depictions in Bontemps' books meant "*freeing*...characters from the heavy dialect." The same thing happens in the depiction of other minority characters—American Indian, Hispanic, or Asian American—they are basically trapped and limited by the language and the behavior the author assigns them (particularly if that author is not from the minority group). So minority children see in these books what they are supposed to sound like and act like, not what they actually sound or act like, which must be really confusing for them sometimes. |

Notice that in this example, the student has pulled quotations she finds interesting and relevant, and she has kept her research in mind when conversing with the sources. Some of her observations, like "The same thing happens in the depiction of other minority characters—American Indian, Hispanic or Asian American—they are basically trapped and limited by the language and the behavior the author assigns them," could potentially be integrated into a paper with minimal adjustments to the language and style.

7.6 Conducting Interviews

Because you are here at the University of Arizona, you have many resources available to you other than the materials in the library. You are surrounded by professors, graduate students, and other members of the university community who are involved in debates currently occurring in their disciplines. A research project can provide an excellent opportunity for you to talk with faculty and graduate students about your academic or professional interests outside the confines of a particular class. In addition, government and non-profit agencies in Tucson may address the concerns you want to research. As you work on your research project, take advantage of these resources. You can use them as general resources to get a sense of some of the controversies surrounding the issue. Or you might rely on them later in your research project when you are seeking more detailed analysis of your specific, narrowed topic. Your instructor may provide you with specific guidelines about using interviews in your research, but here are some general guidelines to get you started.

Conducting the Interview: Some Guidelines for Success

While interviews can be valuable research tools, they also require preparation, organization, and attention to detail in order to be successful. Successful interviews happen when the interviewee (the person being interviewed) feels comfortable enough with the interviewer (the person conducting the interview) to share his or her knowledge, experiences, and opinions freely. If you are interviewing someone for a research project, then, part of your job will be to create a comfortable interview environment, and doing so requires much more than simply choosing the best table at your favorite coffee shop.

You will also want to make sure that you come to the interview prepared and on time, with your materials organized and ready to go. Advanced preparation is crucial because it signals to your interviewee that you take the process seriously and value his or her time. The more effort you put into preparing for the interview, the more effort your interviewee will be likely to put into his or her responses. Approaching the process in three phases—before, during, and after the interview—can help you stay organized as you move through the interview process. In addition, the following guidelines can help you ensure a successful interview:

Before the Interview

Write Interview Questions: The most important task you will complete before the interview will be to write interview questions that relate to your research project. Keep in mind that effective interview questions are keys to a successful interview, and the questions you ask will determine the kinds of responses you receive from your interviewee. While closed questions—those that can be answered with a single response, such as "yes" or "no"—can be useful, you will want to frame most of your questions in ways that elicit more detailed responses. Open-ended questions—those that can't be answered with a simple "yes" or "no"—are useful in interview situations because they give the interviewee room for discussion. For example, an open-ended question like "In what ways has the U.S. economic crisis affected the University of Arizona?" will lead to a more detailed response than a closed question like "Has the University of Arizona been affected by the U.S. economic crisis?" You should plan to write between 10–20 interview questions, though you should anticipate only having time to ask 5–10 of these. To practice writing interview questions, revise the following closed sentences to make them more open-ended:

- Do you think that the U.S. policy on immigration is fair?

- Should parents prevent children from watching too much T.V.?

- Is global warming a proven phenomenon in the scientific community?

Gather Interview Materials: Before the interview, you will also want to gather and organize any materials you will need during the interview, including a tape recorder, notepads, pencils, pens, and so forth. As you collect materials, try to think of everything you will need during the interview, and organize it in a way that will make it easy for you to access it. For example, recording an interview is helpful because it will enable you to focus your attention on the interviewee, rather than on taking notes. While you will want to take notes during the interview, you don't want to be so consumed by your note-taking that you fail to really *listen* to what your interviewee has to say. If you do decide to record the interview, you will need to make sure that you have sufficient batteries and storage space for your recording device, and that your technology works properly. Most importantly, you need to make sure and ask the interviewee for permission to record *before* starting the interview—only record the interview if you have gained permission from your interviewee.

Conduct a Mock Interview: You will also want to practice asking your questions before you go into the interview. Practice asking your questions out loud, preferably with someone else. Doing so will ensure that you are comfortable with the phrasing and pronunciation of your questions before the interview.

During the Interview

Arrive Early: You will want to plan on arriving to the interview about 10–15 minutes ahead of time to set up for the interview. During this time, you can go through your questions, set up your recording devices (in case the interviewee agrees to be recorded), and prepare for note-taking.

Set a Positive Tone: Setting a positive tone for the interview is the first step in creating a comfortable environment, and it also serves to create a connection between you and the interviewee. To set a positive tone, begin by establishing a context for the interview—what you're researching, what you hope to find out, and why you're interested in the topic. In other words, you want to give your interviewee a sense of why he or she has been asked to participate in this research, and you want to show her or him that you have a vested interest in the subject. You also want to make sure and thank the interviewee for taking the time to participate in the research. You can also set a positive tone by greeting the person with a friendly handshake, smiling, and making eye contact.

Listen Attentively: Throughout the interview, make it a point to really listen to what the interviewee has to say. While note-taking is an important part of conducting interviews, listening is even more important; thus you should strive for a balance between your impulse to take notes and your role as a listener. For instance, one way to show your interviewee that you're listening is through body language. Nodding your head as the interviewee talks, making eye contact, leaning in to hear what he or she is saying, and simply smiling at an insightful comment can show your interviewee that you care about what they have to say. In addition, asking follow-up questions in response to something your interviewee says can create an organic, conversational dynamic that not only shows your engagement with the interview, but also helps maintain the positive tone you set at the beginning of the interview.

Ask Follow-Up Questions: Part of being an effective interviewer means being flexible and working with the material that comes out of the interview. This means that even though you have prepared a list of questions to ask during the interview, you will want to adapt your questions to suit the development of the interview. For example, let's say your interviewee has just given you an insightful response to a question, causing you to consider a point you haven't yet considered in your research. Instead of switching topics and asking a new question, you may want to follow up with a statement like "I find your statement about X really interesting. Can you elaborate on that?" or "That's a really intriguing point that I hadn't thought of. Can you say more about that?"

Request Clarification: If you do not hear or do not understand something, ask your interviewee to repeat it or to clarify the point. You want to make sure to capture as accurately as possible the interviewee's statements, and these requests are one way of doing so.

Offer to Share Your Transcript and Research: At the end of your interview, you may want to offer to send your interview transcript (the typed notes from your interview) to the interviewee to check for accuracy. Doing so will help assure you have thoroughly captured the details of the interview and can help you refine your notes, especially if you feel you have missed something. If you feel comfortable doing so, you may want to offer to share your research with the interviewee once it's completed. Finally, remember to thank the interviewee for his or her time and participation!

After the Interview

Transcribe the Interview: You should transcribe the interview while it's still fresh in your mind—within one or two days after the interview. This will help you remember to include important details that you may forget over time. To transcribe an interview, you will need to type your notes from the interview. If you recorded the interview, then your transcription will require you to go back and listen to the interview, typing out the parts of the interview most relevant to your research project. You should also include your own observations during the interview—for instance, you may want to note instances where your interviewee was particularly engaged or excited about a question.

Analyze the Data: After you have prepared your interview transcript, you will go back and study it carefully, noting the points that you will want to include in your research project. As you study this data, it is important that you let the research speak for itself. While you can certainly analyze the information you obtain during the interview, you must be careful not to impose subjective interpretations of what the interviewee meant by a certain statement. In other words, you have to be careful not to misrepresent your interviewee or the information they give you to serve your own research agenda. Instead, you may want to include excerpts from the transcript in your research paper and then provide follow-up analysis that uses hedging to pose possible interpretations of the data.

For more on hedging as a writing strategy, see "Chapter 2: Academic Discourse as Writing for Specific Audiences and Purposes."

Thank the Interviewee: The most important thing you will do after your interview is send a formal thank you to the interviewee because it leaves them with a positive impression of the experience. You may do this via email, or you can send a hand-written card to the interviewee if you have obtained a mailing address. If you have offered to send your completed research to the interviewee, then you may send this along with your thank you. However, you should try to send your thank you within one or two weeks of the interview so that you do not forget this important step.

While these guidelines provide you with the tools necessary for conducting effective interviews, you (the interviewer) play the most significant role in the success of this research method. Remember to relax, breathe, smile, and listen—these simple things alone can help you make a positive, lasting impression.

To cite the interview for your paper, you would follow this format:

Last name, first name of person interviewed. Personal interview. Day Month Year.

An Overview of the Interview Process

- Research potential interview participants.

- Contact potential interviewees and explain project.

- Arrange time for interview.

- Prepare interview questions.

- Practice questions in a mock interview.

- Conduct interview.

- Write up interview notes.

- Ask follow-up questions if necessary.

- Send a thank-you note to the person you interviewed.

- Provide interviewee with copy of final paper (optional).

7.7 Research Checklist

The following checklist can help you remember and keep track of all the stages in the research process and assess your progress as you work through the process.

- [ ] Do the weekly modules in the online Research Lab—this class will go into more detail about doing research.

- [ ] Brainstorm topics.

- [ ] Form a list of possible topics.

☐ Browse a site like *CQ Researcher,* the *Hot Topics* part of the *English Composition research guide,* or one of the subject encyclopedias on the library's website to gather ideas about topics.

☐ Narrow down list of possible topics to one or two ideas.

☐ Get more details and sources on your topic or topics using keyword searches in the Library Catalog and databases like Academic Search Complete. Remember you can also find other good sources from the bibliographies of the books and articles you find.

☐ Record promising sources (links to full-text articles, call numbers, etc.).

☐ Get books from the stacks. Skim for appropriateness. Check out the best sources from the library. When you find good books for your topic, browse the shelves around your book.

☐ Photocopy, print or download articles from scholarly journals and periodicals.

☐ Formulate focused research questions.

☐ Read though your sources. Take notes and summarize your best sources.

☐ Keep track of your sources. Keep a research journal. You may also want to use a service like RefWorks or Zotero to help you with this.

☐ Schedule an interview with an expert on the issue you're interested in. Prepare questions and talking points ahead of time.

☐ Meet with a librarian, either at a reference desk or by appointment.

☐ Double-check that you have all of the sources you need. Check, also, that you've written down all information needed for your own Works Cited list.

☐ Begin writing your first draft!

PART III

Assignments

8
Analysis

Goals

Your textual analysis essay should:

✓ Demonstrate that you have read a text closely, carefully, and critically.

✓ Show a critical awareness of the author's choices and strategies.

✓ Develop a clear and specific thesis that invites the reader to read the text in the same way that you do.

✓ Provide a vivid description of the text (if applicable).

✓ Analyze elements that contribute to the overall meaning or effect of the whole.

✓ Integrate evidence from the text to support your thesis.

✓ Provide a clear and persuasive argument for your interpretation of the text.

✓ Develop well-organized paragraphs.

✓ Provide meaningful feedback to your peers during the revision process.

✓ Incorporate peer and instructor feedback in the final version.

8.1 Analysis: Reading with a Critical Eye

All of the assignments you will be asked to complete in your first-year writing courses require analysis. In fact, in much of the writing and work you do at the university, you will be asked to analyze *something* and to pose your own understanding of it. In your English class, that "something" might be a written text, an image, or an audience; in your Art History class it might be a particular social or historical context, an artist's technique, or a particular medium. In your Biology class, you might analyze cellular function, an ecosystem, or the life cycle of a particular organism; in your chemistry class, you might analyze the chemical properties of a compound or the results of a chemical reaction. Regardless of what "something" you are analyzing, you are essentially performing the same cognitive task: closely and carefully examining the subject in an attempt to understand it better. That is, any type of analysis asks you to *examine*, to *read* "something" with a critical eye. Analysis plays a significant role in any field of study, and it will likely play a significant role in your success as a college student since you will do it in almost every class you take.

In this chapter, you will consider the different methods of analysis you will use in your first-year composition courses, including written textual analysis, visual analysis, and spatial analysis. While these analytical methods study very different types of texts, all analysis shares some common strategies. We will spend the rest of the chapter illustrating how to analyze written, visual, and spatial texts.

In your first-year writing courses, analysis requires an ability to explain how and why a written or visual text works to make meaning using concrete examples from the text. The skills you will need for analysis in first-year composition are fairly consistent and can be applied to all types of texts. But before we move into our discussion of analysis, let's take a moment to define some key terms for this chapter:

For more information on analysis and to see a sample student analysis, see *Rules for Writers*, pages 352–57. For more information about the differences between summary and analysis in academic writing, see pages 130–31 of the *Student's Guide*.

- **Analysis:** The ability to explain *how* and *why* a written or visual text does something and whether the choices made are effective. This goes a few steps beyond summary/description, as summary/description explains *what* is happening with a topic, while analysis explains *how* and *why* something is happening with the same topic. It is the act of breaking a text into parts and examining how those parts create meaning and affect a reader's or viewer's response.

In your first-year writing courses, you will want to be careful not to confuse analysis with summary. Unlike analysis, summary is a statement of the facts about a text, not a critical examination of it. When you summarize a text, you are not engaging in analysis. Instead, summary functions as a way of familiarizing your reader with a given text so that she or he can understand your analysis of it. For example, if you were to write, "This morning's *Daily Wildcat* included an Opinion piece that criticized the president for his foreign policy," you would be summarizing because you are stating what the article is about. To make this statement more analytical, you would need to move beyond summary. For instance, you might write, "The author of the Opinion piece in today's *Daily Wildcat* provides misleading evidence to support his argument that the president's foreign policy is in need of reform. The author's lack of careful attention to the evidence he cites results in an unconvincing argument and undermines the credibility of the *Wildcat*." Notice how the analytical statements reveal a careful consideration of the text beyond just its main point and open up a space for dialogue.

- **Text:** Any "something" that you analyze—whether written or visual. In your first-year writing courses, you'll be dealing with a variety of texts. For example, a text might refer to a book, a newspaper article, a short story, a poem, a speech, a movie, a picture, a videogame, a person, an event, a space, a place, and so on.

For an outline of a visual text, see *Rules for Writers*, page 349–51.

- **Strategies:** How writers, artists, architects, and other creators of texts decide to present their texts and ideas. Strategies include repetition of key terms, use of extended metaphors, arrangement of the text, choice of color and medium, and so on. For example, we have decided to use bullets in this chapter to outline definitions. Why did we do this instead of writing paragraphs for each item? What is the effect of this writing strategy?

When applying these terms to analysis, maintaining focus is essential. In other words, you should have a particular focus when doing analysis because no single essay on a particular text can pretend to say everything there is to say about that text. If you try to take on too much in your essay, you will find that the thesis will lack specificity and the paragraphs will be unfocused. Therefore, you will want to read the assigned texts for the unit carefully, paying attention to particular choices and strategies. What you notice about a text could be any element that conveys a message to an audience. In fact, sometimes what is *not* said is as important as what is said. For example, when you watch a CEO boardroom scene in a movie, you might see eight older white men, a younger white man, and one older African-American man. Think of what is missing from the scene: other races, women, younger people, people who look like they are from a lower socio-economic status, and so on. What does this tell us about power in this situation—and what are the broader implications of presenting the corporate world in this way?

In addition to being a focused study of a text's strategies, analytical writing must also be persuasive in order to be effective. In any type of analysis, you are inviting the audience to see the text in the same way that you do. However, your goal is not to uncover the one "true" meaning that the artist/writer intended. As film scholar Greg M. Smith argues, "One of the first steps that the budding critic should avoid is thinking that a film can be understood as having a single message that we either 'get' or don't get. To think that way is to treat film as a telegram" (66). Films aren't telegrams, and neither are other forms of text, whether visual or textual. In other words, texts do not consist of a singular message; rather, they comprise several potential messages and meanings that the viewer or reader works to uncover in the act of analysis. Texts are complex expressions that invite many interpretations. How you interpret a text will depend on your unique interests, cultural background, experience, knowledge, and perspective. In analytical writing you are enhancing the complexity of the text's meaning by inviting an audience to see the text through your perspective. Therefore, it is important to think about what *you* see in a text that others might not.

As you interpret the text, consider the following questions posed by composition scholars Rosenwasser and Stephen:

- Which details are significant and which aren't? Why?

- What is the significance of a particular detail? What does it mean?

- What else might it mean?

- How do the details fit together? What do they have in common?

- What does this pattern of details mean?

- What else might this same pattern of details mean? How else could it be explained?

- What details don't seem to fit? How might they be connected with other details to form a pattern?

- What does this new pattern mean? How might it cause me to read the meaning of individual details differently? (5–6)

For more information about organizing your ideas, see "Chapter 4: Writing as a Process" in the *Student's Guide*, and *Rules for Writers*, pages 11–16.

Once you choose a focus, you need to devise a strong, clear **thesis** that you can support with specific references to the text. Although different methods of analysis require writers to focus on different features, all methods of analysis are similar in that they provide a way to look closely at selected aspects of the text. Keep in mind that analysis always goes beyond mere observation. You should aim to articulate the significance of your observations in a coherent argument. In an analysis essay, you should demonstrate your ability to develop a clear interpretation of a text based on **evidence** from the text itself and from the method of analysis you use. For instance, a literary analyst might notice the images in a poem and develop an interpretive analysis of these images' significance to the poem's overall meaning.

For more information on writing an effective thesis, see the *Student's Guide* pages 85–88 and 166–67 and *Rules for Writers*, pages 21–24. To see a sample thesis statement in a student's analysis, refer to *Rules for Writers*, page 354.

For more information on using evidence, see *Rules for Writers*, pages 363–66.

For examples of what an analysis essay may look like, please refer to the essays in "Part IV: Sample Essays" in the *Student's Guide*. Also see pages 354–357 in *Rules for Writers*.

When you write an analysis, begin by reading carefully and closely, looking for something in the text that sparks your interest, whether it be portrayals of family relationships, representations of women in social life, or recurring symbols. After you have carefully read and annotated the text several times with your focus in mind, the next step is to attach significance to your observations. By identifying strategies you are addressing the "how" question, examining how the author chose to the construct the text. Then, by attaching significance to those strategies, you are answering the "why" question and therefore broadening the meaning of the text.

Works Cited

Rosenwasser, David, and Jill Stephen. *Writing Analytically*. Fort Worth, TX: Harcourt Brace College P, 1997. Print.

Smith, Greg. "'It's Just a Movie': A Teaching Essay for Introductory Media Classes." *Writing as Revision*. Ed. Beth Alvarado, Barbara Cully, and Michael Robinson. 2nd ed. Boston: Pearson Custom, 2003. 64–71. Print.

8.2 Textual Analysis: Written Texts

We mentioned earlier in the chapter that all the analysis you will do in first-year composition will involve some kind of text, and we also said that "text" in your first-year composition courses can refer to anything from a book to a photograph. However, there are significant differences in the ways you read written texts versus the way you read visual ones. In this section, we will focus on the analysis of written texts, although we want to emphasize that the term "textual analysis" is not specific to only written texts. When you engage in textual analysis, you could be examining something written, like a poem or short story; something visual, like a photograph, a film, or a 3D text; or perhaps even something oral/aural, like sounds within certain spaces and places.

The thing you want to remember about textual analysis is that it focuses primarily on the text and may not consider factors outside of the text—things like the author's or artist's background, the audience for whom the piece was intended, or the historical period in which it was created. When you write a textual analysis paper in your first-year writing courses, you will likely be asked to examine the text alone, in isolation of these outside factors.

When examining written texts, you are looking for **entry points** into the text that will help you understand it better. Entry points can be anything from repeating patterns, extended metaphors, vivid descriptions of certain scenes or characters, or even moments in the text that caused you confusion or any other emotional response. In order to find these textual entry points, you must engage in close reading.

For more on close reading, see "Chapter 3: Close Reading and Interacting with the Text," pages 43–67.

Analyzing written texts begins with close reading—and reading closely means reading a text actively: annotating the text, underlining key ideas and phrases, posing questions, and responding to the ideas presented in it. It also means reading the text multiple times, because each reading will grant you a new way of seeing it that you may not have considered in your previous reading. You can think of actively reading a text like talking back to the text—like you are actually having a conversation with it. If the text were able to hear you, what would you say in response to the words you read? Of course, we don't actually expect you to talk aloud while reading, but imagining yourself engaged in a dialogue with the text can help you to narrow in on some of the text's most significant details: those that incited *your* response.

After you have read a text closely multiple times and annotated it, then you can begin the real work of making connections among some of the patterns and ideas you noticed while reading. At this point, you can turn to Rosenwasser and Stephen's guiding questions, noted in the previous section. These questions will enable you to work toward making the kinds of connections you will aim to make in an analytical essay, including finding supporting details to support your interpretation of the text you are working with.

In the following section, Beth Alvarado discusses the process of reading a written text for the purpose of textual analysis, and she models what it means to find entry points into a text. As she explains, writing itself can be a process of discovery that has the potential to lead to new understanding.

8.3 Writing as Inquiry

By Beth Alvarado

> [W]hen students raise meaningful questions about incongruities in their
> own worlds, they gain genuine motivation and direction for writing, and...
> when students discover new understanding through writing, the writing
> becomes valuable to them and worth sharing with others.

—Janice Lauer, from "Writing as Inquiry: Some Questions for Teachers"

In order for writing to become a process of inquiry or discovery—rather than an act of setting down the obvious or what is already known—Lauer suggests that we start with something that disturbs us or causes us cognitive dissonance. She explains that cognitive dissonance is a term psychologists use to describe

> the perception of a gap between a current set of beliefs or values and some
> new experience or idea that seems to violate or confound those beliefs.
> This clash engenders puzzlement, curiosity, a sense of enigma, sometimes
> of wonder, a pressure to restore equilibrium. While some people suppress
> such tension, the inquirer, the learner strives to resolve it by searching for
> new understanding, by going beyond the known. (20)

In other words, when you are confronted with a text that is off your mental radar, when you experience that dissonance or static in your thinking, you have a starting point for an essay. Instead of ignoring or dismissing your reaction, go on and explore why you are experiencing the "puzzlement."

This approach to analysis is based on several assumptions:

- A text does not have a fixed meaning;

- Each reader, based on his/her own assumptions or experiences, will "read" a text differently; and

- Analyzing a text is like figuring out a puzzle: You have to go back and forth, from your reactions and inferences about the text to the pieces of text to figure out the puzzle for yourself.

What I'm asking you to do, then, is to trust your own reactions to a text and write those down, but then to suspend judgment about the text (or author) and see if you can locate the parts of the text that elicited the strongest responses. Then do a closer reading of those parts. You might look at any number of characteristics of the text: word choice, tone, implications, metaphors, etc. Try to figure out why you had that reaction: What in the text caused it?

Also, how did your own assumptions or background influence your thinking? This tension or dialectic between your responses and the text, if explored, can help you come up with unique ideas for a paper and perhaps a new understanding of the text, one that will teach your reader something she might not have seen for herself.

Let me give you an example of how this might work. When students read Gloria Anzaldúa's essay "The Homeland, *Aztlán/El Otro Mexico*," many feel silenced by her tone; perhaps they feel unjustly accused by passages like this:

> The Gringo, locked into the fiction of white superiority, seized complete political power, stripping Indians and Mexicans of their land while their feet were still rooted in it. *Con el destierro y el exilo fuimos desuñados, destroncados, destripados*—we were jerked out by the roots, truncated, disemboweled, dispossessed, and separated from our identity and our history. (471)

Two things might bother some readers about this passage: One may be that they feel she is making sweeping generalizations about white people (or is retelling history in a biased way) and one may be that they don't understand Spanish. This gives those particular students two things to note in their re-reading of the text: where are the places they feel accused or that she's being biased? and where and how is she using Spanish? If they go back to the text and note evidence, they'll see that either reaction would give them plenty to investigate. In other words, if these are their reactions, they now have a choice of two topics for a paper.

Let's say you are the writer and you choose the use of Spanish as your topic. In the passage above, for instance, as is *not* true in other parts of the essay, Anzaldúa translates the Spanish—so that gives you two specific strategies to investigate: When does she translate the Spanish and when does she not? Then, let's say, you remember from class discussion that someone brought up the family stories, where she switched from Spanish to English, sometimes in the same sentence. Now you have at least three ways she uses Spanish or **three possible patterns to investigate—where she translates, where she doesn't, and where she switches back and forth in the same sentence**—and use as possible organizing principles for your paper. You also have **a central question to guide your inquiry**—or, as Lauer would put it, a "known unknown"—which is: Why does Anzaldúa use Spanish in the three different ways she does? Is there some kind of significance to the patterns? Is she trying to exclude readers?

This leads you to the issue of audience. In class, some people, like you, said they felt excluded, and so you might conclude that she *is* trying to exclude some readers—non-Spanish speakers? whites?—or, perhaps, you think, she is using the piece to recreate for her readers feelings of exclusion she has experienced. On the other hand, readers who understood Spanish said they felt included by the very strategy that others cited as alienating. In fact, there were people in class who loved the family stories because they were reminded of the way their grandparents talked. Maybe, you think, the ways Anzaldúa uses *both* languages illustrates something about her heritage and identity. Or about her conflicts? Or the border region?

Now you have a few possible **hypotheses**: "Anzaldúa uses Spanish in her essay to recreate for non-speakers the feeling of being an outsider in the hopes, perhaps, that the reader will come to understand the injustice she feels." Or: "Even though Anzaldúa risks alienating some readers by not translating from the Spanish, she is using both English and Spanish to illustrate her conflicted identity." Or: "The use of Spanish and English in the essay replicates its use in the border region." You can see how the process of inquiry can lead to different—but equally valid—positions on the same text. The next step, now that you have a tentative thesis, is to go back to the text, where you can gather and arrange your evidence, test it against your hypothesis, and begin to write a draft of your paper.

Works Cited

Anzaldúa, Gloria. "The Homeland, *Aztlán/El Otro Mexico.*" *Writing as Revision*. Eds. Beth Alvarado, Barbara Cully, and Michael Robinson. Boston: Pearson, 2003. 546–53. Print.

Lauer, Janice. "Writing as Inquiry: Some Questions for Teachers." *Writing as Revision*. 19–23. Print.

8.4 Visual Analysis

Like written texts, visual texts consist of a variety of potential interpretations and meanings. But unlike written texts, meaning in visual texts is made primarily through images, illustrations, and design. Because meaning is made differently in these two types of texts, they require different strategies of reading. That is, as a reader, you will look for and notice different things about visual texts than you would about written ones. For example, in written texts, a comparison using the words "like" or "as" signals a simile. In visual texts, where words may or may not be present, such a comparison would be made through visual gestures within the text—perhaps by juxtaposing two images in an unexpected way. You would have to read the visual elements of the text closely, as you would a written text, in order to pick up on such a message.

Put simply, what you examine in visual texts is quite different from what you examine when reading written ones. Visual texts have different ways of creating emphasis. For example, instead of noting word patterns and character descriptions like you might in written texts, you might consider the placement of images in the text (grounding), the artist's choice of colors (color scheme), or the materials that comprise the visual text (medium). Authors of written texts may also bring emphasis to certain features of their writing, but

Analytical Thesis Statements

By Amanda Brobbel

To analyze something is to ask what that something means. An analytical essay answers how something does what it does or why it is as it is. Therefore, a thesis statement in an analysis paper should be answering a *how* or *why* question.

A strong thesis makes a claim about the subject that needs proving. It provides the writer (and the reader) with a clearly focused lens through which to view the subject. A weak thesis either makes no claim or is an assertion that does not need proving. It is a fuzzy lens that will not help the writer (or the reader) be guided to a better understanding of the subject.

Most weak thesis statements suffer because they are overly broad (or not specific enough). Their grammar is often an indication of why they don't help the writer to bring their subject into clear focus. The following example from Rosenwasser and Stephen's *Writing Analytically* shows us how this works:

Broad Noun	+ Weak Verb	+ Vague, Evaluative Adjective
The economic situation	is	bad.

Specific Noun	+ Active Verb	+ Assertive Predicate
The tax policies of the current administration	threaten to reduce the tax burden on the middle class	by sacrificing education and health-care programs for everyone.

they do so with strategies that might differ from creators of visual texts—for instance, through repetition, bold description, or comparison.

Visual analysis, like textual analysis, presents opportunities for varying perspectives and interpretations. In other words, when you engage in visual analysis, you should not be searching for the "right" answer, since there can be any number of effective interpretations of a visual—a number of ways to get it "right." Individual interpretations of visual artifacts can be informed by several factors, including a person's cultural, social, economic, and educational background; the perspective from which s/he is viewing the artifact; her or his knowledge of the medium in which the artifact is presented; and

An example of a textual analysis thesis statement might look like:

Broad Noun	+ Weak Verb	+ Vague, Evaluative Adjective
Kate Chopin's story	is	about a woman who doesn't love her husband.
Specific Noun	**+ Active Verb**	**+ Assertive Predicate**
Mrs. Mallard's husband	represents	the oppression of woman in the nineteenth century.

The best way to remedy the problem of over-generalization is to move toward specificity in word choice, in sentence structure, and in idea.

"By" or "because" are words that show you are answering a *how* or *why* question.

Analytical Thesis Statement for the Text-in-Context Essay

For text-in-context, your thesis needs to interweave references to the text and its context to be considered clear and specific. Look below at the example from UA undergraduate writer Siwei Shen:

Specific reference to a context

Specific reference to a pattern in the text

Contextual explanation of its meaning

From the Marxist view, **the process of the metamorphosis** symbolizes the class struggles of the proletariat to break out of a life of being exploited. Such representation is displayed [in *The Metamorphosis*] in the *similarity* between the causes, nature, and ending of Gregor's transformation and those of proletarian struggles.

Comparison Between Text and Context

In this case the *how* is still defined by a pattern in the text, but the *why* is defined by a context that is implicit in the novel, but not obvious without research.

Work Cited

Rosenwasser, David, and Jill Stephen. *Writing Analytically*. Forth Worth, TX: Harcourt Brace College Publishers, 1997. Print.

so forth. As you investigate visuals, you want to look for aspects of the text that pique your interest and then ask yourself why those particular aspects had an effect on you. You will also want to consider the ways in which the visual artifact works to make meaning (design choices, areas of emphasis, symbolic representation, and so forth), as well as the underlying meaning— or meanings—you see being conveyed in the text.

For example, take a minute to study the following pictures, taken of the "Border Dynamics" sculpture located on the Southwest side of Harvill. Although each picture represents the same sculpture, the way in which the sculpture is represented differs from picture to picture: The pictures on the left and bottom of the page show only a partial perspective of the sculpture,

while the one on the right shows the sculpture as a whole. How do these differences in perspective change the meaning(s) conveyed by the visual? Further, how would this meaning change if you were actually able to go to the sculpture and view it from multiple perspectives?

Now, take a moment to focus on just one of the pictures. Using the questions located on page 180 as a guide, practice analyzing the picture you've chosen. Write a brief, one-paragraph response that addresses the following questions:

- What meaning(s) are being conveyed in the picture? (*Posing an interpretation*)

- What specific design choices lead you to this interpretation? (*Presenting evidence*)

- What aspects of the picture did you find most interesting and why? (*Identifying personal responses*)

In the next section, U of A writing instructor Amy Parziale provides some strategies for finding entry points into visual texts, and she provides an example of what it means to analyze a photograph.

8.5 Reading Visual Rhetoric

By Amy Parziale

While we may not know it, we all interpret and analyze visual messages every day. This section's purpose is to make you more aware of visual rhetoric so that you may be more critical of the messages you see. Why is understanding visual rhetoric important? Consider the controversy over the versions of a single photograph, O.J. Simpson's 1994 mug shot. In 1994, both *Time* and *Newsweek* ran O.J. Simpson's mug shot on the cover of the magazine after he was accused of murdering Nicole Brown Simpson and Ronald Goldman. The editors of *Time* altered the photograph, darkening Simpson's skin. Many argued this was done to stereotype Simpson as the "violent black man" in order to imply his guilt. By thinking critically about the images around us, we become more aware of the ways in which such images attempt to manipulate our perspectives.

Visual rhetoric is a form of communication in which visual elements create meanings and arguments. Advertising is the most obvious form of visual rhetoric in the contemporary world, but works of art, photographs, websites, brochures, even bumper stickers contain visual rhetoric. Think about the meaning(s) and argument(s) created in a stained glass window at a local church, a political cartoon in *The New Yorker*, or the brochure sent to prospective students by the University of Arizona. Each creates a specific message that the visual elements of the piece are meant to communicate to the intended audience.

Some elements that can be a part of visual rhetoric include:

- Types of visuals (text, images, clip art, photographs, etc.)
- Color palette (individual element's color, background, contrast, etc.)
- Font choices (size, color, typeface, etc.)
- Organization and arrangement of the elements in the work (foreground, background, top, bottom, etc.).

For more information on rhetorical analysis, see "Chapter 10: Rhetorical Analysis."

Just like textual rhetoric, the author's purpose in using visual rhetoric is to best persuade her audience to her position—whether it is which shampoo to purchase or who to vote for in an election. Like textual rhetoric, you should consider:

- Who is the author's primary audience? Does she have any secondary audiences?
- What is the work's purpose? What is it attempting to persuade its audience to do/think/feel?
- Are there potential secondary purposes? (These can be conscious or unconscious.)
- How does the work employ rhetorical appeals?
- How successful is it in achieving its purpose(s)? Which elements work in harmony together?
- How could it be improved? Which elements are less successful? Are there elements that seem to contradict or challenge the message or purpose?

When examining a work's visual rhetoric, start by writing down everything you see.

- How do you think the piece was created (photography, painting, film, computer-generated techniques, etc.)?
- What elements make up the piece? How are they arranged? How are they related?
- What is in focus and what is out of focus?

- What size are the objects in comparison to each other? Are the objects to scale?

- How does your eye move around the piece? What elements draw your eye and how is that accomplished?

- What shapes, colors, texture, lighting, shadows, and types of lines are used? What is lightest? What is darkest?

- What sense of space is created? Do objects overlap? What is in the foreground, middle ground, and background? What is in each third of the piece—top, middle, bottom, left, middle, and right?

- What vantage point is the piece created from? How is the piece framed? What is included? What do you think lies beyond the edges?

- Do the elements compliment or contrast with each other? Is a specific element repeated? Is there variety in the elements?

- Does the piece feel balanced? Is there a sense of unity? What feeling and mood best summarize the piece?

Once you've described the many aspects of the piece you can begin to consider how it creates meaning and how well it persuades its audience with its argument.

- What is the overall message? How persuasively is that message communicated? Do any of the elements feel as if they are in opposition to that message?

- Does the work create a sense of credibility? Does it include facts and figures? Is there a narrative or story? Does it appeal to you on a specific emotional level?

- Who is the intended audience? Who does the intended audience include/exclude?

- Does the piece interact (consciously or unconsciously) with issues of culture, language, class, race, ethnicity, country of origin, gender, or sexual orientation?

- What is left out of the piece?

- Are you persuaded by its rhetoric? Do you agree with its message?

Applying Visual Analysis

Let's take a look at a photograph and consider some of the elements that contribute to its visual rhetoric.

Here's a photograph used for marketing purposes by the University of Arizona. Notice how the students are posed. The two students do not look like they were just sitting there and someone took their picture. Instead, it looks like they were asked to sit in this particular position at this particular location. Looking at their body positions, it becomes clear that if they were talking, they would not be facing each other. Look at the expressions on both of their faces. While they are both smiling, they do not look very comfortable having their picture taken. All of these elements support the claim that this photograph was not a candid photo, but was posed for the purpose of using it in marketing.

After determining that the photograph is a marketing tool, we might want to consider the choice of these two students. Why two male students? Why do they both have backpacks on? What does that tell us about them as students? Why these two students? Is it important to consider the fact that one of the students is of Asian heritage, especially since Asian males make up less than 3% of the UA student population (UA Fact Book)? What do we make of their clothing? Why are the students sitting in front of the Student Union? What's going on in the background and how does that affect our reading of the photo? What message do you think the University wishes to portray through this photo? Is the image successful in representing the desired message?

Understanding visual rhetoric allows us to engage with the multitude of images we are bombarded with each day on a more critical level. The next time you are driving by a billboard, strolling through a museum, or flipping through a magazine, pause and consider how the image constructs its meaning through visual rhetoric.

Works Cited

UA Fact Book. Fall 2006. Web. 12 March 2008.

8.6 Reading a Film

By Amy Parziale

Like visual rhetoric, we tend to interpret films without acknowledging that we are thinking critically about the images we see. When asked about a film, you might answer, "I really liked that film" or "I hated it." You may not immediately be able to articulate why you had such a reaction, but if pressed, most people will actually give a close reading: "The dialogue was stilted and unrealistic" or "The main character wasn't fully developed so I didn't care about her." These close readings are the beginning of film interpretation. In this section we will go over some basic filmic terminology and techniques in order to assist you in improving your ability to analyze film. All elements of a film are carefully chosen and constructed in accordance with the filmmakers' vision. Because they are made by people, films express those individuals' personal and cultural ideologies. By being able to examine a film critically, you will be able to analyze the messages being expressed. As with other types of analysis, you will need to come up with a unique argument about the film and substantiate your claims by interpreting specific details.

Shot: what is captured during an uninterrupted period of time by one camera. An **establishing shot** is an initial shot that establishes the setting and orients the viewer to the world of the film. **Shot/reverse shot** is an editing technique often used between characters or actions. This technique is most often used during conversations in order to capture both the speaker and the reaction of the person being spoken to. Establishing shots, shot/reverse shots, **eyeline matches** and **match on action shots** are all components of Continuity Editing (see below).

Cut: during editing, the process by which two shots are joined; in the finished film, the instantaneous transition from one shot to another. The cut is the most common technique used to transition between shots. Other transition techniques include wipes, iris open/close, dissolves, fade-in/fade-out, and fade to black or white. **Continuity editing** is the system by which most films' shots are combined. Continuity editing uses cuts and other transitions to establish the reality of the world of the film, construct a coherent sense of time and space, and tell stories efficiently and effectively. A **take** is the amount of time a particular camera rolls without stopping. In continuity editing, filmmakers tend not to use overly short or long takes. But, a filmmaker may decide to build suspense by quickly cutting between the same shot/reverse shot over and over again, or she may decide to use a **long take** in which viewers will become uncomfortable because they are not used to watching from one position for a long period of time. *In the Bedroom* and *Secrets and Lies* are two films that use extremely long takes for dramatic effect.

Diegesis: the world of the film. The diegesis does not need to follow our understanding of reality but needs to be consistent throughout the film to create a sense of time and space, a world that the viewer can believe in during the viewing. The diegesis of a film includes things that are situated in both on-screen and off-screen space. **On-screen Space** is the space seen within the frame, what is on the screen. **Off-screen Space** is the space not seen within the frame. When a character or object is off-screen, the viewer will continue to believe in its presence.

Framing: the use of the camera's limits to determine what appears on screen and what does not. **Mobile framing** is framing in which the camera moves. Some common types of mobile framing are: **handheld shots, crane shots, dolly or tracking shots, panning** (in which the camera moves on a vertical axis), and **tilting** (in which the camera moves on a horizontal axis).

Shot Scale: the distance of framing in a shot or how much is captured by the camera. There are seven generally accepted shot scales. An **extreme long shot** can capture more than the human body; it may show a landscape, building, or crowd of people. A **long shot** is capable of showing the entire human body at once. A **medium long shot**, called an **American shot**, captures the human body from about the knee up. The **medium shot** will show a person from the waist up. The **medium close-up** shows a person from the chest up. A **close-up** can be of any object shown up close so it appears quite large and fills the majority of the screen. Many close-ups are of the human face, generally from the neck up. An **extreme close-up** shows a part of a larger object, a part of the human body, or a very small object. The object or part of an object appears very large taking up the entire screen. Shot scales vary; it is possible to have a shot that is in between a medium and a medium close-up, for example. Naming a shot's scale is not an exact science but should follow these widely accepted definitions.

Shot Angle: the angle of the camera lens relative to what it is capturing. A **high angle shot** looks down at its subject from a higher angle. A **low angle shot** looks up at the subject from below. Using different angles can create meaning in the film. A character who is always shot from a high angle may seem powerless and trapped while a character who is always shot from a low angle may seem powerful and imposing. Of course, this interpretation of the angle depends upon the other elements of the film. Like all cinematic elements, shot angles do not have specific, set meanings.

Mise-en-scène: literally "put on stage" in French. In films, mise-en-scène is created by four components: **lighting, setting/props, make-up/costume,** and **figure behavior**. These are elements within the frame that the filmmaker has the power to control.

Lighting: the type of light used in a particular shot or sequence of shots. The most common lighting technique is **three-point lighting**, which consists of a backlight, key light, and fill light. By using these three points of light, the human face can be lit in such a way that there are no shadows on the face, thus allowing the viewer to see even minute changes in the actor's face. **Backlighting** is a technique used that illuminates the set from behind. **Key lighting** is the brightest light in three-point lighting and generally illuminates the face from the front. Because this bright light creates shadows, three-point lighting also uses a **fill light**, which fills in the shadows created by the key light. The fill light is generally positioned to one side of the character and near the camera in order to eliminate shadows. **High-key lighting** refers to a scene with a very bright key light causing the scene to have almost no shadows. **Low-key lighting** refers to a noticeable difference between the brightness of the key and fill lights, creating deep shadows.

Setting: the location of the film. The setting can be on-location, on a set, or created digitally. Many filmmakers attempt to create an authentic setting for their story. A film's settings can move across several spaces, even several countries, or a film can have a more restricted setting, for example one room of a house. Alfred Hitchcock's *Lifeboat* is a good example of a restricted setting as the film takes place in a lifeboat. The setting sets the mood and can affect how we interpret the plot of the film.

Props: any object in the setting that has a function or meaning within the film. "Prop" is actually short for "property" and is a term borrowed from the theater. Props can act as catalysts for action, as a motif, or as foreshadowing. A famous example of a prop used as a foreshadowing motif is the use of oranges in *The Godfather* trilogy to symbolize death and betrayal.

Costume and Make-up: how the characters are dressed and stylized. Costume and make-up also tend to be aspects in which the filmmaker wishes for authenticity within the diegesis of the film. Costume and make-up can help an actor's performance seem more believable. Choices in color palette, patterns, and contrasts have meaning and affect the overall effect of a film.

Figure Behavior: the movement and behavior of an actor or other element (animal, object, etc.). Figure behavior includes expression, movement, and posture as well as acting style and degree of realism.

Sound: There are two major types of sound in film: diegetic and non-diegetic. **Diegetic sound** is produced by something within the world of the film. **Non-diegetic sound** is produced by something outside the time and space of the film, such as voice-over narration or soundtrack. A great example of the difference between diegetic and non-diegetic sound occurs in *Blazing Saddles* when music is heard while the main character rides his horse through the desert; the audience assumes the music is non-diegetic until the character comes across the musicians playing the music out in the desert.

Film Genres: There are many different genres and sub-genres of film that have particular narrative and thematic conventions. Some examples of genres are: western, horror, musical, comedy, action, mystery, and romance. Because viewers understand the conventions of each genre, filmmakers can play with audience expectations.

Now that we've walked through some cinematic terminology, let's examine the opening sequence from *Star Wars, Episode IV: A New Hope*. When analyzing a film, it is helpful to try to write down what happens in each shot, where people and objects are placed and any themes, motifs, or patterns that emerge.

After the now infamous text crawl that sets the scene along with the **non-diegetic soundtrack**, the camera **tilts down** through space to show viewers a planet with two moons. A spaceship enters from the upper right portion of the screen to the center of the screen, capturing viewers' attention. Quickly, another spaceship enters the screen from the same direction. This ship is massive compared to the one it chases. The ships exchange fire. This **long take** sets up the central conflict: the Rebels against the Empire.

The film then **cuts** to a closer shot of the small ship. We see a green flash strike the ship causing a large explosion. The film finally cuts to the interior of the Rebel ship and our first two characters are introduced in a **long shot**: C3PO and R2D2. We see the hallway they are in shake due to the explosion just witnessed. The **mise-en-scène** of the shot is quite stark. The hallway **setting** is all white with grey floors. The lighting is **high-key**; we can see many details and light reflects off of the robots as they move down the corridor. The shot cuts from an **American two-shot** to a **medium shot** of C3PO, who finally speaks the first line of **dialogue**: "Did you hear that?" The conversation is made up of **shot/reverse shots**. Through dialogue we get a glimpse into the character of C3PO, a neurotic, worry-wart robot.

The Storm Troopers then force their way into the Rebel ship. After a shoot out between the two sides, the film cuts to our first glimpse of Darth Vader, the villain. The **slightly low camera angle** causes Vader to seem even larger and more menacing. The **music** signals his entrance with loud horns and we hear his mechanical breathing. His **costume** becomes more clear as he walks toward the camera; we can see his long black robe and full helmet as well as the circuitry on his chest, signaling that he is not human. He stands over the bodies of dead Rebel soldiers with his hands on his hips; this **figure behavior** is aggressive and indicates his power. By constructing these shots in this way, the filmmaker seems to be emphasizing the inhumanity of the Empire, especially Darth Vader.

These shots are immediately followed by a close up showing an arm reaching out to R2D2. The bare feminine arm is in stark contrast to the previous shots of Vader, thereby marking the humanity of the rebels. Without even showing whose arm it is, the contrast immediately causes viewers to see this person as the complete opposite of Vader, making her a leader for the Rebels and potentially the hero of the film. We get a quick glimpse of Princess Leia. She is crouching down, showing her vulnerability and desire to hide. Her costuming is also the exact opposite of Darth Vader's; she is wearing a white, flowing gown. Her femininity is emphasized by the fact that she wears a long dress and her hair is tied up on each side of her head in intricate buns.

Having seen only the first few minutes of the film, it becomes quite clear whom viewers are meant to root for and against. If we were to analyze the entire film, we may pay attention to the ideas touched upon during this opening sequence. For example, we may decide to trace how gender is constructed in the film: Is Princess Leia a "damsel in distress," or is she a hero? Do characters follow traditional gender roles, or do they play with social expectations? We may also continue to trace the contrasts between the Rebels and the Empire: Is the Empire always portrayed as inhuman, or are there moments in which their humanity is made clear? Are the Rebels always portrayed as morally superior to the Empire, or are there moments in which their morals can be questioned? In order to answer these questions, you would need to watch the film several times, especially scenes that are the most important to your argument. You would most likely need to pause to take notes about the various cinematic elements that construct each scene.

By utilizing the film terminology discussed in this section, we are better able to support our claims about the film through analyzing how it is constructed. Film analyses that ignore the ways in which the cinematic elements are organized and constructed tend to talk around a film rather than closely reading it. Such analyses generally fall short when compared to papers that base their argument and claims on carefully analyzed details. Being aware of how films are constructed will allow you to think more deeply about film as an artistic medium.

8.7 Spatial Analysis

While much of the analysis you do in your first-year writing courses will focus on written and visual texts, your instructor may also ask you to think critically about the spaces and places you inhabit on a regular basis. In this section, you will learn about methods for space- and place-based analysis, as well as what these methods of analysis can tell you about human relationships, identity, and social constructions of class, politics, culture, race, gender, and so forth. In order to understand these methods of analysis, you will need to know the following key terms:

- **Space:** Space can be understood as the area in which social action takes place. Space is formed out of the connections that you make between what you see happening in the world, how you understand and interpret what you see happening in the world, and how you live in the world. Space is both relational (meaning it depends on relationships between people, places, and objects) and situational (meaning it depends on contextual factors like history, politics, religion, and so forth). In other words, the connections you make between what you see, how you understand what you see, and how you live are always changing, and they are produced by different aspects of society.

  A person's understanding of space depends on a variety of factors, including the context in which she or he is examining the space and the practices that bring her or him to that space. Although space *seems* invisible, it can be represented visually by distance, location, and/or interactions between people or objects.

- **Place:** Up until now, you have probably understood place to mean a fixed location, but like space, place is a situational and relational concept. Places are made when people use a certain space in a way that becomes accepted and habitual. You can think of place as a kind of space that is formed by the way people use it and experience it in their everyday lives, as well as the emotional attachments they form to the place through these experiences.

For instance, a home becomes a place where people gather together as a family to sleep, eat, and store belongings because that is how people have used their homes over time. Since each person experiences and uses a place differently, places will hold different meanings for different people.

As you think about the distinctions between space and place, you will want to note that place is made out of the way people use space; thus the concepts are closely related. For instance, let's say you go to the beach in Mexico one year for Spring Break. You notice that the beach is barren—you see nothing but white sand for miles and miles—and only a few people are swimming there. You go to this same beach every year for Spring Break while in college, but you notice that every year, more and more people populate the beach. Gradually, the empty space along the beach becomes littered with trash, and the once-barren land along the shoreline has now been developed with rows of hotels. This example illustrates the concepts of *space* (the space of the once-barren beach) and *place* (the hotels that were built because people became accustomed to using that area of the beach for recreational purposes).

But why should you be interested in space and place? Why can you learn about the way the world works by closely reading spaces and places? Many people who study space and place, including students and teachers of geography, know that space and place affect the way we think about society, culture, and politics. Students and teachers in other disciplines, like engineering, architecture, women's studies, and sociology, also study space and place. For example, if you were interested in learning about the American political system, you would investigate the spaces and places where politics play out—state capitol buildings, community meetings, the office of your local senator or congressperson, and even the White House. Carefully examining how people interact and work within these spaces and places can give you insights into how political systems are formed by people.

The idea here is that social structures like classism, racism, and gender discrimination come into being through and within certain spaces and places. By analyzing people's interactions and experiences within these sites, we can come to understand the social structures that operate within a society.

Place plays an important role in the formation of identity and culture as well. If your instructor were to ask you to analyze a place that holds significance for you—the house where you grew up, for example—you would want to think about how you use and experience the space of your home, as well as the kinds of emotional attachments you have formed in relationship to it. You might also consider how home has been defined in society—what kinds of spaces function as "home" for people and how do these homes change depending on the cultural, political, social, and economic context? What do people do in these spaces? What kinds of cultural practices happen there? Finally, you might even consider the ways in which your own identity has been shaped by your experiences in this place. What did you learn in your home that has informed who you are today?

Because place is formed out of people's accepted and habitual uses of a space, studying places can tell us a lot about cultural practices, social "norms," and individuals' personal connections to certain locations. When studying places, your aim is to explore the individual and collective experiences that make that place a *practiced space* (a space that people have created and use for certain purposes) and to analyze the larger social structures working within it.

Applying Spatial Analysis

To illustrate how space- and place-based analysis might work, let's return to the pictures on pages 168 of this chapter. These pictures represent both space and place, but the spaces and places represented in these photographs may be differently understood by different people. In your earlier examination of these photographs, you probably noticed that the figures in these photos are being separated by a large physical border. Each figure reacts to the border in a different way—some push and some stand nonchalantly. You might have also noticed that these figures appear to be without skin, all similar in color and build. Yet, what else can you glean from these photographs?

To understand these photos from a spatial perspective, you might consider the following questions:

- How are the figures interacting with one another?

- What do you understand these interactions to mean?

- How is space being represented visually in the photograph?

- What does the depiction of space tell you about the relationships between these figures?

- How are figures in the photos using this space? What about their experiences in this space?

- Based on the figures' experiences in the space, what place(s) do you think are being represented here?

- What are these figures' connections to this place? What clues in the photos tell you so?

- Finally, what can these representations of space and place tell you about larger social issues that might connect with the ideas in these photographs?

Answering these questions requires "reading" this photograph with a critical eye, applying the strategies for analysis you've been reading about in this chapter. Since close reading necessitates an interaction with the text, you might even want to annotate the photograph like you would a poem or a short story. Since our focus right now is on spatial analysis, your annotations should pay particular attention to the concepts of space and place in this photograph and how people are interacting within these spaces. For example, your annotation might end up looking like this:

"Border Dynamics" Sculpture on the UA Campus

The neutral colors give me the sense that these figures could represent anyone—and the fact that the fence looks like any other steel fence I've seen implies that it could be anywhere.

It's hard to tell from the picture, but it looks like the figure is really close to this wall, pushing with the entire weight of its body.

The border itself represents a place—borders exist between countries, but also within individuals (emotional, mental, etc.). Because it's on a border campus, this makes me think of the U.S./Mexico border and the fence that will soon go up there.

Large wall represents an obstacle, as shown by the figure to the left who is pushing against it. When I look at the height of the figure in relation to the wall, it seems like the figure is tall enough to climb over it—maybe a symbolic overcoming of the obstacle?

The buildings and trees in the background imply an urban landscape, but the sculpture itself seems to be removed from the urban—there is no landscape, only bodies and a fence.

The two figures are positioned near each other spatially, but do not seem to be interacting with each other. They have completely different responses to the wall—one is engaged, the other seems to be pretty removed from whatever's happening.

Concrete tiles again suggest an urban landscape.

Now that you have closely read and interacted with the text, you can begin analyzing and interpreting it, using the previous questions as a guide. To further investigate the use of space in this sculpture, you may even want to visit it, walk around it and through it, and experience it in its full dimensions. As you do, consider how your perceptions of space and place changed, if at all, once you had a chance to experience its spatial mass in person. Finally, remember also to think about what your interpretation might tell you about human relationships, identity, and the social structures you notice there.

Clearly, your first-year writing classes will require you to read, write about, and even compose different types of texts. You will be challenged to think beyond the surface-level meaning of the texts you read in class in order to

Analysis

uncover the more complex interpretations you can bring to them. In order to uncover the hidden intricacies of any text, you must read it closely, interact with it, locate sites of inquiry, and use your own lived experiences to guide your responses.

9
Text-in-Context
(Contextual Analysis)

Goals

Your contextual analysis essay should:

✓ Exhibit a careful analysis of primary and secondary texts.

✓ Smoothly incorporate research materials and correctly document them to support your analysis.

✓ Incorporate and document quotations, summaries, and paraphrases.

✓ Support your thesis with examples from primary and secondary materials.

✓ Anticipate the expectations of your specific audience and address its concerns.

✓ Provide meaningful feedback to your peers during the revision process.

✓ Incorporate peer and instructor feedback in the final version.

✓ Reflect correct use of grammar and mechanics.

9.1 Text-in-Context: An Overview

Text-in-context (which may also be referred to as "contextual analysis") essays build on the skills that you began to develop with the textual analysis paper. Your textual analysis essay assignment asked you to look at an isolated text closely and interpret it with descriptive evidence from that text. Text-in-context adds a new layer of complexity to your analysis. In this essay, you are still analyzing a text, but you are asked to use additional sources to enrich your analysis and understanding of the text. Some people choose to call this use of outside sources "building a context" or "building a framework." Some of the terms used for this assignment are similar to one another, so in the following list, we have tried to clarify the terminology that is often used when discussing text-in-context essays:

- **Primary text:** This is the text that you are analyzing—the main focus of your analysis. It can be a book, an article, a movie, a photograph, a painting, or even a place.

- **Secondary texts:** These texts create the context or framework—they add to your understanding of the primary text by introducing historical, philosophical, theoretical, and biographical information that casts the primary text in a new light. For instance, if you are analyzing Charlotte Perkins Gilman's story "The Yellow Wallpaper" as your primary text, your secondary texts might be articles about psychoanalytical practice in the late nineteenth century or about the techniques of literary realism or expressionism, as these would enrich your close reading of the story with new contextual information.

The secondary text may also be called a "lens text," since you can look at it in order to discover new things about the primary text that you might not see otherwise. Remember those children's books that came with red-tinted glasses? The pictures in the text were obscured and meaningless, but when you put on the red-tinted glasses, a picture emerged. Those red-tinted glasses are like the secondary text in that they give us a new perspective on the primary text.

A secondary text does not necessarily have to be about the primary text (although sometimes it is). For example, if you wanted to analyze the film *The Matrix* as your primary text, you might choose to use Joseph Campbell's book *The Hero with a Thousand Faces*, which was published in 1972, as a secondary text. In this book, Campbell writes about archetypes and hero-types, so this would enable you to talk about Neo as a hero archetype, and the different ways that Neo is not a radical hero, but rather a stereotypical one. The secondary text in this instance may allow you to shed light on and read the primary text in a different way. However, take note that Campbell's book was published over twenty-five years before the making of *The Matrix*.

Two additional terms may also be used as part of the Text-in-Context assignment: primary and secondary sources.

- **Primary source:** Primary sources are considered original productions, such as a novel, poem, painting or photograph, a movie, an interview, and so on.

- **Secondary source:** These are sources that comment on and have a secondary relationship to the primary source. Some common examples of secondary sources are an analysis of a literary text, a critique of a painting or photograph, a movie review, or an opinion about an interview.

For more information on finding and evaluating sources, see *Rules for Writers*, pages 382–404 and "Chapter 7: Research as Part of the Writing Process" in the *Student's Guide*.

An easy way to think about primary and secondary sources is the difference between movies and movie reviews: the movie is the original work, the primary source. The movie review is critiquing and talking about the primary source, making it a secondary source to the movie.

The text-in-context essay invites you to place a text in a broader framework (disciplinary, historical, theoretical, and so on) in order to see things you wouldn't notice if you only looked at the text itself. These frameworks might derive from historical, theoretical, biographical, social, or cultural information, and they serve as contexts in which you can analyze your primary text. Consider the following example:

Imagine that your teacher has asked you to analyze a primary text that is relevant to the status of women in society—for example, Karen Brennan's short story "Runaways" or Charlotte Perkins Gilman's "The Yellow Wallpaper" in *Writing as Revision*. You can build a context by using a secondary text that discusses issues that many women face in society; for example, sociology books that explore male-female relations, or historical studies of social movements involving women during the period in which these texts take place. Applying the ideas from these new contexts lets you think about the women represented in the primary text in a different way: Do the women in the primary text seem to experience what others have talked about in the secondary texts? Is their experience unusual? The ideas from the secondary texts should continue to add to your understanding of the primary text because they add new and different information. To write your own essay effectively you'll need to read closely, analyze, perhaps do some research, argue, and, of course, revise.

The contexts you can apply to a text are various, and they can be used in different ways. The list we present here is not exhaustive, but it does offer a start for thinking about different possible contexts:

- **Historical:** What are the historical events and facts surrounding your primary text, and how does this affect how you read your text? Here, you might want to think about when the text was written or composed, the time period in which a short story or novel takes place, or other factors concerning the time period of a text.

- **Biographical:** What occurred in the author's life? What were the author's beliefs, values, experiences, and so on, and how do these affect the ways that you understand the author's purpose in your primary text?

- **Social:** This context is very similar to historical context because it asks that you look at the social influences of the time. What were the social values, events, discourses, and so on, and how are these social contexts reflected in the primary text?

- **Cultural:** What kinds of culturally-specific values, beliefs, and patterns do you see in the primary text? How has the primary text been shaped by cultural influences, such as religion, nationality, family traditions, and so forth?

- **Critical:** What have other people, such as literary, film, or art critics, said about the primary text, and how can that influence or change the text's meaning?

- **Theoretical:** This is a huge category! There are many different theories that enable people to critically examine the features of society—feminist, Marxist, social, modernist, post-modernist, cultural, and so on. Here, you might draw upon the theories of a certain scholar or movement to examine your primary text.

- **Literature or film texts:** A primary text in some cases can become a secondary text, depending on how it is applied. For example, you can read Gilman's "The Yellow Wallpaper," which is a short story, and apply it to your analysis of Andrea Yates, the Texan woman who killed her five children in 2001.

Getting Started on Your Text-in-Context Essay

The text-in-context essay gives you practice with analysis and prepares you for the type of writing that you will be doing in future English classes and in other disciplines. Text-in-context asks you to include secondary texts to support your assertions, a skill that you need in order to successfully write any type of persuasive essay. In order to successfully complete the text-in-context essay, you need to do the following:

- Argue a controlled thesis using contextual evidence (e.g., evidence collected from your secondary texts) for the points that you make.

- Find specific evidence to support your claims from both the primary and secondary texts.

- Examine *how* the secondary texts create a new context (or contexts) in which to read a primary text. Explain the primary and secondary texts and how they relate to one another.

- Explain *why* this new context is important and/or significant to the understanding of your text.

For a more in-depth discussion on writing your essay, see "Chapter 4: Writing as a Process." For specific information about incorporating research into your documented essay, please see examples in "Chapter 11: Exploring a Controversy and Writing a Public Argument."

Like analysis essays, contextual analysis essays are persuasive. How you decide to present the text and what evidence you decide to include convinces your reader to analyze the text in the same way—it asks the reader to believe that your analysis is effective and credible. Therefore, your thesis should come from your own ideas, taking an analytical stance that invites the audience to read the text in the same way that you do. Use secondary texts only to bolster your points, not to structure your essay or make your arguments for you.

In incorporating secondary sources, it is essential to remember the importance of analysis. When using outside sources, it is all too easy to end a paragraph right before the analysis begins. A writer may open a paragraph with a topic sentence, create the context by drawing on the secondary text, and apply the context to the primary text, but then fail to explain the significance of her observations. For example, a writer might point out in a topic sentence that "The Yellow Wallpaper" illustrates common attitudes toward women's mental health in the late nineteenth century, paraphrase one of the articles used as a secondary source to explain what those common attitudes were, quote from the story, and then move on to another point, instead of explaining how the quote from the story illustrates the attitudes discussed by the secondary source and why it should be of interest to the reader. It is important to always anticipate the "So what?" question. Why does this new reading matter? What do you want the reader to take from it? In other words, what's the point? You do not have to agree with the context or the text. You can apply the context, note how it relates, and then discuss how the contextual knowledge changes our interpretations. This is not an exercise in brainwashing; it is an exercise in critically applying an academic convention by synthesizing multiple sources and ideas in a cogent, unified manner.

For more information on analysis, please see "Chapter 8: Analysis."

Using secondary sources: One resource for you to start using right away, even as you begin preliminary reading for your text-in-context essay, is Chapter 6, "Working With Sources: Summary, Paraphrase, and Quotation." This chapter discusses how to introduce your sources to your readers, to quote carefully and sparingly, and to follow up your quotations or paraphrases with commentary of your own to situate the source material in the logical flow of your essay's argument. Pay particular attention to the appropriate forms of documentation. Incorporating research and discussion will add to your credibility in that your stance will be more precise, discerning, and convincing. This is not just true of academic audiences—whenever you support claims with other perspectives and evidence, people tend to find what you have to say more convincing.

For examples of what a text-in-context essay may look like, refer to "Part IV: Sample Essays."

In the next two sections, Abra McAndrew explores different ways to consider a primary and secondary text together before beginning the writing process, while Christiane Buuck offers steps and strategies on how to critically read texts and how to apply a lens text to an essay. These are actual essay assign-

Tips on Writing Introductions for Essays

Make the first words of your essay count. You may think the evidence found in the body of the paper ends up being what gets weighted the most. Having a solid, well-developed essay matters, true enough, but it is the introduction that catches your readers' interest and sets up your discussion, guiding them to see things as you do. Your writing is always competing for the interest of readers, and that is something that merits your attention. Even if you are operating under the assumption that you are only writing for your teacher and maybe peers, you are still competing for that instructor's attention, those peers' attentions. The opening section of your essay needs to be sharp, thoughtful, and relevant. For something different, try writing the introduction last, after you have explored the significance of the expe-

rience. Before you write, come up with a plan for how you want to reach your audience. Here are a few basic strategies to try out (although you will probably recognize these as approaches you already have tried out from time to time, perhaps not consciously or for effect).

The Funnel Introduction—This style is the most standard introduction format. A funnel moves from a general statement of your topic (this serves to situate your reader) to specifics (this outlines the specific points). The aim of the funnel is to move from general discussion of a defined idea or problem and then become increasingly specific as the introduction progresses. By the end of the intro, we've reached your particular interest and focus—the thesis. How you begin a funnel influences its quality and effect. Make your starting point on a level of knowledge that you think your readers will be familiar with. Don't start too generally because

ments that these instructors used in their classes and may help illustrate how the text-in-context essay may be approached.

9.2 The Many Faces of the Primary Text

By Abra McAndrew

Have you ever seen those pictures where the image looks like a face, but the face is actually spelling out a word like "liar," or the picture looks like a vase, but it's actually two faces looking at each other? Or even the magic eye pictures that were so popular in the 1990s, where the picture looked like a bunch of fuzzy colors until you focused in such a way that you were able to see a ship or a bird? Appreciation of optical illusions comes from our ability to set aside our first impressions and see an image in a new way. The text-in-context assignment asks you to perform a similar re-vision of your primary text in order to reach a deeper understanding of its complexities; when you see both the word and the face, you can appreciate how the text was constructed to produce two very different responses in those who give it only a superficial glance.

readers will not be interested in obvious observations or sweeping generalizations. One of the more common problems with the opening lines of a funnel is that they could be the opening words to virtually any essay—for example, "Since the beginning of time," or "Throughout history, people have fought with one another to control natural resources."

The Anecdotal Introduction—One effective alternative to the standard funnel is to craft an anecdote that brings to light something essential about your topic while capturing the attention of your readers through vivid detail. People relate to stories, even if they are abbreviated, so think about how you could use a story to kick off your paper with human interest. Your anecdote can be something you've discovered in your research, something you learned during an interview, perhaps even something that you have experienced yourself. Design the story so

that it intrigues your readers, without using so much detail that you belabor your introduction. You will want to be sure that you develop a sufficient bridge to get you from your anecdote to the main idea and position of your paper, so that the reader doesn't have to do all the work in determining what's most important to take from the story. For example, if you're writing a reflective essay about the written work you've done throughout the academic year, you might begin your essay with a colorful, purposeful description of the drafting process of your first essay of the year: What did you do that worked well? What could you have done differently? What images seem most memorable from that experience? How will telling readers about this experience get readers interested and "set the table" for the rest of the essay?

See the introductions to the essays in Chapter 13.

One way to approach this assignment is to first broaden your perspective. Look away from the primary text for a moment and glance at the secondary texts that are assembled for your consideration. Read the titles and skim the abstracts, introductions, and conclusions of a few of those texts. Which pique your interest? Select a few that you would like to read more closely. Don't worry about how the sources might relate to each other at this point. Although you may be required to use a limited number of sources in your paper, it is a good idea to plan to read more than that number so that you'll be sure to find some that interest you—if you must use two, make sure to select at least four potential sources; if you must use four, select six, or even eight sources to read. As you read, apply the techniques of close reading that work best for you in order to make sure you understand the main points of the texts you've selected.

A helpful strategy is to write a journal entry in which you explore the connections between the main ideas of the secondary (or lens) texts and your primary text. Identify and briefly summarize the primary text and think about which characters, relationships, scenes, ideas, or specific quotations from the primary text are brought to your mind by the ideas in the secondary text. Consider the following questions:

- How does the secondary text help you to see some aspect of the primary text in a new way?

- What questions does it help you answer?

- What is the significance of a new contextual understanding? Does the context bring out issues of difference or inequality that you might have missed?

Write for a while to explore these connections as concretely as possible.

After you've done a journal entry for each secondary text, you will have some potential material for your text-in-context essay. Review your journal entries and see which connections you've made that seem to speak most clearly to you about the meaning or implications of the primary text. Is there a theme or a pattern among your journal entries? Think about how you might creatively combine the information from a couple of your sources in order to see the primary text in a new way, and you'll be on track for a unique and original interpretation supported by solid evidence. For example, a 1993 *Newsweek* article entitled "White Male Paranoia," which discusses the white male reaction to the false perception that they are losing economic and other powers to women and people of color, can help you to understand a possible motivation for Lester's midlife crisis and his relationship with his wife in the movie *American Beauty*. Another source that analyzes the reasons why older men often fantasize about younger women yet often do not act on those feelings can further illuminate Lester's character. Combined, these sources provide you with an interpretation of the film in the context of contemporary American society that extends beyond what is obvious from the movie itself.

9.3 New Lenses and Complex Readings

By Christiane Buuck

Like the analysis essay, the text-in-context essay will require you to interpret a text using close reading strategies. However, in this essay, you will work with multiple texts. A secondary or lens text will help you see the primary text in a new way and develop a more complex reading and analysis of the primary text. The key to a successful text-in-context analysis is focus. You will become an expert on one specific facet of the primary text. In the end, your essay should teach readers something about the primary text that they had never considered before. Don't be afraid to explore something small that really interests you. Perhaps you have always wondered what different animals might represent in *Apocalypse Now* or why characters' faces are lit in specific ways at different portions of the film. The easiest mistake to make in this kind of essay is to fall into comparing and contrasting the primary and lens texts. Remember to keep this paper an analysis.

Here are some key terms and ideas you will need to write this paper:

- **Primary text:** the document or film you will analyze in this assignment;

- **Secondary or lens text(s):** the document(s) that will help focus your analysis of the primary text; and

- **Dialectical journal entry:** a way of documenting your close reading and beginning the process of analysis. To make a dialectical journal entry, draw a T-graph on a sheet of paper. At the top line of the T, write the name of the text you are reading and a short guiding comment. For example, "Le Ly Hayslip 'Prologue: Dedication to Peace'—an essay about the author's childhood in Vietnam. She explains how she became a Viet Cong fighter. Hayslip explains the Viet Cong's indoctrination techniques and her motivations, and ends by calling for peace among the survivors on all sides of the Vietnam War." Next, label one side of the T-graph "details" and the other side "inferences." On the left side of the graph, you will record details from the text. On the right, you will make inferences. See the following examples.

While the process of arriving at a thesis may seem frustrating at first, it works and leads to some very strong essays. If you follow this process, you will be doing the work of the essay in reverse; that is, you will find all of your evidence and analysis first and come to a thesis statement last. Then, when you are ready to write your essay, all of the pieces will be clearly laid out before you.

Step 1: What is your primary source? (I will use *Apocalypse Now* as an example.)

Step 2: What questions do you have about the primary source? List ten. *(For example: Why do the American soldiers kill everyone in the Vietnamese fishing boat when the Vietnamese people were unarmed? Where do the events in the film take place?)*

Step 3: Can any of these questions be answered by the primary text alone? If so, cross them off the list. *(For example, we know that the American soldiers were nervous when they encountered the Vietnamese people in the fishing boat, but that doesn't explain the murder of everyone aboard. This question cannot be answered by the primary text alone, so keep it on the list. As to the second question, we know that the events in the film happen in Vietnam and Cambodia, so the second question listed above can be crossed off.)*

Step 4: Pick the question that is most compelling to you and write it above the T-graph of the dialectical journal entry below. Complete the dialectical journal entry, adding paper as necessary.

Question = *Why do the American soldiers attack the Vietnamese civilians in the fishing boat without provocation?*

Dialectical Journal Entry	
Details	*Inferences*
American soldiers begin to fire when the young Vietnamese woman makes a subtle movement toward a tall basket.	Perhaps she moves out of fear. There is something hidden in the basket. The soldiers might think there are weapons in the basket. (Notice how many inferences can be made for one detail.)

Step 5: Now that you have completed the dialectical journal entry, you have begun to see some patterns emerge that will help you refine the initial question. Remember the key questions in reporting: *who, what, when, where, why* and *how*. Write your revised question (or questions) below.

After watching this scene closely, you learn that a puppy was in the basket. The young woman reaches for it and this movement triggers the soldiers to fire. At the end of the scene, the young woman is wounded while the rest of the people on the boat are dead. Willard defies orders and shoots her instead of taking her to a hospital. In the process of analyzing, you begin to notice a pattern. Perhaps you notice that the Vietnamese people's lives are not valued highly by the American soldiers in the scene. You may also notice that the American soldiers are edgy around Vietnamese civilians, and wonder why. You may remember other scenes in the film that play this dynamic out.

Revised question: *Why are the American soldiers visibly edgy and quick to shoot around Vietnamese people?*

Step 6: Propose a few answers to your question(s). These answers are the first step to a paper thesis.

> *The soldiers are far from home and surrounded by unfamiliarity.*
> *In war everything gets confused.*
> *The soldiers are afraid.*

Step 7: Decide on a lens text. The information/insight you glean from your critical reading of this secondary text should add complexity to the answers in Step 6. Remember that the secondary text should not provide you with answers. Instead, it should help you think about a primary text in a new way that can help you develop your own original argument.

Lens text: *Le Ly Hayslip, "Prologue: Dedication to Peace"*

Step 8: Complete a dialectical journal entry for the lens text, focusing on the details that shed light on your question and proposed answer.

Question: *Why are the American soldiers visibly edgy and quick to shoot around Vietnamese people?*

Proposed answer: *The soldiers are afraid.*

Dialectical Journal Entry For Lens Text	
Details	*Inferences*
p. 656: "My father taught me to love god, my family, our traditions, and the people we could not see: our ancestors. He taught me that to sacrifice one's self for freedom [. . .] was a very high honor."	A sense of history and continuity is very important to Vietnamese culture. Sacrifice is a worthy ideal. Freedom is highly valued. Hayslip's cultural education happened at home and was very personal.
p. 656–57: Viet Cong leaders came to Hayslip's village and talked about the importance of independence from outside powers such as China, France, and the U.S.	The American soldiers in the film may never have learned about Vietnamese culture. The Viet Cong's ideas are related to Hayslip's father's words. The Viet Cong related to people in understandable terms.

Step 9: Modify your answers and conclusions in light of the lens text. How does your understanding of the primary text change? How does the lens text help focus your argument? In this paper, you want to become the specialist of one particular way of reading a text. If everyone would agree with your conclusions, then there is little reason to write a whole paper about them. Don't be afraid to go out on a limb, to be controversial or innovative, so long as your argument is grounded in textual analysis.

The Viet Cong's motivation for fighting the Americans is deeply rooted. The Viet Cong operates secretly, at night, and without uniforms. The American soldiers are fighting a very different war, psychologically speaking, than they are prepared for. To the characters in Apocalypse Now, *the enemy has many faces, all of which are Vietnamese.* Apocalypse Now *is filmed from an American perspective, which relegates the Vietnamese to hollow and stereotypical roles, but every so often a slight movement, such as that of a woman to protect a puppy, allows a Vietnamese character to transcend the stereotype and take on human dimension. Hayslip's essay helps us interpret those subtle moments when stereotype becomes character.*

Step 10: Now you are ready to start your paper. Notice that in Step 9 you have written a tentative thesis *(underlined)*, and in the preceding steps you have already noted down many of the supporting arguments. The thesis of this paper may be two or even three sentences long. The major work of your paper (that is, the thinking and the new ideas) is now mostly done. Now you need only organize these thoughts into sentence and paragraph form and build a solid argument. Remember that you might need to tweak your details and inferences, adding some and deleting others, in order to make the strongest argument possible.

9.4 Culture: Another Kind of Text

Some of your instructors may assign you a different kind of text-in-context, one that asks you to incorporate notions of "culture" into your analysis. The difficulty, of course, is that we may live inside of certain cultures but feel distinctly excluded from others, so the mechanisms of culture are sometimes difficult for us to discern and analyze. This is one of the possible goals of this assignment—refining your analysis skills while making culture visible.

For more information on analysis, please see "Chapter 8: Analysis."

Some instructors will ask you to use culture as a lens text through which you analyze a primary text (such as reflecting about your reading/writing experiences or writing about how a book or poem is influenced by culture). Analyzing culture asks us to step outside, examine, and discover culture as a text. Through cultural analysis, you will become more aware of the ways a text and its reception reflect the ideologies—values, assumptions, conflicts, desires, anxieties, and so forth—of the culture that produces them. The underlying assumption of cultural analysis is that "any cultural product [...] carries, implicitly or explicitly, ideas about how the world should be seen" (Corrigan 88). This is extremely difficult because the structure of culture can become invisible, and the task of cultural analysis is to discover the structures of culture and make them visible again. In other words, you want to take what is familiar to you and make it strange—to do so you have to work hard to perceive cultural aspects in a different light.

No matter what the text, effective analysis always strives to understand the complexity of a subject. Cultural analysis, then, asks you to analyze the many layers of meaning that influence the writer's construction of a text and/or the reader's interpretations of a text. Culture, in other words, becomes a context for the ways in which we understand ourselves and each other. We have included a list of terms used by cultural theorists. Your instructor may choose to use some of these theories and not others in order to focus your research. However, if you do research or reading in the area of cultural studies, you will often see these words used (and sometimes used and defined in different ways).

- **Ideology:** underlying values, assumptions, conflicts, desires, anxieties, and so on. The beliefs that people hold; the prominent ideas that tell us what should be, must be, needs to be, or what seems normal. Sometimes called "cultural values" when in reference to a popular or widely held belief. For example, the idea of *democracy* in the United States is an ideology—it assumes that everyone should have a voice, and everyone's voice should be equal, whether people are uneducated or college professors, politicians or people who never read the news, religious or atheist, and so on. Other ideologies might include capitalism, religion, and education.

- **Assumptions:** the beliefs that a person takes to be true/false, good/bad, interesting/boring, and so on, reflecting that person's worldview. For example, imagine that a man who works at the university has a sister who is a single mother, working at a fast-food restaurant. As a member of a university, the man might assume that his sister's job would be boring and hard on the body. But his sister looks at the job that the university employee has and assumes that he never really works because he is at a desk all day. He might think that a person working at a fast-food place would want out, whereas his sister, who has just received a promotion and now makes more money than he does, assumes that he will leave the academy for a business job where he can make more money. One of the next steps in analysis is discovering where these assumptions come from, such as within concepts like the nature of work, the love of one's job, the desire for money, the desire for cultural prestige, and so on.

- **Rhetoric:** the art, practice, or study of the persuasive functions of language. For example, when you were in high school, maybe you had to ask your parents for permission to use the car whenever you wanted to go out. What if you wanted to go across the state and hang out with a friend? In this situation, you had to use rhetoric—you had to persuade them by assuring them you would be careful. Perhaps your arguments were based on the fact that you had not gotten into an accident, you had not seen this friend in a long time, you had your own money for gas, and you would be home before they needed the car again. All of these pleas were rhetorical strategies. When you analyze culture, you need to explore how culture affects rhetorical strategies. For example, when you watch an "Old Navy" clothing commercial, you will notice that the commercials often use nostalgic music from the 50s and 60s, that the models are always thin, smiling people in that clothing line, and on top of that, the models represent different ethnicities, such as African-American, Caucasian, Asian, and so on. What is persuasive or rhetorical about these choices? How are these rhetorical strategies reflecting the target culture of this commercial?

For more discussion on rhetoric, please see "Chapter 10: Rhetorical Analysis."

- **Semiotics:** the study of sign symbols; an analysis of signs to understand the ways that they convey meaning; the process of conveying meaning in human communication; the structure of language as a matter of symbols, both spoken and written. For example, consider the heart symbol ♥. This symbol does not look like a real heart, yet it represents a heart. Also, when you see a heart symbol, you understand the cultural meanings attached to it—love, Valentine's Day, romance, and so on. Words are like this as well. Consider the word *love* for example. What does this mean when you say "I love you" to your partner, your friend, your parents, your aunt, your dog? Are any of these feelings the same as when you declare that you love a movie?

- **Power and institutional structures:** the ways in which power can only act within social structures that support them. The French theorist Michel Foucault discusses how power is always situated in historical movements that create institutional structures. These institutional structures create, reproduce, and maintain power. This is actually a fairly difficult theory. In order to think through this, consider sexism as an example: the idea that women are weaker than men, subordinate to men, or not as capable as men. Arguably, this form of oppression is maintained in the workplace (where women hit the "glass ceiling" faster than men), in school (where women are not always encouraged to excel in math and science), and in the media (in which women's sexuality is used to objectify them for commercial purposes). These structures work together to maintain power over women; however, Foucault argues that these power structures cannot be practiced unless there are *points of resistance*. When women and men resist these forms of power, their acts of resistance affirm that the power exists and is able to act in concrete ways. Questions that you might want to ask are: Who is being disempowered? What institutional structures are disempowering those people/things? What forms of resistance are being offered and what is the effect of the resistance? Who, then, is being empowered?

- **Inequalities:** the structures in our society that privilege some and oppress others. This is intimately linked with the previous definition of power and institutional structures. Once power acts on a situation, whether that situation is a person or a political event, power is unequally distributed and therefore creates hierarchical relationships. Those in power then attempt to find ways to maintain and reproduce their power through different strategies such as representation, litigation, and so on. You can then look at the ways in which inequality is formed and maintained.

- **Sameness:** the ways in which people share similarities in worldviews, life-styles, social interactions, and so on. These similarities can be constructed for certain rhetorical (persuasive) means. Think, for example, about those bumper-stickers that say "Aren't we all human?" or "Many people, one world." The rhetorical strategy here appeals to sameness. Sameness is a very strong strategy that can be misused. For example, when the Japanese attacked Pearl Harbor during WWII, America reacted by placing all Americans of Japanese ancestry into internment camps. These people were grouped in with the enemy because of their sameness, and as such, were forcefully taken from their homes and jobs. When you consider sameness then, you might want to think about how it is used both positively and negatively in our society and how that affects your perceptions of certain peoples or events.

The above list is by no means comprehensive. In fact, the term "culture" is almost impossible to pin down, since there is not one culture, but many cultures. Furthermore, cultural analysis is extremely difficult because we have been living in our culture, so it has become natural to us and we no longer think about it. It is good to remember though, that culture maintains both positive and negative structures in our society. Even when we question negative structures, they do not always go away. Think about the Civil Rights movements of the 1960s, when Dr. Martin Luther King, Jr. challenged the inequities between African American and Caucasian people in America. Unfortunately, these inequities have not vanished—there are still structures within our society that support racial inequity. Arizona faces these problems, particularly with people of Latino and Native American heritage. You might want to question why the English language is privileged over Spanish, and why there is not more racial diversity in your classrooms when the city itself is incredibly diverse.

Getting Started on Your Cultural Analysis Essay

For a more in-depth discussion of writing your essay, see "Chapter 4: Writing as a Process." Also, for more information on writing thesis statements and using evidence, please see *Rules for Writers*, pages 21–24 and 361–64.

There are many similarities between the other forms of analysis that you have done in your first semester writing class and cultural analysis, which also has similarities to rhetorical analysis. Cultural analysis asks you to look at the tools that culture uses to enforce ideologies and practices; rhetorical analysis brings this down to a language level and asks you to look at symbolic tools (language, images, and so on) that writers use to persuade an audience. Nevertheless, the tools of analysis for all of these papers are the same. You will need to do the following:

- Narrow your topic to something manageable.

- Find specific evidence to support your claims.

- Examine *how* a cultural element works or what it means in your text (mere description of a cultural element is not sufficient).

- Explain *why* the cultural element that you examined is significant.

While engaging in cultural analysis, you will be looking for ways in which texts and culture are intricately connected, the ways that culture affects audiences' readings of a text, and/or the value that is placed on cultural texts. You need to also consider whether the text you're analyzing challenges or accommodates dominant beliefs—who is being empowered/disempowered and how? Doing this form of analysis is necessarily persuasive. By making visible the structures within your cultures, you are able to convey your new understandings to other people, potentially changing their worldviews.

Work Cited

Corrigan, Timothy. *A Short Guide to Writing about Film*. 6th Ed. New York: Longman, 2006. Print.

9.5 The Writing Classroom as a Context

While looking at a text through historical, theoretical, social, or cultural lenses can yield interesting insights, the writing classroom can also provide you with new ways of considering texts. Class discussions are especially important in helping you understand a text, since your instructor may bring in information about the background of the text or introduce new terms, theories, or concepts not covered in this chapter. In addition, what your peers say in large and small group discussion can provoke constructive ideas that can lead you toward a working thesis.

As you get ready to write your text-in-context essay, you should reflect upon your class discussions of your primary text and revisit the notes you took in class. Thinking about these details can serve as an important invention strategy, since they take you back to the moments when you first engaged in conversations about the text. These first impressions can often lead to important discoveries about the emotional responses you had to certain texts, especially when you challenge yourself to ask *why* your responses may be unique or different from others in your class. Finally, if you are dealing with a controversial text (a text characterized by social tensions), you will want to think about how these social tensions played out in the classroom. Oftentimes pondering over these classroom experiences can be a generative activity that can deepen your knowledge surrounding the text. Below are some questions you might want to ask as you think back on these moments in the classroom:

- What class activities has your instructor used to help you understand the text? In what ways do these activities affect or change your understanding of the text?

- What are some of the major issues and observations that came up during class discussions of the text? Do you agree or disagree with these issues and observations? Why?

- What new terms, concepts, or theories has your instructor introduced to help guide class discussions of the text? Which of these are most useful to you? In what ways have they guided your reading of the text?

- What questions about the text were left unanswered after these discussions and activities?

- Based on class discussions and activities, how does your reading of the text compare to your peers' and instructor's responses? In other words, how is your reading similar or different? What factors might account for these similarities and differences in interpretation?

- Did moments of tension arise in discussions or activities surrounding the text? If so, what factors might have accounted for this tension? What have you learned about the text in talking about this tension?

For more about tension in the writing classroom, read "Embracing Difference, Promoting Equality," an essay written by instructors who teach in the Writing Program, in "Chapter 13: Sample Essays."

Using these questions can guide you through the process of using the writing classroom—particularly, those discussions and activities that were pertinent to your primary text—as a context for analysis. Once you have considered these factors, then you can build upon your findings by adding layers of historical, theoretical, social, cultural, or biographical content, depending upon which of these seems most resonant with your findings.

The possibilities for analyzing a text in context are extensive and stimulate the production of new knowledge, which is why this method of analysis is so widely used in academic writing. The more ways we look at texts and the more contexts we apply to them, the more our understanding of them grows. Text-in-context essays enable us to broaden our purview outside of the text in isolation so that we may promote ongoing creative interpretations and ensure that meaning is always evolving, never fixed.

10
Rhetorical Analysis

Goals

Your rhetorical analysis should:

✓ Effectively appeal to your chosen audience.

✓ Provide a clearly defined thesis and focused argument.

✓ Identify the relevant arguments in the text.

✓ Systematically analyze the relevant arguments in the text.

✓ Evaluate the overall effectiveness of a text to persuade an intended audience.

✓ Effectively incorporate peer and instructor feedback in the final version.

10.1 Rhetoric: An Overview

Over the course of your English 101 course, you were likely asked to look beyond the surface information in a text to make critical evaluations of the author and text. You may have looked at theme, characters, and the general message the author intended for the audience. Rhetorical analysis continues these types of investigations by focusing specifically on the arguments of the author as presented in the text. A rhetorical analysis involves you, the critic, making evaluative claims about the effectiveness of the text while using the tools of rhetorical analysis to explain to your audience how you reach these conclusions about the text. This task seems easy at first, but as you will soon find out, arguments are complex, nuanced, and sometimes contradictory. Your job is to critically analyze these elements of the text and provide your audience with a better understanding of the text, the audience, and the purpose. In the process of your analysis, you too are making an argument about how the text ought to be read.

The majority of this chapter describes a *type* of rhetorical analysis often called Aristotelian or classical rhetorical analysis. This type of analysis focuses on the form of arguments and how an author persuades (or dissuades) the intended audience. This requires that the critic (you) understand the author, the nature of the text, and the intended audience. Other types of rhetorical analysis hone in on other areas argument, identity, power, and consequences. For more information about these types of rhetoric see section 10.7, refer to your English 102 or 109 textbook, or ask your instructor.

10.2 Foundations: Purpose, Audience, and Context

Purpose

Every text you read in English composition contains various meanings and interpretations. However, when working toward a rhetorical analysis you can look at the specific goals of the author for the text and audience. You can ask questions like:

- What message did the author intend the reader to understand from this text?

- What response or reaction did the author intend the reader to have concerning this text?

Notice the repeated term, *intend*, indicates what the author desires of the text. Often the author's purpose or intent for the text is not successful or readers have different reactions to the text that the author did not anticipate. Can you think of any examples where a speaker or writer intended one thing, but the audience interpreted it differently? Finding the general purpose of a text is only one element of fully understanding the text. Already, you should notice that *audience* is a key factor in interpreting the purpose and later in evaluating the success of the author in achieving that purpose.

Purpose:
The goal(s) of the text that you are reading or writing.

Audience

Writers often make rhetorical choices based on how they think about their audience. They pay attention to their audience's educational level, age, class, gender, race, ethnicity, and presumed political beliefs. Thinking about audience helps writers choose what tone and level of vocabulary to use as well as which strategies of argument to use. For example, magazine ads in *Good Housekeeping* primarily target married mothers with a middle-class income, whereas ads in *Cosmopolitan* aim at young career women who are dating men and are interested in heterosexual companionship. You can often guess a lot about an audience by thinking about who usually reads a magazine such as *Cosmo* or *Good Housekeeping*. These audiences differ in major ways from the audiences for professional journals such as *Psychology and Aging* or *Engineering and Mining Journal*. While some individuals may read a popular magazine such as *Good Housekeeping* one day and a professional journal such as *Psychology and Aging* the next day, they will be in two very different frames of mind when reading each of these journals and will have very different expectations about the content and format of the writing. Audiences read a magazine and a research journal for different purposes, and attending to those differences can make you a more effective reader as well as writer. Knowing the type of publication, then, tells you a lot about the audience and larger context.

Audience:
The person(s) who is reading or listening to the text. This person might be a **Primary Audience** (the person for whom the text is generated) or a **Secondary Audience** (the person who has an interest in the topic because that person is connected/interested in the speaker, Primary Audience, or topic).

With few exceptions, texts have more than one audience, whether or not the writer or speaker intended a certain audience. However, the first audience to identify is the intended audience of the author. Then you can focus on secondary audiences, for whom the effectiveness of the text may differ from the primary audience.

Context

Although we read many texts in the English composition classroom these texts do not exist in the vacuum of the classroom. These texts were created in the real world among real-world issues and the people faced with these issues. Each text interacts with the world around it. When George W. Bush addressed the Joint Session of Congress and the American people shortly after 9/11, his audience members were not the same people he would have addressed on 9/10. The audience was deeply influenced by the context; therefore, making a full analysis of his speech must include a clear understanding of the context in which the speech was delivered. Although the context is not always as obvious as 9/11 for former President Bush, every text exists in a unique context that contributes to how the author wrote the text and how the audience understood it.

Context:
The many circumstances surrounding a text that shape what the text means to a specific audience.

Context, then, includes the many circumstances surrounding a text that shape what the text means to its audience. There are many sorts of contexts. Contexts can vary and shape the purpose and audience of a text. Think about the various contexts you can identify, if you consider these dimensions of a text:

- The date and type of publication;

- Recent events that may have shaped how people think about the topic;

- The specific associations that readers of the publication may have;

- Social movements (like civil rights) that are related to the topic; and

- The cultural and linguistic backgrounds of the primary and secondary audiences.

When a text exists in a different *time* or *place*, its meaning can change. As an example of how context changes, consider Martin Luther King, Jr.'s "Letter from a Birmingham Jail." King's descriptions of police brutality toward African Americans had a different effect on his 1963 readers than they have on readers today. At the time, his account of police brutality was intended to raise his readers' consciousness and mobilize them to correct this injustice. Because King wrote in the social and historical context of the Civil Rights movement, he described the police abuse bleakly, as an example of the wrongs he and his supporters felt society should eradicate through his campaign of non-violence. However, Dr. King's words would have a different effect on contemporary readers who had just seen a news report about a police beating of an African American such as Rodney King. In this case, the effect of Dr. King's description would not be to make readers aware that police brutality exists. Rather, readers might read his words and wonder how much the Civil Rights movement really accomplished. As you can see, the context defines how a text can affect the reader, and those effects change as the rhetorical situation changes.

People's cultural values, beliefs, and expectations are strongly influenced by their ethnicity, language, religion, history, gender, sexual orientation, and many other factors. As a result, it is important to think about the cultural assumptions that lie beneath a particular argument. The following diagram shows the relationship among the components of a rhetorical situation. When you analyze or create your own text, consider the dynamic elements of the writing situation and the elements represented. Remember that the *contexts* of a text may vary, but they generally have the same basic elements: **author**, **audience**, **context**, and **topic**.

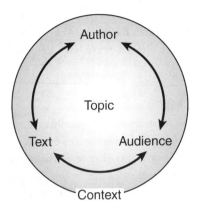

Notice that the arrows go both ways. The **author's** background and stance interact with the target **audience**. The **text** is shaped by both the author and the audience. The **topic**— that is, the issue or controversy— sits in the middle, and *how* it is discussed depends on the surrounding variables.

10.3 Getting Started: Finding Purpose, Audience, and Context

Before you begin making evaluative claims about a text, you should make sure you understand how the audience, purpose, and context construct the text. In Chapter 3 the full text of Martin Luther King Jr.'s *I Have a Dream* provides an ideal text to begin this process. This text obviously was intended for a primary audience that no longer exists, but you can still speculate King's intent/purpose, identify the primary and secondary audience, and describe the complex context of then and now. Use the questions below to help guide your thinking about the text. Remember, your answers should reflect the complexity of the text and the questions you ask of it.

- What is the general purpose of King's speech?

- Who was this speech initially intended for?

- Who reads/listens to it now?

- In what context did King deliver this speech?

- In what context is King's speech invoked now?

- How does this context influence the audience's interpretation of the speech?

- How might this context have influenced how King presented his ideas?

- Now identify:

  o Purpose:

  o Audience:

  o Context:

As you begin to identify the elements in and around a text you soon see that some texts are more persuasive or successful than others. One of the challenges of rhetorical criticism is describing the *how* and *why* that differentiates one text from another in persuasion.

10.4 Evaluation: Tools for the Job

Rhetorical critics use many different tools or strategies to critically evaluate a text. In this section you will learn some general guidelines for evaluating a text. Since this chapter focuses on a more traditional style of rhetorical criticism, the focus of these tools is on the argument of the author. You can use these tools to determine how well the author achieves his/her purpose through the text. This evaluation requires that you first understand the text and these tools. These tools are not mutually exclusive of each other, just as the interchange between the text and context are not separate. Also, these descriptions are not comprehensive of each tool; much more has been written on each. The next section provides you with more direction in the application of these tools to a text.

Credibility

One of the first questions you might ask about a writer/speaker is what are her qualifications to write on this topic? The question seems simple at first, but often depends on the types of claims the author is trying to make in the text. You may believe a review about the latest movie by one of your friends, since the consequences of your friend being wrong are minor. However, if this same friend advises against taking a certain type of medicine your doctor prescribed, you would be wise to question your friend's qualifications to make this claim about the medicine.

If an author is a professor of political science, you allow him/her to make broader claims about politics without citing as many sources, but if the author is a biologist, you may question his/her political expertise. The biologist may need to utilize some sources or other forms of evidence to convince you of his/her credibility. This type of credibility focuses on what you may know or assume about an author's expertise in the subject of the text.

In addition to the author's expertise, you may evaluate another form of credibility based on the character and associations of the author. One way that an author establishes character is through the style and tone of her writing. Have you ever had an experience where you agreed with someone in theory but were so put off by the person's delivery that you could not take the person's side? This is where tone becomes especially important. Writers can easily lose credibility by using an inappropriate tone. For example, a writer who seems to be addressing her readers as if they were young children may find that she loses credibility. Likewise a writer who uses jargon and terminology that will be unfamiliar to the audience may also lose credibility with readers. Even if an author is an expert in a field, the relationships the authors has and/or mistakes the author has made may influence his/her credibility.

For example, if a scientist is an expert in climate change, you may consider believing his/her argument that fossil fuels do not contribute to global warming. However, if you find out that the scientist's studies were funded by ExxonMobile, the statements then seem biased or at least a little less credible. This type of credibility is based on the associations the author makes to groups, organizations, or even philosophies about the world. Included in this character-based credibility are the actions of the author. Each time someone evaluates Bill Clinton's presidency, the famous testimony in which he lied influences the evaluator's estimation of his presidency. In these cases, the credibility is not the sole indicator of the effectiveness of the argument, but a contributing factor in the overall evaluation.

Logical Argument

A major element of a traditional rhetorical analysis is evaluating the logical arguments an author makes in a text. Depending on how your instructor prefers to frame this assignment, you may learn technical argument evaluations including logical fallacies and syllogistic reasoning. For the purpose of this section, a more foundational understanding of logic will allow you to evaluate a text.

The conclusions people make in their arguments generally follow one of two types of reasoning: inductive and deductive. At the most basic level, inductive reasoning draws from individual experiences or examples to make more general claims. For example, the statement "All cacti I've touched hurt my hand; therefore all cacti will hurt my hand" would be inductive. The persuasive strength of inductive claims relies heavily on the experience of the listener/reader, and the probability of the claim. Claims like "I like chocolate ice cream, therefore all people like chocolate ice cream" fail to persuade since counterexamples are easy to imagine, if not demonstrate.

On the other hand, deductive reasoning draws conclusions about specific examples from greater truths. The classic example:

> All men are mortal.
> Socrates is a man.
> Therefore, Socrates is a mortal.

This example demonstrates the simple relationship between the different parts of the argument. However, if all men are not mortal, or if Socrates is not a man, then the conclusion of the argument would be invalid.

Whether the argument is inductive or deductive, it relies on whether or not the audience shares the same belief about the argument. If the audience finds the premise(s) of the argument reasonable, then they may be inclined to believe it. Otherwise, they may doubt the logical reasoning behind the argument. In rhetorical analysis, we are evaluating the effectiveness of the arguments of a text for a particular audience. Logic is one element of that effectiveness, one connection to the audience. It is definitely a powerful connection, but logic and facts alone do not make a text persuasive.

Emotional Appeal

In addition to building a strong argument, authors often include emotional appeal in a text. An emotional appeal adds to the credibility and logic in a text by relating the topic to a story or language charged with meaning and feelings for the audience. In the 2008 Presidential election, Barack Obama and John McCain often used stories of individual people to help connect with the

Revising for Transitions

Transitions are words, phrases, and sentences that guide readers as they move through a text while signaling connections among ideas. These transitional words, phrases, and sentences guide the reader in much the same way as road signs guide a driver. Writers use transitions both within paragraphs and between paragraphs, and these transitions act as bridges between different ideas, connecting them.

Within paragraphs, you can use transitional words, such as "therefore" or "moreover," or you can use transition sentences that directly explain the connections between two ideas in the same paragraph.

You can use transitions to link ideas with the paragraph, but try to limit use to only those that are necessary to make your ideas clear. Too many transitions distract the reader from your message and slow down the rhythm of your language. Therefore, use only those that you need. In the following paragraph, transitions are effectively used:

Although these devices contribute to the persuasiveness of Plato's argument, a weakness develops in that Plato tends not to address the opposing contention. Plato does not recognize that by attempting to prevent the imperfections in mankind through eliminating pain and error, he destroys the natural balance that enhances the very pleasure he attempts to

audience. Sometimes these individual stories became the central focal point of the discussion instead of the policies and issues. Emotional appeals can come in the form of a story, individual words, or a change in tone and pace of a speech. Stories connect to the audience and make the audience feel like the speaker/writer better understands them. Language can emotively direct the audience's attention in one direction rather than another. Consider these two sentences:

- The increase of carbon emissions potentially leads to high amounts of greenhouse gasses.

- Our cars are choking the planet to death.

Both sentences argue for essentially the same thing, but the second sentence uses emotionally charged language to further the argument.

As you can see, an argument needs to at least combine some element of credibility, logical appeal, and emotional appeal to reach and convince the intended audience. Although you do not always need to analyze all three elements in an argument, you should recognize how the rhetorical elements can mix and influence each other.

create. **Essentially**, Plato **not only** suppresses creative growth vital for the mental health of a young child **but also** creates a society unable to express fault, prohibiting their ability to learn from circumstance. **Additionally**, how can pleasure be measured if a comparison, or opposite emotion, is non-existent? Plato's entire thesis is constructed upon balance and equality, **yet** in this one discussion, he creates societal division and simultaneously disrupts a harmonic balance established by naturally dependent emotions.

—Nikki Ing, Student

Paragraph-to-Paragraph: Use transitional expressions in essays to connect ideas from paragraph to paragraph. Usually in effective paragraphs, writers can use transitional sentences in the lead sentences and/or in the last sentence to make clear the preceding or following paragraph's connection to the one being written. If the essay is logically arranged, the transitions simply emphasize that logical organization. Consider the first sentence of the previous student example: "Although these devices contribute to the persuasiveness of Plato's argument [...]." In this paragraph-to-paragraph transition, the writer reminds us what the topic of the previous paragraph is and then introduces the topic of this paragraph, which is "[...] a weakness develops in that Plato tends not to address the opposing contention."

10.5 Organizing the Analysis

Since a text contains many different arguments and examples, you don't need to analyze everything in the text. Rather, you should purposefully choose the arguments you will focus on in your analysis. This makes your rhetorical analysis follow the arguments of the author and keeps you focused on the text rather than the tools for rhetorical analysis. Breaking the argument up into logical appeal, emotional appeal, and credibility divorces those elements from each other, leaving a fractured understanding of the argument. By analyzing the rhetorical elements as they appear in each claim you have a better chance of providing a thorough explanation of the complex relationship between these elements in the argument.

Now that you know what you will analyze in the text (the main arguments of the text), you need to focus on how you will go about the analysis. Depending on the preferences of your instructor, this format may provide you with a successful way to approach each argument. Assuming that your audience is familiar with the text, a full summary of the text is not necessary, but a brief summary of each argument you are about to analyze can help your audience remember the text and understand your evaluation of the text.

Although a rhetorical analysis structured around the major claims in a text will add clarity to your analysis, your instructor may request a different style of organization. One method or organization isn't necessarily superior to another, since your goal ought to be to clearly and systematically express your points.

10.6 Sample Rhetorical Analysis

Look at the Rhetorical Analysis, "Money is My Monkey Wrench: A Rhetorical Analysis" in Chapter 13. The author focuses on the main arguments presented in Kasser's text and throughout the essay continues to return to the effectiveness of the argument.

In writing this essay, Owan recognized the complexity of Kasser's arguments and sought to argue for the effectiveness of those arguments. Notice that Owan briefly summarizes each of Kasser's arguments and then analyzes the argument. He attempts to explain why the arguments are effective to the intended audience, and then moves to the next argument. Owan is asking his reader to reread Kasser's text and see the complexity of the argument.

Although Owan chose to focus mainly on logical arguments in the Kasser text, you could be equally successful focusing on the credibility and emotional appeals in the Kasser text. Kasser taps into common threads of experience (religion and ethics) to point out the duality in materialism in our culture.

As you approach your rhetorical analysis, remember that you are writing to your own audience. You are asking readers to interpret and reinterpret a text in a unique way, dictated by the types of analysis you provide. In many cases, the focus will be on argument. In such cases you are asking your readers to evaluate the effectiveness of a text's arguments. Just like the text you are analyzing, you need to know your audience and context and provide logical, emotional, and credible arguments for your conclusions about the text.

10.7 Beyond Aristotle: Other Types of Rhetorical Analysis

In this chapter you've learned about a basic type of rhetorical analysis: Aristotelian. The main focus of this type of criticism is the effectiveness of an argument as measured through predetermined categories. We evaluated arguments on the grounds of logic, credibility, emotional appeal, context, and audience. However, the field of rhetorical analysis spans several disciplines (English, Communication, Political Science, History, and Gender Studies, to name a few) and manifests in many different forms.

Although we looked at the effectiveness of an argument in this chapter, different forms of criticism look to different qualities that emerge in texts and analyze the argument beyond the surface to discover messages of power. These types of rhetorical analysis can be classified by the power relationships investigated (sex/gender, race, religion, sexuality, political systems) and/or specific devices as they relate to those investigations.

For example, a metaphoric analysis may analyze the immigration metaphors in a popular politician's speeches. Instead of arguing for or against the effectiveness of the text, a writer could identify the relevant metaphors and then make claims about the meaning and effect of using the metaphors. Let's say the politician always claims, "immigrants are flooding across the border." On the surface, the politician is making a simple observation: a lot of immigrants come to the United States. However, the politician chose to use *flood* as a metaphor for how immigrants cross the border. *Flood* refers to a rushing of water that is uncontrollable. By using *flood*, the politician characterizes the manner in which immigrants cross the border: too fast. We could continue the analysis by pondering the specific implications of a flood versus other fast moving waters, like a *gush*, or *river*. *Flood* has some inherently negative (destructive) connotations that are not carried with *gush* and *river*, making *flood* both uncontrollable water and bad water. This characterization of immigrants, we might reason, lumps all immigrants into one giant, uncontrollable mass working in unison to cause harm to the United States. Turning our attention back to the politician, we can say that the surface arguments of the speech seem innocuous, but the subtext presented in the metaphors offers a much stronger message to the audience.

As you can see, we can easily analyze texts beyond the basic arguments. Your textbook for English 102 offers a more detailed explanation of other types of rhetorical analysis.

11

Exploring a Controversy
and Writing a Public Argument

Goals

Your controversy analysis should:

- ✓ Effectively appeal to your chosen audience.

- ✓ Provide a clearly defined thesis and focused argument.

- ✓ Incorporate research materials to explore the multiple perspectives surrounding a controversy and correctly document them.

- ✓ Demonstrate that you have conducted thorough research.

- ✓ Employ analytical and rhetorical skills to demonstrate your understanding of key arguments surrounding a controversy.

- ✓ Effectively incorporate peer and instructor feedback in the final version.

Your public argument should:

- ✓ Effectively appeal to your chosen audience.

- ✓ Provide a clearly defined thesis and focused argument.

- ✓ Articulate a clear position within the controversy you previously researched.

✓ Provide your audience with a clear call to action.

✓ Employ analytical and rhetorical skills to demonstrate your understanding of key arguments.

✓ Effectively incorporate peer and instructor feedback in the final version.

11.1 Controversy Analysis: An Overview

Turn on any major news channel and you'll soon realize the ubiquity of controversy in the world. Whether you're listening to political pundits argue over the timeline for troop withdrawal in Iraq, or watching historians debate the events surrounding John F. Kennedy's assassination, you're witnessing argument, and argument is the driving force behind today's most pressing controversies. While controversy can be generally defined as debate, contention, or dispute, you might also think of a controversy as a social issue or topic that is steeped in disagreement. With any controversy, there is something "at stake," a larger relevance that has an impact on a society or those living within it. If there were no larger relevance, then the issue probably would not be controversial; without anything "at stake," chances are it wouldn't be worth arguing over. Thus when considering a controversy, you want to ask yourself "What's at stake for those involved?" Answering this question will help you get a sense of why the issue is being debated—why it matters.

> **Controversy:** a contentious social issue that has a larger relevance for a society or those living within it.

To understand what a controversy is, think about some of the hot button issues you hear about on a regular basis. For example, the issue of water conservation is one especially relevant to those living in the desert, since drought is typical in such an arid landscape. Environmental advocates have argued for the necessity of restricting water use. They might advocate such actions as taking shorter showers, landscaping with drought-tolerant plants, fixing leaky faucets, implementing gray water systems, and so forth. However, others might argue for unrestricted water usage, noting that they have the right to use as much water as they want, as long as they have the means to pay for their water usage. Still others might fall in between these two extremes—perhaps they understand the importance of water conservation, but don't always live by these principles. Here is how this might look if we represent it visually as a continuum—a line that demonstrates the range of positions available concerning the issue of water conservation:

100% convinced about water conservation: infrequent use of car washing, use low-flow shower, recycle bath and dish water, desert landscaping at home.	Somewhere in the middle: partial awareness and conviction; they may agree with some principles of water conservation but don't always live by these principles.	100% convinced about unrestricted water use: corporate lawns, long showers, weekly visits to car wash, running the water constantly and liberally.

But what's at stake? For one, water is necessary for the maintenance of all life. Yet, the issue also holds relevance for those involved in different ways. Environmentalists, for instance, might argue that we need to use water in ways that ensure we have enough to sustain a population of people over time. Thus using an excess of water might eventually result in a water shortage that could have negative effects for desert ecosystems. On the other hand, those who support unrestricted water use might say that their individual rights are being jeopardized because restricting water usage takes away their right to choose how much water to use and how to use it. In either case, something is at stake.

Most controversies are more complex than simple pro/con, for/against, and yes/no distinctions. Determining these binary distinctions is the first step in understanding a controversy, but rarely provides a full understanding of the actual issues. When you explore a controversy, part of your goal will be to ascertain the in-between areas that exist within a controversy—the arguments that fall in the gray area and that may not be as simple as "for" or "against." Finding and understanding these gray areas will take time and research, and the more you research a controversy, the more you will be able to comprehend the arguments made on *all* sides, by *all* those involved.

But why explore a controversy? As part of your English 102 course, you are analyzing arguments, researching arguments, and making arguments. The controversy analysis researches an argument, which will inform the argument you make in your third essay, public argument. Many instructors require students to use the research gathered during this paper as the basis for the public argument. Since you'll be spending so much time on one topic, you ought to pick a topic that interests you. While you research your controversy analysis, keep in mind that you will eventually write an argument of your own on this same topic. Such an understanding will enable you to anticipate **counterarguments** as well as to create a more educated standpoint on the issue. Comprehending the multiplicity of viewpoints surrounding an issue will better prepare you to engage in discussions surrounding the issue, even with those who may not hold the same opinion as you.

Counterargument: An opposing argument to your position on an issue. In a controversy analysis, you want to explain all the relevant arguments and counterarguments, even if you disagree with one of the positions.

In this chapter, you will learn strategies for writing a controversy analysis, including locating a line of inquiry, creating a research proposal, conducting research, and annotating key sources. You will also learn essential principles of persuasion, including how to create public arguments that draw upon the research you've conducted into the controversy. Your instructor may require you to do some or all of these beneficial exercises.

11.2 Getting Started on Your Controversy Analysis

Controversy analysis:
An analytical essay that incorporates research to trace the key arguments made by people who have a stake in an issue. Controversy analyses evaluate the validity of key claims, examine the persuasive strategies employed by key groups or people, and explore the similarities and distinctions between diverse viewpoints.

A **controversy analysis** is an analytical essay that incorporates research on the key arguments made by people who hold a stake in an issue. More than just outlining these arguments, however, a controversy analysis should evaluate the validity of specific claims, examine the persuasive strategies employed by key groups or people, and explore the similarities and distinctions between diverse viewpoints. The purpose of a controversy analysis is *not* to assert a position on the issue but instead to demonstrate a thorough consideration of a variety of viewpoints and to elucidate the arguments made by others.

Another goal for your analysis is to initiate a conversation among the various texts you cite: By showing how these sources develop their lines of argument surrounding a controversy, comparing these lines of argument, and evaluating the effectiveness of their persuasive strategies, you are essentially beginning a conversation regarding the range of opinions that figure in to a controversy. The difficult part of initiating this conversation, however, will be to let your own voice control your analysis. Because you will be relying heavily on your research in your controversy analysis, it can be easy to let these "voices of authority" dominate your essay. But a well-written controversy analysis should forefront the voice of its author, stressing the author's analysis and evaluation of the sources—not the sources themselves. Keep this in mind when you get ready to draft your controversy analysis.

To write a controversy analysis, you must first locate a controversy and, more specifically, a line of inquiry surrounding that controversy. For instance, let's say you are interested in exploring the topic of stem cell research. Once you begin researching this topic in the library and online, you realize just how broad the topic is; so much information is available on the subject that you would likely have a difficult time trying to outline key arguments surrounding the issue. In order to make your topic more manageable, you need to focus on one area of stem cell research. You decide to look at how stem cells have been used in cancer research, and you are particularly interested in whether or not stem cells have proven potential for finding cures for cancer. As you move forward in your research, you will want to consider the following questions:

- What do you want to find out? What is your purpose for exploring this controversy?

- What is at stake in the issue? What is its larger social significance?

- Who are some of the key groups or people who have a stake in the issue?

- What else do you know about this issue?

The next section will help you locate a **line of inquiry** and will guide you through the process of invention and discovery. This will be the first step you will take in your controversy analysis, since it will help you determine a strategy for conducting your research.

Line of inquiry: Guiding questions to help develop positions and arguments on a topic. In a controversy analysis, the line of inquiry ought to help you discover complexity in your controversy.

11.3 The Importance of Invention and Discovery

Sharon Crowley and Deborah Hawhee explain that the word *invention* comes from the Latin word *invenire*, which means "to find" or "to come upon," and the Greek word *heuriskein* meaning "to find out" or to "discover" (20). As these definitions indicate, invention is an active process. The invention process involves finding existing arguments and ideas pertaining to your topic and then discovering ways in which you can contribute to the conversation. Basically, invention is the part of the research process where you seek out all sides of the argument but also explore how all of those sides work (or fail to work) on their intended audiences. Whereas analysis deals with *how* and *why* questions, invention examines the *what* and *how* of arguments.

In "Chapter 4: Writing as a Process," you learned various *invention* strategies to help you develop ideas. When you write a controversy analysis, you sometimes have such a strong opinion about an issue that you can be tempted to skip the invention process entirely. However, if you don't think about opposing points of view, you risk overlooking productive counterarguments that might lead you to modify your position. You also set yourself up to conduct one-sided research that results in a one-sided essay. Because a controversy analysis should provide a comprehensive overview of key arguments surrounding an issue, being too one-sided will undermine the effectiveness of your essay. Also, when you get ready to assert your own position, readers will be more likely to agree with your argument if you acknowledge the complexity of your issue.

For more ideas about invention, please see *Rules for Writers*, pages 11–17.

For example, suppose you want to write about the issue of animal rights. Your research question might be, "Is it ethical to conduct medical experiments on chimpanzees?" Going into the research process, you might strongly believe that animal-rights activists are ethical guardians or violent extremists. However, if you answer your research question in two seconds without first setting foot in the library or conducting research online, you blind yourself to the complexities of the issue. If you hold to your initial impression, you'll be tempted to find only those sources that agree with your opinion, rather than seeking a rich array of sources. If you support the use of chimpanzees in medical research, you might overlook the fact that chimps have DNA that is 99 percent human. If you oppose such research, you might overlook important advances in medicine that have resulted from the practice. Think of your initial opinions as hypotheses and then test them against the diverse evidence and arguments you encounter during your research. The more you learn about your issue, the more you'll be able to write a comprehensive controversy analysis and, later, to create a well-informed public argument.

Entering the Conversation

One way to enter into a conversation with your sources is to actively make notes in the margins, underlining or copying excerpts for future reference, and writing down your reactions to the claims you encounter. The conversation becomes analytical when you then return to your annotations and notes to study both the content and underlying assumptions in what you wrote. In addition to encouraging you to look at your own perspective with a critical eye, the following questions ask you to consider the other perspectives that are present in your issue:

- What are the various viewpoints on the issue you are studying?

- Who might support these viewpoints and why? (Describe these people's values and beliefs, then analyze what you included/excluded in your descriptions.)

- Where among the various viewpoints do you stand and why?

- In the conversation you are studying, what are the various groups' unstated, underlying assumptions? What are yours?

- How did the issue get to be an issue? What is its history and how have the viewpoints and arguments changed over time?

- Whom does the issue affect and why? How would you characterize the viewpoints of those who are immediately affected?

- Who are the experts? What do the experts present as "facts"? What "facts" are open to interpretation?

- What new and/or slightly different positions or strategies can you imagine people creating in the future to advance or derail the argument(s) within your issue?

- What is likely to happen in the future? Will the issue have more serious effects? Will more people be affected? What will happen if we do nothing? (Different groups may forecast different scenarios, so there may be multiple answers to these questions.)

- How do the various groups present themselves and each other? Are there particular appeals that different groups rely on to reach audiences?

- Where does your own stance on the debate come in? Who agrees with you? Who disagrees? Who partially agrees with you and why?

Answering these questions during your research process will help you to understand the spectrum of arguments that form a controversy and will also help you develop your stance when you get ready to create your public argument. In addition, your instructor may ask you to write a proposal during the invention/discovery stage. This document will help you plan your work, select your sources, and organize your research. Your teacher will use the proposal to help you shape the research and writing process in an organized way.

Work Cited

Crowley, Sharon, and Debra Hawhee. *Ancient Rhetorics for Contemporary Students*. 3rd ed. New York: Pearson, 2004. Print.

11.4 The Research Proposal

Proposals help people in various fields plan complex research and collaborative projects. Scientists write proposals for grant money, instructors for new courses, students for changes in policy, manufacturers and designers for new products, and managers for reorganization. Likewise, when freelance writers hope to sell articles, they must query magazine editors by sending in brief descriptions of the articles they would like the magazines to purchase. Even an artist might write a proposal for an installation. The purpose of the research proposal assignment is two-fold: First, it gives you practice in writing a brief and concise projection of your intended work; second, the process of writing your proposal will force you to think about your upcoming essay and make decisions about which writing strategies to employ. Your research proposal, then, should address both what you wish to learn about (your topic) and how you plan to increase your knowledge of the topic (your research process).

Research proposals aid in the research process by requiring that you narrow the scope of your topic and express that scope in a single document. Additionally, your research proposal will enable you to receive feedback early in the process about important matters, such as the quality of your sources, the feasibility of your topic, and the overall coherence of what you plan to investigate.

Research proposals for argumentative academic writing often include the following components:

- The topic or problem that you plan to investigate;

- An awareness of the range of arguments or positions that exist;

- A set of preliminary research questions to which you hope to respond;

- Research that has been completed (sometimes you include an annotated bibliography of this); and

- Questions that you have for your peers and instructors.

The checklist above is for writing an exploratory research proposal. Some instructors may want you to write the research proposal after you have had time to research and pre-write some of your ideas, in which case, you will need to think through a tentative argumentative stance. Once your proposal has been approved, you can start organizing your research. You may also be asked to write an annotated bibliography, which is explained below. The annotated bibliography helps you summarize the various viewpoints you've read about concerning your research and provides a useful resource to reference during your writing process.

11.5 The Annotated Bibliography

One of the assignments that will help guide your research process is the annotated bibliography. Instructors assign the annotated bibliography to provide a helpful step in the research process and to acquaint you with a form that is often used in research projects. The annotated bibliography, which consists of alphabetical lists of topic-related sources each with a summary paragraph, provides a useful way for researchers to share their information.

Putting together an annotated bibliography will help you gather and analyze information before you sit down to write. When working with many sources, it can be very helpful to have brief summaries of each article as a quick resource guide. Often, teachers will distribute annotated bibliographies among students in a class as a way to share ideas and sources. Since students sometimes need the same kinds of sources, another student's annotated bibliography can make you aware of other material that might be useful for your particular project. For these reasons, it is important to realize that your classmates as well as your instructor are your audience for this assignment. To that end, take care to write in a voice and style that appeals to this general, non-expert audience, translating technical material into your own words where you can. If you are too brief in your annotations, those summary paragraphs may not help you recall the details of the articles, and they may not give others enough information to assess the usefulness of the articles. Your annotated bibliography should include a short discussion of how each reference will be useful for your writing.

Below is an annotated bibliography that was written by UA student Stephenie Mirka. Please note that the citations are in MLA format and in alphabetical order, and that in each entry, Stephenie considers not only what the source is about, but also how it could contribute to her research.

Annotated Bibliography

Hardesty, Dawn Wotapka. "Long Island landlord group: Sex offender law goes too far." Long Island Business News (Nov 17, 2006): NA. InfoTrac OneFile. Thomson Gale. University of Arizona Library. 24 Feb. 2007 <http://find.galegroup.com.ez-proxy.library. arizona.edu/>.

In her article, "Long Island landlord group: Sex offender law goes too far," Dawn Wotapka Hardesty claims that a bill in Long Island, regarding landlords renting to sex offenders, is ridiculous. The author utilizes many quotes from people, who agree and disagree with her claim. By including the both points of view in her argument, she strengthens her essay. She also explains the disadvantages of this law, and how it victimizes sexual offenders. Her purpose is to show that some sex offender laws are too extreme. This article will provide a point of view different than mine for my persuasive essay. It will give me an example of a sexual offender law that is creating problems for landlords. Hardesty provides information from the creator of the bill, which will be useful to back up my claims. I found this source using InfoTrac One and chose it because it gave a good example of why some laws do not work against sexual offenders.

Longo, Robert E. "Safe As Houses?" Community Care. 1634 (2006): 32. Academic Search Premier. 24 Feb. 2006 <http://web. ebscohost.com/ehost/>.

In "Safe As Houses?" Robert E. Longo claims that the development of Megan's Law has not been proven to decrease the number of sexual abuse cases within the United States. The author proves this by including background information, statistics, and examples. He discusses

---

the many implications of Megan's Law, such as cost and victimization of sexual offenders. This victimization has caused many to become offenders again because they are not able to live normal lives after their release from prison. Longo's purpose is to show his readers that the only way to put an end to sexual abuse is to stop it before it occurs. Megan's Law does not aid in this since no evidence exists to prove that it has prevented reoccurrences of sexual abuse. This article will aid in my research question of deciding whether sexual offenders should be integrated back into society. It shows examples and statistics that could be used in my paper.

Miller, Kathleen. "Wyoming Worries About Attracting Offenders." Fox News. 24 Feb. 2007 <http://www.foxnews.com/wires/2007Feb20/>.

Kathleen Miller discusses the number of sex offenders that are moving to Wyoming as a result of the harsh laws in other states in her article, "Wyoming Worries About Attracting Offenders." Miller uses quotes from a representative of the U.S. House of Representatives, sex offenders, a police officer, and many others. These add substance to her article, when used with background information and other facts regarding laws in Wyoming. Miller's purpose is to inform people of the lack of laws for sexual predators. She wants this to change so that more sexual predators will have to be registered, and harsher laws will be created. In my paper, this article can provide me with an opposing point of view. This will help me to draw my own conclusions about the opposing viewpoint.

Seipp, Catherine. "The Sex-Offender Lobby." The Wall Street Journal. 25 Feb 2007 <http://www.opinionjournal.com/>.

Catherine Seipp states in her editorial, "The Sex-Offender Lobby" that laws regarding sex offenders and landlords in California do not coincide well. She proves her point by explaining Megan's Law. Also, Seipp's article contains quotes from opponents and advocates of Megan's Law. By including the views of a landlord who is unable to move a sex offender out of his mobile-home park, but still needs to inform angry residents of their presence, she makes her case far more understandable to the reader. The author's purpose is to let people know that lawmakers should not oppose Megan's Law. This applies to my research question by showing the opposing point of view. I can use this in my persuasive essay to show readers what others think regarding the issue of sex offenders. Seipp includes various quotes, which could be added into my paper to expand on the opposing viewpoint.

Sullum, Jacob. "Zoned out: sex offender residency restrictions." Reason 38.10 (March 2007): 9(2). InfoTrac OneFile. Thomson Gale. University of Arizona Library. 24 Feb. 2007 <http://find. galegroup.com.ezproxy.library.arizona.edu/>.

Jacob Sullum's article, "Zoned out: sex offender residency restrictions," suggests that laws restricting where sexual offenders live are unnecessary and create stress for prior sex offenders. Sullum does this by describing how the majority of the laws apply to people who committed crimes when they were teenagers. He also says that restrictions for where these offenders reside may end up making them less likely to register, which would make it impossible to track their whereabouts. The author includes some quotes from officials and statistics, as well. This article demonstrates that sexual offenders should not be segregated from the rest of the community. It will help to answer my research question by providing me with statistics that prove that laws against sex offenders should not be as harsh.

Wing, Arthur. "Housing and Sex Offenders." Child Abuse Review 7.6 (1998): 449-452. Academic Search Premier. 24 Feb. 2007 <http://web.ebscohost.com.ezproxy.library.arizona.edu/ehost/>.

In his review, entitled "Housing and Sex Offenders," Arthur Wing argues that sex offenders need to live somewhere in the community, but also need to live somewhere that minimizes their risk of offending children again. He develops his claim by providing many detailed solutions to the problem. Also, he includes the advantages and disadvantages to each solution. Wing's purpose is to convince people that local authorities should be involved in the housing of registered sex offenders. He desires this change to come about while still protecting the children in the surrounding community. The author basically sums up my view of my research question. I believe that sex offenders should still have rights because they are citizens, but the safety of children should also be taken into consideration when housing these former criminals. The author discusses various acts, such as the Crime and Disorder Act 1998, which will help the authorities and health professionals to work together in finding suitable programs and housing for offenders. This will definitely provide much of the needed information that I will use to back up my claims.

The Rhetorical Précis

Amy Kimme Hea, a professor in Rhetoric, Composition, and the Teaching of English, uses an assignment in her courses that is called "the Rhetorical Précis." According to Dr. Kimme Hea, the purpose of the rhetorical précis is to offer a short account of an article that does more than summarize the content. The rhetorical précis, which is generally four sentences long, accounts for the author's main assertion as well as an explanation of how the author develops or supports the thesis. The précis also includes the author's purpose in writing (how she wants to change her audience), a description of the intended audience, and the relationship the author established with that audience (Woodworth 156–64). Examining issues of audience and purpose is essential to writing descriptions that analyze rather than summarize the content of a source.

Sentences of the Précis

1. Name of author, [optional: a phrase describing author], genre and title of work, date in parentheses; a rhetorically accurate verb (such as "assert," "argue," "suggest," "imply," "claim," etc.); and a THAT clause containing a major assertion (thesis statement) of the work.

2. An explanation of how the author develops and/or supports the thesis, usually in chronological order.

3. A statement of the author's apparent purpose, followed by an "in order" phrase indicating the change the author wants to effect in the audience.

4. A description of the intended audience and the relationship the author established with the audience.

Sample

Douglas Park, in his essay "Audience" (1994), suggests that teaching audience is an essential but elusive aspect of teaching writing. Park develops this idea by exploring different definitions of audience, looking at how a text itself can delineate audience, and then discussing specific strategies writers can use to create contexts for audience. His purpose is to help teachers of writing understand and teach the different aspects of audience in order for them to help students improve the sense of audience in their writing. Park establishes an informal relationship with teachers who are interested in strengthening their students' weak writing.

The Abstract

An **abstract** is a summary—usually of an academic text—that stands on its own as a piece of writing rather than as part of an essay. Abstracts are similar to annotated bibliographies in that they make it easy for you to keep track of your sources during the writing process. If your instructor asks you to write a summary or abstract that stands on its own, summarize the text's main ideas and also include the following:

For a sample abstract, please see *Rules for Writers*, page 516.

1.   Author's full name.

2.   Title of the text.

3.   Publication information such as when it was written and where the text was published.

4.   An introduction to the context in which it was written; i.e., the issue, debate, recent discovery, etc.

Work Cited

Woodworth, Margaret K. "The Rhetorical Précis." *Rhetoric Review* 7.1 (1998) 156–64.

11.6 Writing Academic Arguments

The way one creates an argument in general and an academic argument in particular can vary widely across cultural contexts. In some cultures, a writer does not necessarily have to acknowledge opposing views or even document sources. This is sometimes because the audience is expected to familiarize itself with those opinions independently, driven by personal interests, and because knowledge is viewed as collective rather than individual property. In the U.S. plagiarism is considered unethical and has concrete disciplinary consequences. A sort of cultural stigma also accompanies plagiarism, in that writers are expected to demonstrate their independence from other sources and to position themselves carefully as individuals. Citing sources properly helps a writer to accomplish this with technical mastery.

Different cultures—both inside and outside of the United States—value different writing styles and patterns of organization. Indeed, there are qualities to appreciate about such ways of creating academic arguments. If you have been educated in such a system your entire life, you are not expected to forget everything you have been taught about writing in your native culture. Rather, you should become aware of the differences between other academic traditions and U.S. norms for academic argumentation. This is the first step toward appreciating both and to using each appropriately in its own context.

In the North American context, argument and research are inextricably linked in the scholarly community. It is important to remember that academia has a culture of its own, as well as numerous subcultures comprised by the various disciplines. Members of the academic community conduct research before they take a stance in order to first find their place in the conversation. For example, before presenting her latest findings on ultrafast lasers, a physicist would read recent articles in *Physical Review Letters*, a leading journal in her field, in order to be up-to-date on the latest work in that area. Then, in her own article, before presenting her particular argument, she would refer to that other work so that others can see that she is aware of the current conversation. Following this, she would move on to present her own carefully researched argument and back it up with experimental data.

Another characteristic of academic arguments is that scholars not only build on what has come before, but also add to that knowledge, so that their articles and books are not mere reports on and responses to other arguments, but presentations of new knowledge. So while research is required for the scholar to be seen as credible, the scholar must also contribute an idea that will further the discussion—some new or different slant that is presented clearly and supported by convincing evidence.

Developing the Elements of an Argument

Once you have carefully considered your sources and understand the arguments surrounding the controversy you're exploring it is time to think about the specific elements that comprise strong argumentative writing so that you can declare your own position. In every good academic argument you should be able to find an **issue**, **claims**, a **thesis** (clearly stated or implied), and **supporting evidence**. Once you have determined where you stand on the issue, it is time to develop claims to support your argument. Good claims are specific and assertive. Once you have a sense of the claims you would like to make, you are close to writing a thesis—the statement that sets the parameters of your discussion and identifies your position. Once you know the thesis and direction of the paper, the focus shifts to the effective use of evidence and supporting materials.

For more advice on developing lines of argument and supporting your claims with evidence, see *Rules for Writers*, pages 362–66.

Issues

The first step in constructing an argument is deciding on an issue to discuss. An issue is a point of concern or controversy within a topic, usually something that is debated in society or a scholarly field. Determining an issue to focus on involves refining a general topic, such as Indian mascots used by sports teams, and creating a question about that topic for which there would be more than one position. It may be helpful to think of your initial formulation of the issue as a yes or no question. There must be at least two sides to the argument—in reality, there are always more than two "sides" to an issue because no complex problem offers only two possible ways to approach it. An example of a yes-or-no question would be something like this:

Topic	Indian mascots for sports teams; e.g., Cleveland Indians, Washington Redskins, Florida Seminoles
Research Question	Should the governing bodies of sports organizations (the National Football League, the NCAA, Major League Baseball, etc.) ban the use of Indian mascots?
Claim: For	Yes, institutions like the NCAA and others should ban the use of Indian mascots.
Claim: Against	No, these institutions should not ban the use of Indian mascots.
Combination	The governing institutions of sports teams should establish strict ethical guidelines for mascots (not quite a ban, but could be used to get teams to engage in dialogue about effects of this social practice).

However, the examples above hardly exhaust the possibilities for claims about this controversy. Rather than pursuing a seemingly straightforward, yes/no approach to argument, you could choose to frame the problem differently, so that the argument you create doesn't directly answer the "yes/no" question or take an obvious pro/con stance. Instead, it explores the *underlying issues* that shape people's opinions and positions. Consider these alternatives to the pro/con format, noting how the research question is more open-ended:

Topic	Historical and cultural factors behind the Indian mascot controversy.
Research Question	What historical and cultural factors have led many to argue for eliminating Indian mascots for sports teams?
Claim	A history of the use of Native American symbols as mascots for U.S. sports teams reveals a longstanding disregard for how these practices affect Native Americans negatively.

Claim	The controversy over the use of Indian mascots demonstrates how most white Americans tend to understand U.S. history very differently than Native Americans do.

In neither case do we have a "yes/no" to a clear-cut question, but there is clearly an argument and a position in each claim. People could disagree with the above claims, and at least some should if it is something worth writing about.

Some of the topics you are interested in may not appear to be suited for argumentative writing. They may seem inappropriate because they lack two obvious and opposing sides, meaning "there's a topic, but I can't find any issues." For example, "people with disabilities" is a topic or descriptive category, but framed as such it is not a "problem" that would lead people to disagree about anything. However, there are topics related to disability that are considered controversial issues.

Topic	People with disabilities and the law
Issue	Should drug, alcohol, and other addictive behaviors be considered disabilities, conferring certain legal rights and services to those who are diagnosed with them?

As this example shows, by refining the general topic of "people with disabilities and the law," you can arrive at a controversial issue.

Claims

The second step in creating an argument is making your claims. When you make a claim, you are declaring that a problem does or does not exist and that a solution is or is not needed. The claims you make in your argument will be for one side of your issue or another—or a reasonable compromise. So in the example of the mascot controversy from above, you could make several possible claims, two of which include:

Claim 1	Using names such as "Indians," "Savages," or "Seminoles" as mascots demonstrates an ignorance of the historical realities experienced by the indigenous peoples of North America.
Claim 2	"Indian" mascots freeze representations of Native Americans in time; they are always "braves," "savages," and "warriors," not people experiencing everyday life.

An author who creates the first of these claims needs to take into account the counterclaims that those who disagree, the "opposition," may propose. The author who argues that Native American mascots are harmful will have to show that the cost of changing the mascots (both monetary costs and public opinion) will be worth the time and trouble because it addresses a subtle racism that is harmful to society. Remember that with research-based academic writing you should not make a claim unless you already have some background knowledge on the issue. That means you have to do some research or at least brainstorm about what you already know about the issue so that you can support your claims.

Thesis

Although arguments tend to have more than one claim, the thesis of an argument is its primary claim. A thesis should clearly and concisely state what the writer is trying to do in the essay. Typically this means identifying the scope of the discussion and the writer's position. As with a claim, a thesis must be arguable. It should not just be based on opinion but should indicate a clear position on the issue.

For more information on thesis statements see "Chapter 4: Writing as a Process" in the *Student's Guide* and *Rules for Writers*, pages 21–25 and 361–62. The former includes exercises on identifying weak versus strong thesis statements.

Thesis   Using "Indian" mascots demonstrates that contemporary U.S. society has an **inadequate understanding** of both the history of Native Americans and their continued presence as active members in local and national communities; therefore, **these "mascots" should not only be challenged,** but the **communities in which they exist should have open forums** in which the histories and current lived experiences of the many Native American tribes are openly discussed for everyone's education.

The preceding example shows that the thesis of the paper often includes a series of claims that then need to be developed in the paper (the three primary claims are highlighted in bold). A good thesis statement will usually give the reader a sense of the direction the paper will take. Some writing instructors will call this a *forecast* or a *blueprint*. As the thesis above illustrates, this gives the reader a framework for understanding the argument and structure of the paper and can be done in one or two sentences without awkwardness. Your instructor might explain alternative approaches to argument that do not require you to write a thesis statement, but in any case, you will need to guide readers along clearly.

Evidence

A thesis has little credibility without evidence to support it. Depending on your audience (see the following section for more information), the evidence used to support a claim may be logical, such as facts, statistics, or references to the law; or it may be emotional, such as the use of personal narrative or emotionally-laden terms. In the case of an academic paper that examines how the Industrial Revolution influenced the writing of the novel *Frankenstein* or a persuasive paper that argues for increased spending on the military, it is important to include evidence from credible outside sources. In the case of the *Frankenstein* analysis, evidence might come from such credible historical sources as *The British Industrial Revolution: An Economic Perspective*, one of the many texts that provide scholarly information on the cultural context of Mary Shelley, or from the actual journals Mary Shelley wrote during her lifetime in which she expresses her attitudes toward the working class. Organizing your evidence also presents you with a challenge. Brian Hogan, a former 102 student, explains:

> I learned how it is important to organize my supporting ideas first for the paper and then to develop each idea. This helped my papers flow better and allowed me to develop strong arguments as opposed to trying to tackle the paper as a whole. I've now learned to make sure each idea is supported properly by evidence from readings. I've also learned how to make my transitions better by relating ideas in my paragraphs.

As you are organizing your evidence, it is important to make sure that your argument remains in the forefront. There must be a balance between the claims and the evidence so that the argument does not rely too heavily on personal opinion or outside sources. A balanced argument features strong claims that are supported by compelling evidence. Of course, when constructing a strong, balanced argument the audience must always be kept in mind.

A Question of Audience

From the beginning, your target audience helps shape your essay's goals and intentions, the tone you adopt, the writing style you use, the persuasive strategies you choose, and the level of sophistication you bring to the conversation.

Think of how, in ordinary conversations, you can express the same opinion differently when talking with a friend as opposed to your professor or your class. In order to simplify the issue of audience, it might be tempting to write for a "general reader," but that general reader might not be the person who can or will help you achieve your purpose. For example, say you are writing as a physiology major with the goal of becoming a physical therapist, and your purpose is to convince insurance companies to extend their clients better coverage, particularly for physical therapy. You should write your essay to people who can make this happen—people who have undergone physical therapy and are willing to argue for better insurance coverage, or people who could persuade the insurance industry to change (patients' rights groups, for example), or to the insurance companies themselves. No matter who you choose, you will need to have a forum in mind—that is, a way of reaching that audience, whether via a letter to the editor of a magazine, a direct letter to the audience, or an article on a webpage. Because you are not yet an expert in your field, you probably won't want to target the readers of an academic journal as your audience. But a general-interest or other non-scholarly magazine is perfectly appropriate: The physiologist might write an article for *Time* or *New Mobility* magazine aimed at people in wheelchairs; or even *PT: Magazine of Physical Therapy*, which provides general healthcare and legislative news for physical therapists. There are different reasons for speaking to each of these groups, and you should target the one you can move to action. Narrowing your audience this way will help you **focus** your paper and choose the most convincing materials to present.

While it might appear that most of the essays you have come across in your research are directed to a "general audience," the fact is that most journals, newspapers, and magazines cater to different populations within the "general public." Advertising companies know this strategy well. The people who commonly read *Time* are different from the people who commonly read *The Wall Street Journal*, who in turn are different from the people who commonly read *People*. While on the surface the writing may appear to reach the same audience, the authors have made choices about the types of topics they will explore, the relative depth of their analyses, the examples that will be most appropriate, and so on. If you were to conduct a comparative analysis of these articles, you would uncover many ways that the authors have shaped their work for the magazines' or newspapers' reader-profiles. Freelance writers often rhetorically analyze magazines in order to understand how to make their work more appealing to the magazines' editors.

Even if you were to write for the "general public," who would that be? The U.S. is made up of so many diverse groups—we come from different racial, ethnic, sexual orientation, religious, language, and socioeconomic backgrounds, just to name a few—so as you know, you can't count on "the general public" to think like you or even to understand where you're coming from. Stretch yourself to think about views that are drastically different than your own. For example, if you identify as a conservative Republican, how might you reach an audience of liberal Democrats? What beliefs would you want to tap into? What information do you need to have to figure out in considering how your beliefs differ? Just as in everyday interactions with people who have backgrounds other than your own, when you're creating an academic argument for a particular audience, it's important not to assume that they will have the same views as you. That doesn't mean you can't write to them—you just have to spend time reflecting and discovering where and, more importantly, *why* your views on a particular issue might diverge from another person's views.

Of course, there are times when you want to reach a very broad group of people. If you are writing to convince insurance companies to change their coverage, for example, you could either write different letters to the bosses or CEOs of different companies, or you could write one letter that targets the common interests among them. But notice that the category "CEOs of insurance companies" still addresses a much narrower group of people than "the general public." By identifying your readers as CEOs of insurance companies, you have indicated a set of values and responsibilities held by your readers. As you write, you can invoke those values to make your work more convincing. Furthermore, you can avoid the combative model of argument that leaves no common ground for you to stand on.

For more on seeing your audience as a panel of jurors, see pages 360–61 in *Rules for Writers*.

Addressing Audience Rhetorically

When attempting to appeal to an audience, all writers must make decisions in order to be as persuasive as possible. These decisions are often made unconsciously, but bringing this decision-making process to the conscious level will help to make your writing more effective. In particular, it is important to be aware of the uses of both emotion and logic in creating an argument.

Readers can recognize both obvious and subtle writing strategies that appeal to their values and beliefs. Obvious appeals include emotionally-charged words and stories. Other strategies include description and repetition (as in Martin Luther King, Jr.'s "I Have a Dream" speech, in which he uses the phrase "I Have a Dream" over and over as he builds to the climax of the speech). Rhythm and figures of speech such as metaphors and similes can also be classified as stylistic devices that create *emotional* appeals in their readers. However, the danger, as UA student Eric Jacobson notes, is that the emotions may guide the work:

> When writing, be careful that your passion for your subject doesn't cloud the content of the work. Be sure to back up your argument with facts. On the other hand, don't let criticism keep you from writing what you believe. Use the criticism to help shape your argument.

Various strategies make sound use of logic but also have to do with how fairly an author presents evidence or frames an argument from the outset. An author can be logical without being reasonable. For instance, authors will often cite statistics or demonstrate that only one solution to a problem is practical or feasible when actually other solutions can work as well. An author may also present only two choices and then logically eliminate one, causing readers to ask: "Were there really only two choices to begin with, or did the author falsely limit the perspectives or evidence at the start?" One task for rhetorical analysis is to identify these various appeals in the way the author has constructed the text.

Authors must also establish their credibility by showing their familiarity with the subject, their broader awareness, their respect for others' values, and their integrity. They establish their credibility by demonstrating this familiarity and awareness to their readers. For example, an adviser at the university who frequently works with students' schedules will have more credibility for you as you determine your own class schedule than a parent who once took similar courses at another college.

For a more extensive description of persuasive strategies, see "Chapter 10: Rhetorical Analysis."

Thus far you've analyzed arguments and researched arguments; your next task to put forward a clear argument of your own. This will require the skills you've developed over the course of the first two units.

11.7 Writing Public Arguments

By Jennifer Haley

You have already explored analyzing and researching an argument, but what does it mean to write a *public argument*? The term "public" derives from the Latin term *publicus*, which meant "belonging to the people."[1] Since then, "public" has acquired many meanings, but it has always carried a sense of belonging to most or all members of a community, rather than being accessible only to a smaller, private group of people. Likewise, the Public Argument unit challenges you to write an argument that will be accessible and persuasive not only within the private discourse community of your English 102 class, but also to a broader audience of people.

As you move from the Controversy Analysis unit to the Public Argument unit, your first concern should be to decide upon your position in the controversial issue you've been researching. Taking a position does not necessarily mean that you have to choose between two sides. In fact, some of the most sophisticated arguments draw from both or many sides of a controversy, creating a new stance that benefits from the strengths of what's already been argued about an issue. Using the example of the water controversy argument from earlier in this chapter, you do not have to create an argument that is 100% pro-conservation or that is 100% pro-restriction. Some of the most persuasive arguments—to the largest *publics*—might be found in the "somewhere in the middle" category. For example, one such middle argument might advocate placing restrictions on water use only during the hot-

1 "Public" *Oxford English Dictionary Online.*

test hours of the day, when water is most likely to evaporate. As you decide on a position, think about angles that haven't already been brought up in the sources you've researched. And, just like every source in your Controversy Analysis essay had a stake in their argument, you'll find that the best arguments you can make are those in which *you* have a stake.

Once you've decided upon a position, the next step is to decide *to whom* you will make your argument. Just like when you write to a "general audience," when you write a public argument you should always keep in mind the nature of the specific "public" that you are targeting. It might be a broad public, such as all *Wikipedia* users, or it could be more narrow, such as students who live off-campus. In either case, the most important step in writing the public argument is identifying your audience and analyzing it rhetorically to understand its members' needs and expectations. Keep in mind that you can't always know or control who makes up your specific audience—that's precisely what makes it public. What you can do is devise a strategy for how to appeal to most of your readers or listeners based on what you can know about your targeted audience. Some of the questions you might ask about your audience include:

- How many viewers/readers/listeners might I have?

- What might my audience members already know about this topic? What do I need to tell them?

- What do I know about my audience? Do I know their age, locations, educational level, race, gender, political tendencies, etc.?

- What do I know about how my audience already feels about the topic? For example, which of my points will likely draw the most contention?

After you have a handle on your audience, there are several rhetorical factors you should consider as you develop your public argument. Below, you'll find the types of questions you might ask as you decide how to make your argument persuasive to your chosen public.

Purpose: The purpose of an argument is usually to move an audience, whether you're moving them to act or simply to react to what you're saying. Most essays you'll write in college share at least one purpose—to earn a certain grade. But public arguments have diverse purposes. For example, if you are making an argument about water conservation laws to a group of Tucson voters, your purpose would be to persuade your audience to vote a certain way on election day. Other public arguments, such as writing an article for the online encyclopedia *Wikipedia*, have less obvious purposes. Some might even argue that writing to *Wikipedia* is not making an argument. After all, aren't you just reporting facts? Even on *Wikipedia*, though, your purpose is to convince many readers that your knowledge of a subject is the best version of that knowledge. Because *Wikipedia* users can edit or even delete your writing if they disagree with it, the pressure is on to prove that you've done your research well enough to convince other users not to change your work. Regardless of your audience, you should always frame your public argument around a specific purpose, and you should be able to articulate what that purpose is to anybody who asks. Ask yourself:

- Am I moving my audience to *act*, to *react*, to *know*, or to *feel*, or all of the above?

- What do I want my audience to *do* in response my position?

- Am I making it clear how my listeners or readers can take the action I want them to take?

Medium: There are many modes of argument besides words on paper that might appeal to your audience, such as a speech or performance, a compilation of images, a digital argument that uses hypertext, and so on. While academic essays and some public audiences would expect to read a twenty-page research paper, many audiences are more likely to pay attention to non-alphabetic communications. For example, an audience of college students rushing to class would be unlikely to listen to a ten-minute speech about animal rights, but they might glance at an installation of large photographs with shorter, "bite-sized" portions of written text. Your medium should complement your purpose—if you hope to evoke your audience's sympathy about animal rights, for example, photographs would be more likely to gain an emotional response than the two-page essay. By considering the purpose, timing, and location of your argument you should be well-prepared to decide the best medium for your claims.

- How much time will my audience have to "read" my argument?

- What kind of format is most likely to serve the purpose of my argument?

- What kind of media are most familiar to my audience members? Will they know how to interact with my chosen medium, or will I have to teach them how to read it?

Persona: In an academic essay, writers often use a formal writing style, a deliberate tone, or a specific series of secondary sources to establish themselves as authoritative about a given topic. Unlike in an academic essay, you are often present in real-time for a public argument and you are often arguing to an audience who has no idea who you are. Therefore, developing a clear persona is an essential step. This persona could be one of neutrality, such as in a brochure that seeks to present unbiased facts. Or, your persona might be humorous, compassionate, angry, or detached. The subject matter, medium, and context of your public argument will help you decide on the most persuasive persona to embody.

- What is my relationship to the issue? Do I have experience that makes me an authority on the subject, or am I relying mostly on outside research?

- Will I be making the argument in person, or will a text make the argument for me?

- What is my relationship to the audience? Do they already know who I am? How will I explain my stake in the issue?

- What kind of persona best matches the subject matter and purpose of my argument?

- How will I convey my persona—through my tone, my words, my designs?

Language: The level of knowledge and expertise of the public you're targeting will ultimately determine your choice of language. For example, if you are seeking to convince your local hospital to buy an MRI machine, you'd likely use technical language about the medical benefits of magnetic

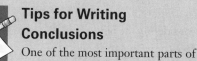

Tips for Writing Conclusions

One of the most important parts of your paper is the conclusion, for it will contribute to the reader's final impression of your essay. In high school, you may have been taught to use the conclusion as a place to restate your thesis and introduction as a way of reminding readers of your main points. This may be appropriate in some contexts, but it also may suggest that the reader didn't read the whole essay or understand the argument, which is generally not the case for the relatively short essays written in a first-year course. A conclu-sion that simply repeats what the writer has already stated in the rest of the essay is not pulling its weight, so to speak, because it does little to contribute to the overall meaning of the essay.

A more sophisticated approach to the conclusion will use it as an opportunity: not just to remind readers of what the main points of the essay were, but to emphasize why those main points were important. In other words, the conclusion can provide the "so what" of your whole essay, placing it in a wider context and showing how and why your argument matters in a larger sense. Some students have been cau-

resonance imaging to a group of doctors and nurses, but that same language might frustrate a more general audience of patients. Both of these audiences might be "public," but they demand very different uses of language. The medium also plays a role in your choice of language—if you're making a documentary, you wouldn't use a plethora of fancy words that your viewer might have to look up in a dictionary, even if such jargon would be perfectly appropriate for a written essay.

• What kind of language will my audience be most comfortable with? Specialized terms/jargon that allow for more precision? Generalized language that is more understandable but less exact?

• How will my language reflect my persona?

• How will my medium affect my language choices?

There are many different publics that you might target for your public argument. Some English 102 teachers will team up, making another section of English 102 your default public argument. If this isn't the case in your class, you might think about addressing an issue you feel strongly about in a discourse community you belong to, like presenting a speech to a UA club or team or submitting an opinion piece in the *Daily Wildcat*. You could envision a very narrow audience with a wide capacity for public change, such as a member of Congress or a special interest group or non-profit agency in Tucson. Or you could look to wider, less controlled public audiences, such as

tioned against introducing new information in the conclusion, and this is certainly an important consideration. Nevertheless, it is possible to "open up" your essay at the end without including material unrelated to the rest of the essay, as long as you provide your reader with the connections between your essay's main argument and those larger issues.

For instance, a writer might argue in an essay that Kate Chopin's "The Story of an Hour" uses imagery associated with the changing seasons and nature to underscore the protagonist's sense of freedom and rebirth upon learning of her husband's death. Instead of simply repeating this idea in the conclusion, the writer could discuss how the issues Chopin explored in this story, written at the end of the 19th century, are still relevant for women in the 21st century. This would connect the essay to modern readers and ensure that the "so what" is made clear: the issues explored by Chopin are not unique to a certain time period, and this might be one reason readers should seriously consider the validity of the writer's claims about the text.

For advice on and examples of conclusions, refer to pages 26–27 in *Rules for Writers*.

writing on a blog, creating a webpage, or even performing your argument on the UA mall. Regardless of what audience you choose, the public argument assignment will require that you think critically about the means of persuasion that will best suit your argument and your audience.

This chapter focused on two very distinct writing tasks. Even though you are trying to provide your readers with a comprehensive understanding of a complex issue in your controversy analysis, you will make clear choices of what to include in your paper. Through these decisions, your writing, like all other writing, is persuasive. You are persuasive in that you will highlight certain areas of the controversy, which takes attention away from other areas. In other words, you're telling your audience what is important to know. Did you make the right choices?

On the other hand, the public argument assignment requires you to make your own argument concerning a controversy. Instead of merely reporting about the controversy, as in the controversy analysis, you will enter the conversation and align yourself with a certain understanding of the controversy. You may convince someone to change his or her mind about the controversy, and even act on that position. Thus, your argument in this assignment has consequences. Do you make a strong argument? What about a strong call to action? Often we can't know what our readers do in response to our writing, but we can still write with an understanding that our research, our arguments, and our actions matter.

12

Personal and Reflective Writing

Goals

Your literary analysis should demonstrate:

✓ Analysis of how a personal experience has influenced the ways in which you think, who you are, or how you read and write.

✓ Detailed and sensory description of your experience(s), using vivid details and specific language instead of vague language.

✓ Careful structuring to convey a central purpose or idea, as well as audience awareness.

✓ Incorporation of peer and instructor feedback in the final version.

Your reflection should demonstrate:

✓ Your ability to think about your writing and yourself as a writer.

✓ An in-depth reflection regarding your process of revision.

✓ A sense of how reflection assists in your continuing development as a writer.

✓ Your ability to collaborate in peer groups to revise your writing.

12.1 Personal and Reflective Writing: An Overview

Writing about yourself may sometimes seem fun and easy. At other times, it may seem intensely difficult. Personal writing gives you the opportunity to grow individually and intellectually. As you write about your life, your beliefs and values, and the choices that you make, you'll likely learn something about yourself or make connections between yourself and others. However, even though self-discovery is an important element of personal writing, it is often important to have an external audience in mind, too. Personal writing requires more than simply creating an inventory or timeline of events; rather, it is a genre in which you can inform, involve, and enlighten your readers through strategic, thoughtful uses of personal experience. It is important to see personal and reflective writing as ways that you can combine the skills and practices of analysis with writing that explores your own life, ideas, and experiences.

Personal writing plays a role in a variety of first-year composition assignments. For example, you might be asked to write a personal essay, such as a literacy narrative or personal/cultural analysis. Some teachers will ask you to do idea-generating exercises, freewriting, or journaling (all forms of personal writing) as a way to brainstorm, or dig deeper into your writing processes. Or, your teacher might assign a research essay that asks you to identify and explore an issue in which you have a personal stake. Also, many of you will be asked to write reflective essays in which you discuss your writing process and final draft. Reflective writing, one form of personal writing, is a key component of your first-year writing courses. Reflecting on your own challenges, strengths, and improvements as a writer will help you to better understand how to further bolster the quality of your writing. Whether it is in an essay, a freewriting assignment, or a reflection, you are likely to encounter personal writing in your first-year composition courses. In this chapter, you will enter the personal writing process and explore the depths and complexities of such writing.

For advice on freewriting or keeping a journal, see *Rules for Writers*, pages 14–16.

12.2 The Personal Writing Process

By Kelly Myers

Composition scholar David Bartholomae refers to personal writing as "a corrupt, if extraordinarily tempting genre" and he's got good reason for concern (71). Basically, he's worried about people like me. I'm a shameless snoop. I'm the kind of person who used to hold a glass up to the wall so that I could listen in on my brother's slumber parties. One summer I read letters from my boyfriend's ex-girlfriend while he was away on a family vacation. I used to spend long hours sitting in my closet with a flashlight reading my sister's diary. I long to both hear and confess juicy secrets—and, if I'm being totally honest with myself, that's why I was drawn to personal writing. But the truth is, even though it is extraordinarily tempting, personal writing is not about confessing secrets or snooping around in people's personal lives.

Personal writing exercises can help to complicate our stories, uncover our motivations, and access our assumptions about the world, all of which can lead to more complex personal writing that moves beyond the realm of confession or therapy. When you approach personal writing assignments, it is important to work toward creating a space between the person (yourself) and the personal (your stories or experiences) so that you can examine the choices you make in recreating your experiences. Since you can never recapture an experience exactly as it unfolded, personal and experience-based writing always involves making choices (consciously or unconsciously) about what to include and exclude. In stepping back and taking the time to examine these choices, you can begin to see the complicated layers that make up your identity and life experience.

Personal Writing and/as Rhetoric

The process of stepping back to examine personal writing involves establishing an awareness of your audience and purpose. In other words, the personal writing process is intricately linked to the rhetorical analysis skills discussed in Chapter 10. Therefore, once you have a central purpose and primary audience in mind for your personal writing, you need to shape your experience(s) and the overall structure of your writing accordingly. For example, as a writer you get to shape the voice or voices that emerge in your writing. Having a "voice" in writing does not mean that you strive to transfer your speaking voice onto the page. Instead, your goal is to construct the voice(s) in your writing to create an *ethos* that suits the overall purpose. Just as credible sources are of primary importance in a research essay, the voice and *ethos* that you create are fundamental to the success of your personal essay. When you create a specific voice, you are establishing a relationship with your audience, working to earn their attention and trust.

> Your instructor may or may not use the term "ethos" but you will definitely be asked to think about the ways writers establish credibility with their audiences. For more information on rhetorical analysis and types of appeals, see Chapter 10.

For example, in his essay "This Is Emo," Chuck Klosterman argues that the actor John Cusack has forever ruined romantic love. *Ethos* plays an important role in making such an argument, as the author could easily come across as simply embittered or pathetic. In the following passage, look at the specific details, tone of voice, and sentence construction that Klosterman uses to create his *ethos* (to do a more in-depth study of this passage, refer to the workshop questions in the next section):

I once loved a girl who almost loved me, but not as much as she loved John Cusack. Under certain circumstances, this would have been fine; Cusack is relatively good-looking, he seems like a pretty cool guy (he likes the Clash and the Who, at least), and he undoubtedly has millions of bones in the bank. If Cusack and I were competing for the same woman, I could easily accept losing. However, I don't feel like John and I were "competing" for the girl I'm referring to, inasmuch as her relationship to Cusack was confined to watching him as a two-dimensional projection, pretending to be characters who don't actually exist. Now, there was a time when I would have thought that detachment would have given me a huge advantage over Johnny C., inasmuch as *my* relationship with this woman included things like "talking on the phone" and "nuzzling under umbrellas," and "eating pancakes." However, I have come to realize that I perceived this competition completely backward; it was definitely an unfair battle, but not in my favor. It was unfair in Cusack's favor. I never had a chance. (2)

In addition to creating voice in personal writing, there is also the role of emotion to consider. As was discussed earlier, personal writing is not simply a venting of emotion; however, just like voice, the audience's emotional experience is a central element of the essay's persuasive power. Maintaining a high level of emotional engagement, such as sustained anger or grief, can be exhausting for a reader and can blur the overall purpose of the essay. Such prolonged emotional commitment can be used as a rhetorical strategy, depending on your purpose; however, more often you will need to zoom into and out of emotionally-intense moments. Oftentimes, a large part of structuring a personal essay involves designing the audience's emotional experience in a way that serves the greater goals of the essay.

Along with its role in persuasion, emotion can play an invaluable role in your writing process. The most powerful writing frequently comes from issues or experiences that have had a profound emotional effect on you. Analyzing your emotional connections, as well as your sources of apathy, can provide important inroads into the personal/analytical writing process, which is essential in assignments such as the literacy narrative.

Finally, in addition to voice and emotion, personal writing is often strengthened by research. It may seem strange to think of personal writing and research papers together, but just as facts and statistics work to strengthen an argument, concrete details and information about people, places, issues, etc., make personal writing more compelling and believable. Logical connections and progressions are important for the overall purpose of the essay and the credibility of the author. As so much of personal writing revolves around the author, rhetorical appeals play a central role in building trust between the reader and the writer.

Revising Personal Writing

Once you have selected the topic or angle for your personal writing, the next step is to dig into the experiences and shape the rhetorical strategies. But how do you move between the personal and the analytical in your writing? One important approach is the involvement of other people in your personal writing process. As we have discussed, audience plays a crucial role in personal writing; therefore, it is important to actively engage an audience throughout your drafting process. Composition scholar Barbara Kamler suggests the following workshop questions as a way to begin the personal-analytical revision process:

- What is powerful in the writing? Identify an image, line, metaphor, or representation of person that is powerful.

- What is omitted? Who/what is absent and/or hinted at or over-generalized?

- What clichés are used to gloss over experience, facts, feelings?

- What doesn't fit? What contradictions, if any, emerge?

- What aspects/issues of [fill in blank] are concealed?

- What common issues, experiences, storylines do the texts [in your workshop group] have in common? (62)

Asking focused questions about what is both present and absent in the writing helps to reveal the ways in which the experience was constructed, as well as the assumptions at work in that construction. Also, looking at moments of specific detail, as well as moments where the writing becomes clichéd or overly general, can reveal levels of comfort and discomfort within the situation. Instead of trying to resolve contradictions in the writing, such tensions are often generative spaces to explore. Finally, it can be helpful to look at your writing within the context of other student writing to identify commonalities and differences in your experiences.

Of course, analyzing a personal experience in order to create thoughtful, rhetorically-savvy writing is difficult work. On an emotional level there is struggle, even grief, involved in confronting and unraveling the roots of our experiences. There is also pain in the revision process when we have to cut out parts of our stories that are really important to us personally but not relevant to the greater purpose of the essay. However, even though such revisions are difficult, they mark a crucial step in moving personal writing away from confession or self-indulgence. Since revision is so important, you will need to be sure to select your personal writing topics very carefully. Most importantly, you will need to be sure that you are ready to return to the experience(s) again and again to constantly revise and reflect on the writing.

In the end, personal writing, like any academic writing, is a *process*—one that calls on your skills in rhetoric, research, and reflection. When engaging in personal writing, it is important to understand that experiences and identities are always in motion, always developing and changing within the context of the moment. Instead of approaching your personal writing as a stagnant text that is beyond critique, this chapter invites you to approach your experiences as an opportunity to better understand the ways in which identities are shaped on both personal and cultural levels.

Works Cited

Bartholomae, David. "Writing With Teachers: A Conversation with Peter Elbow." *CCC* 46.1 (Feb 1995): 62-71.

Kamler, Barbara. *Relocating the Personal: A Critical Writing Pedagogy*. Albany: State University of New York Press, 2001.

Klosterman, Chuck. *Sex, Drugs, and Cocoa Puffs*. New York: Scribner, 2003.

12.3 Why Personal Writing?

We sometimes think of stories as made-up, pretend, childish, or peripheral. However, as Erec Toso, a creative writer and instructor in the UA English department, discusses here, stories often have powerful social and cultural meanings. We are not always aware of how much certain stories affect the ways we live our lives. Stories can be personal, but they are also social. In "Stories," Toso reminds us of the broader importance of examining the personal and cultural stories that are always operating on and around us.

Stories

By Erec Toso

> The stories we tell ourselves about ourselves determine the quality of the selves we imagine we are. The stories we tell about others determine the quality of our relationships with them.

> —Rami Shapiro in *Hasidic Tales: Annotated and Explained*

Let's start with a premise: humans see the world through a veil of stories. These stories interconnect with one another to weave a screen through which we filter experience, make judgments, and define ourselves. They contain beliefs, assumptions, values, hopes, fears, and desires, and add up to a network of understanding that we use to order reality. In short, stories shape our identities. If they form some of the base of who we think we are, they are worth examining.

Stories are a kind of spontaneous human response to things we can't understand. They are with us and will be always, which means they are also hard to change. For one, the stories we live by are buried deep in the mind. We don't even know they are there. We see only fleeting glimpses of them, the tips of giant icebergs. For another, we identify with them, and will fight to keep them. They are "right" and we cling to them like life itself.

The job of a reflective personal writer is to become aware of both personal and social stories, to identify them, to name them, and to evaluate them. Some stories have worn out their usefulness and need to be revised. Just because we use stories to organize and explain the mysteries of experience does not mean that all stories serve us. Sam Keen writes in his preface to *Your Mythic Journey* that:

> The organizing myth of any culture functions in ways that may be either creative or destructive, healthful or pathological. By providing a world picture and a set of stories that explain why things are as they are, it creates consensus, sanctifies the social order, and gives the individual an authorized map of the path of life. A myth creates the plot-line that organizes the diverse experiences of a person or a community into a single story.

> But in the same measure that myth gives us security and identity, it also creates selective blindness, narrowness, and rigidity because it is intrinsically conservative. It encourages us to follow the faith of our fathers, to hold to the time-honored truths, to imitate the way of the heroes, to repeat the formulas and rituals in exactly the same way they were done in the good old days. As long as no radical change is necessary for survival, the status quo remains sacred, the myth and ritual are unquestioned, and the patterns of life, like the seasons of the year, repeat themselves. (xii–xiii)

By becoming aware of personal and cultural "myths" and then reframing them, you can change stories to better fit the problems and challenges you confront. If you "author" your own stories, you are not living the stories of others, or the stories you inherited. For example, you tell yourself stories about who you are as a writer, what you can (or can't) do, how writing works, what the best ways are to cut corners or to "get by," or how important writing is to the rest of your life. Improving your writing implies making your writ-

For more on the reflective writing process, see "Chapter 14: The Portfolio Process and Reflective Writing."

ing stories visible, looking at them for the myths that are working, and that form the basis for making decisions about how to compose, revise, research, and edit. If the "stories" about writing are keeping anyone from learning or succeeding as a writer, those stories need to be revised, to be replaced with stories that allow for growth and improvement as a writer.

Work Cited

Keen, Sam and Ann Valley-Fox. *Your Mythic Journey: Finding Meaning in your Life through Writing and Storytelling.* Los Angeles: Jeremy P. Tarcher, 1989.

The story is just one aspect of personal writing. Another way you can approach personal writing is by considering your own memories. In the next section, Mary Woo provides an exercise that demonstrates the way memories, like stories, can help you come to important realizations about your own writing. Woo shows that memories can be explored first through the senses, using *description*. But as this activity demonstrates, you can take the sensual memories and vivid description a step further through analysis.

12.4 Turning Memory into Meaning

By Mary Woo

When you are introduced to textual analysis, one of the first distinctions your teacher will most likely make is between summary and analysis. You learn how to move from summary, which may be something you are familiar with from high school (the book report), toward analysis.

Most of you will do some sort of personal writing in your first year writing classes, whether it is a personal narrative or a reflective essay. Personal essays often become confused with "journaling" or simply writing an autobiography of one's life. It is difficult to fully understand the difference between description and true reflection. Students tend to be natural story-tellers (think of how many stories you tell your friends in one day!).

Remember a time when you told your friends about an incident, let's say the time you went to the mall? You described who was there, what you bought, what you ate. Essentially you summarized your experience for them. But did you reflect on it? Probably not, because it was a casual conversation that didn't require reflection. However, in personal essays, you are not looking to summarize an experience for your reader. You are trying to create *meaning* out of your experiences. In order to create meaning, you must put your experiences into a context. For instance, let's say you went to the mall, and ran into an old boyfriend/girlfriend. This wouldn't mean anything to your listener unless you explained who the old boyfriend was, and what he or she meant to your life.

One of the most difficult parts of personal writing is having the distance to look back on your experiences and understand what they mean in the context of your life. That is also part of the process of writing—the attempt to understand. The following exercise may be helpful in distinguishing the real difference between summary and analysis, and to transform description into a reflective narrative about your transition into college.

First, think about your dorm room or apartment. Describe the setting, using all five of your senses. Some guiding questions might be: What is on your wall? What does the room smell like? What furniture was provided by the school? What did you have to buy? What is on your desk? How messy is the desk? What kind of pictures do you have? How is the space divided?

Your writing should be purely descriptive, simply detailing the facts of your living space. For instance, "There is a poster above my bed, and on my desk I have several textbooks, a laptop, potpourri," etc.

Read your descriptions aloud to your classmates. Make note of the descriptive nature of the writing and the common observations you shared.

Then, focus in on one aspect of the room that you mentioned. It can be a picture, the loud music coming from the neighbors, the scent of old food. Whatever it is, just pick one object.

Now, try to move towards a more rhetorical approach to this object. More than just the *what* of the object, ask *why* and *how*? How does the object in some way encompass your college experience?

Let's take one example. You have a can of Clorox wipes sitting on your desk. It is the first cleaning item you have ever bought. Before coming to college, your parents always cleaned up after you at home. You would identify yourself as a "messy" person at home. However, in coming to college you were placed with two roommates who were in fact even messier than you, thus causing you to be the "clean" one.

The descriptive sentence would sound like this: There are Clorox wipes sitting on my desk.

Now begin to ask some rhetorical questions of it: How do the Clorox wipes represent something of your identity? How has coming to college changed your identity in some respects? How is your identity different at home than here? Why did you choose to buy Clorox wipes, as opposed to paper towels and cleaning spray? How have your roommates made your identity more distinct? Notice the "how" and "why" in all the questions. Just as analysis asks *how* and *why* of a text, so does personal writing ask this of your memories.

Perhaps you have discovered that your identity shifts depending on your surroundings. Perhaps coming to college has brought you a new sense of independence and maturity. Either way, in asking these questions, you have begun the transition from summary to analysis, and to creating meaning out of your experience.

The analysis of personal objects and personal experiences can be used in many forms of personal writing. You might do this type of analysis when writing a literacy narrative. The literacy narrative is one genre that you may have the opportunity to work with in your first-year-composition classes. Literacy narratives are essays that examine an individual's experience with language and various forms of literacy. In this type of essay, personal writing has a unique role. In the following section, Laurie Morrison describes the process of constructing a literacy narrative. Notice that story and memory, which were important components of the previous sections, also play a part in identifying and analyzing a literacy experience.

Vivid Description

In *On Writing* Stephen King describes writing as a form of telepathy, a "meeting of the minds" in which an image is transmitted from one person to another. After providing an elaborate description of a strangely painted rabbit in a cage, King writes, "[W]e all see it. I didn't tell you. You didn't ask me. I never opened my mouth and you never opened yours. We're not even in the same *year* together, let alone the same room...except we *are* together. We're close" (106). Vivid description and concrete details can bring people closer, creating a moment of telepathy in which an image or a moment travels from one mind to another. Or, as is the case in Dave Eggers' writing, description can carry personality, fostering a connection between author and audience. For example, when looking at San Francisco through Dave Eggers' eyes, the traffic over the Bay Bridge becomes "a string of Christmas lights being pulled slowly, steadily" and foggy mornings in Berkeley are "filmstrip white" (51). His unique descriptions allow readers to experience the city in a new way.

Description becomes especially vivid when an author uses sensory detail to breathe life into places and personalities. For example, in *East of Eden* John Steinbeck does not simply tell readers that the Salinas Valley in Northern

12.5 Identifying and Analyzing a Literacy Experience

By Laurie Morrison

The literacy narrative assignment includes two main tasks: as you write your essay, you'll narrate the story of an experience you've had with language, and you'll also use that experience to make a clear point about how language works or how it has affected you. Consequently, you'll employ narrative strategies such as dialogue, pacing, and sensory detail to tell your story in a compelling way, but you won't stop there. You'll also analyze your experience to figure out what it can tell you, your teacher, and your classmates about literacy.

Sometimes, these two aspects of the literacy narrative—telling a good story and conveying a central point about language—can be difficult to bring together. But in an excellent literacy narrative, the writer thoughtfully examines an experience to come up with an insight about language and constructs a narrative essay that builds to that insight. You don't need to finish analyzing your experience before you begin writing; you might go back and forth between drafting the story of your experience and examining its significance. You also have space to be creative with style and organization. You can experiment with storytelling techniques, and you might play around with starting in the middle of the action or holding off on stating your central point until the last paragraph. While you have some flexibility in crafting your essay, you'll want to make sure that you ultimately bring your storytelling

California is a beautiful place in the springtime. Instead, he pulls his audience directly into the landscape where the "splashes" of California poppies "are a burning color—not orange, not gold, but if pure gold were liquid and could raise a cream, that golden cream might be like the color of poppies" (4). Through his word choice, Steinbeck paints a picture that can be seen, felt, even tasted. Concrete and sensory details create living moments on the page, moving a reader to see, feel, or experience something differently.

Of course, it is important to keep in mind that there is a fine line between effective detail and description abuse. Unless the description is strategic and purposeful, it can easily clutter your writing. Figurative language (e.g., metaphors and similes) can enliven writing; however, if overdone, the details become roadblocks that interrupt the flow of the writing.

Works Cited

Eggers, Dave. *A Heartbreaking Work of Staggering Genius*. New York: Vintage, 2001.

King, Stephen. *On Writing: A Memoir of the Craft*. New York: Scribner, 2000.

Steinbeck, John. *East of Eden*. New York: Penguin, 1992.

and your analysis together. Try to avoid narrating your experience and then tacking on a moral at the end. Your essay will be much more cohesive if you have a carefully-thought-out main point and if all of your narrative details advance it.

The trick to developing an insightful central point and creating a unified literacy narrative is to slow down and really commit to the process of identifying and analyzing the experience you'll write about. Wendy Bishop, a respected scholar and teacher of writing, emphasizes the importance of analyzing a language experience. She explains that students have plenty of material for writing literacy narratives because we all have complicated experiences with language. After all, we are bombarded by words that come at us from parents, teachers, friends, advertisements, songs, and T.V. shows, and we use language to connect to some people and to distance ourselves from others. But as Bishop points out, language affects us in such subtle ways that we need to stop and reflect on our experiences in order to understand how language shapes our identities and interactions. Therefore, slowing down and asking yourself questions can help you to understand the role language plays in your life and to reach a strong central point for your essay.

The following questions can help you to identify and analyze a rich literacy experience and, ultimately, to write an insightful, unified literacy narrative. Keep in mind that you can return to these questions at any point in your drafting process.

Questions to consider as you identify an experience:
- Can you think of a significant event that helped or hurt your progress toward becoming a reader or writer? If you think of a generalized event, such as your parents forcing you to read for an hour every day when you were in middle school, push yourself to think of a particular moment within that larger event. Identifying a specific, one-time experience will help you to focus your storytelling and analysis.

- Can you think of an influential person in your life who has helped or hurt your progress toward becoming a reader or writer? Again, go for specifics: can you identify a particular instance in which that person influenced you?

- Can you think of a moment that somehow changed your views about language?

- Can you think of a time when you judged someone for the way he or she spoke or wrote? Can you think of a time when you felt judged for the way you speak or write?

- Can you think of a time when you had to switch back and forth between different ways of speaking or writing?

- Can you think of a time when you had to "learn the lingo" to be accepted into a certain group?

- Can you think of something you said, wrote, read, or heard that really *worked*—that had exactly the effect it was supposed to have on the people who heard or read it?

- Can you think of a time when you felt unable to communicate your ideas or feelings?

Questions to consider as you analyze your experience:

- Why does this experience stick out in your memory?

- What lessons can you, your classmates, and your teacher learn from this experience?

- What could a wider audience, such as parents, college students, children, teachers, or aspiring writers, learn from this experience?

- How is the current "you" different from the "you" who is a character in the experience? What can you see about the experience now that you couldn't then? How would the current "you" handle the same situation?

- How has your experience affected your attitudes toward reading, writing, and communicating? What are the implications of your attitudes toward reading and writing? In what ways might your attitudes serve you well in college? In what ways might they get in your way?

- How do you think your life experiences, cultural affiliations, race, gender, and/or religion have influenced this experience and your attitudes toward reading and writing?

- In what ways is your experience comparable to the experiences that your classmates are writing about? In what ways is it different? Why do you think those similarities and/or differences exist?

- In what ways is your experience similar to or different from the experiences of the published authors whose stories you've read in class? Again, why do you think those similarities and/or differences exist?

Students often protest that they don't have anything to write about because they haven't had any significant experiences with language. But you don't need to have had a particularly juicy, hilarious, or traumatic experience to write an interesting literacy narrative. Don't worry if you haven't worked to overcome the limits of a disability like Helen Keller, or if you didn't teach yourself to read while you were locked up in jail like Jimmy Santiago Baca or Malcolm X. You just need to identify a specific experience that involved reading, writing, or communicating and that seems worth reflecting on. You might have some inkling about what the experience means, or you might just feel like it buzzes with potential meaning. Either way, the experience doesn't need to be objectively significant: your *interpretation* of the experience will make it significant to you and to your readers.

For an example of a literary narrative, see Chapter 13.

Works Cited

Bishop, Wendy. *On Writing: A Process Reader*. New York: McGraw-Hill, 2004.

12.6 Reflective Writing

In your first-year composition courses, the term *reflection* has a very specific meaning. Reflection is a fundamental component of the revision process. Writers use the term "reflection" for a variety of purposes. In the context of the first-year writing courses, reflection means careful, sustained exploration and analysis of an experience. For example, if you do an analysis of a literacy experience, you may have an opportunity to explore an achievement or a failure that changed the way you think about yourself. In the reflective essay at the end of English 102, you may choose to look back on a developmental process, such as completing extensive, multiple revisions of an essay or essays over the course of a semester. Whatever the case may be, your reflective

Personal Writing Exercises

by Stephen Brooks

Although a literacy narrative is a very important form of personal writing, and one that you are likely to see in your writing classes, it is only one way that academic writers engage with the personal, and perform personal writing as a part of the academic writing process. In this activity, Stephen Brooks provides several prompts for personal writing. By starting with writing like this you will discover ideas that you may want to develop further, perhaps in more formal academic writing. You might work with these writing exercises in class or on your own.

1. Your Choice:

   I. Write about something that's important to you (maybe the first thing that pops in your head): your father, your mother, your dog, your first kiss, your car, your shoes, your model train set, your nails, your future, your present, your ... anything.

   Be honest.

writing needs to convey more than your memories of an event—it requires an extended effort to push beyond the recollection of details and explanations with which you have grown comfortable, so that you can arrive at a new understanding of a past experience. To reflect means to contemplate what you were thinking and feeling when a pivotal experience took place in order to better understand what that experience has meant for you and possibly others. How did you change through the experience? How did it affect your relationships, identity, or worldview? What did it help you understand about your culture or the culture of others?

Reflecting upon Your Writing

The aim of reflection is to create meaning, much like another process discussed extensively in first-year writing courses: analysis. Reflective essays ask you to **analyze** what you did, why you made certain choices, and what effects these choices may have had on audiences. When you write a reflective essay on your writing experiences, you analyze your writing process and yourself as a writer.

Try to remember that reflective essays are really just another form of analysis. In "Chapter 8: Analysis," we defined analysis as "the ability to explain how and why a text does something and whether the choices made are effective." Analysis, as it is used in reflective essays, asks you to explain how and why you made certain choices when writing and whether the choices you made were effective. In the reflective essay, you can even go a step further,

Or

II. Start writing with a feeling and see where it takes you—**inspiration**.

Be patient...let it come to you before you start writing. Slow down, clear your mind. Let the first words ring.

Go.

2. Write about an experience in your life that has changed you—something that happened, no matter how small or large, after which your perception was never quite the same. Be sure to include the before and after. Most im-portantly, bring the reader up to the present as you wrap up this mini-essay.

3. Write about something that makes you angry. Work from observation outwards. This can be serious, humorous, or both. Let the ending be natural—find it.

4. First, read Bob Dylan's "Last Thoughts on Woody Guthrie." Then, write a poem or prose piece about a person, directly or indirectly, that has powerful influence on you—good, bad, or both. Be prepared to share with your classmates.

explaining what you chose to do, whether the choices were effective, and what you would do the same or differently in the future.

Topics for Analysis

When writing a reflective essay, it is important to remember that the analysis should focus on the process—the writing process, the process of becoming a writer, the peer-review process, and so on. Textual analysis focuses on the text (your finished essay); reflective analysis of your writing focuses on the writing process, a topic on which only you can provide special insight.

Reflective essays that focus on you as a writer have many possible topics. You can choose to focus only on the writing process in the classroom, or you can talk about your writing experiences throughout your life and how those experiences shape the ways in which you define yourself as a writer now. Consider the following list as the beginning of a brainstorming session in which you are trying to narrow your topics for analysis:

• The ways that prewriting did/didn't help.

• The peer review process, what you gave and what you received.

• Conferences with teachers.

• Global revision choices.

• Local revision choices.

• Talking about your paper to other people.

• The act of revision itself.

• The different style/word choices that you made.

• Your understanding of different writing options.

• How college writing fits into your life.

You may draw from your own learning and writing experience to add even more ideas for topics.

Once you have generated some topic ideas, you might want to think about what was effective/useful or ineffective/not useful about certain choices, events, or experiences. What did you learn? Did the choices, events, or experiences reinforce something you already knew? If you did not gain as much from a particular project as you hoped to gain, what are the possible reasons for this, and what might you do the next time around? In other words, this is an excellent time for you to analyze yourself in the process, noting your own responsibilities within the larger scope of the writing project, the course, or your ongoing development as a writer. It is as important to address any disappointments or even failures in your experience as it is to discuss the successes and achievements. Most writing processes include a combination of good and bad reactions and effects. Exploring the complex relationships between these reactions and effects can be the most interesting and useful part of writing a reflective essay.

Writing About Writing

Before you even begin to write, you might want to revisit "Chapter 4: Writing as a Process" and "Chapter 5: Re-Visioning Your Work." They will provide you with terms and models to talk about writing. Discussing your own writing can be very difficult because many of the strategies that you used might have been compulsory (your teacher required you to do something) or unconscious (you just did something because you always have). The reflective process asks you to think critically about what you did and why you did it. Why did the teacher ask you to do something in the writing process, and was it useful to you? Why or why not? Did you talk with your friend about the paper before you started writing it? Why? Once you consider choices that you made and how those choices affected the final product, you are ready to begin writing your reflective essay. Consider the following paragraph, taken from student Andrew Mora's reflective essay:

> Even with this new understanding of peer revision, I am still aware of the fact that much help can come from other people. Another set of eyes can see something completely different than mine do. One problem with my writing that has been noticed by both my professors and my peers includes the way I start sentences. I tend to have generalized statements that do not make the paper sound as strong as it could be. These local revisions, which are within sentence revisions, were found on almost every page of my papers. For example, in one of my earlier drafts of the persuasive paper about globalization and the effect it is having on youth, I wrote, "It is estimated that 17 million people would have died if this way had taken place." After discussing my paper with my professor, we noticed that I often started sentences with "It is," "There was," "They are," etc. Openers like these typically do not make strong points. This statement later became "In June of 2002, the U.S. Defense Intelligence Agency estimated that as many as 17 million people would be killed during the first few weeks." Though I can see how this error changed, I still feel I might not be able to catch myself using these words as I write in the future. It is one of the many areas that I will need to continue to work on.

In the above paragraph, the author of the piece discusses his experiences with local revision, specifically the word choices made at the beginning of sentences. He talks about how he became sensitive to the issue, why it is important, and what he did in order to address the problem by looking at both his rough draft and final draft. Andrew gives specific examples from the text, enabling the reader to clearly understand what he is discussing. Furthermore, he doesn't just talk about the text but what he does in relation to the text. We can see this in phrases like "I tend" and "I still feel." Finally, the writer acknowledges that this is a challenge that he will continue to face, acknowledging his responsibility to employ the strategies learned in this class to future writing projects.

Whatever choices you make in your reflective essay, you will want to consider the following guidelines:

- Analyze the process of writing the paper or papers (not just the final drafts), or of becoming a writer.

- Give concrete examples from your process (either quotations from your writing or rich descriptions of specifics in your writing process).

- Explain *why* certain choices were made (not just "my teacher told me to") and whether those choices were effective.

- Use the language of writing. For example, if you explain that you revised something, then what sort of revision was it (local, global, stylistic, and so on)?

In the end, reflection is a practice that helps you to take responsibility for your own development as a writer. After you have completed your required writing courses, you will often have to write for new situations, audiences, and purposes. Only when you have reflected upon the strategies that you have previously used will you be able to analyze whether they will be effective in these situations. Only by reflecting upon your writing will you be able to continue to learn how to improve your writing in courses in your major, on the job after you graduate, and in your life outside the classroom.

PART IV

Sample Essays

13
Sample Essays

13.1 Sample Essays: An Overview

This chapter includes essays written by first-year writing students at the University of Arizona along with a four-part essay written by instructors of first-year writing. You can approach the student essays included in this chapter in a number of different ways. Like most writing, they contain features to emulate and learn from, as well as areas that could be improved upon with further revision. Consider them, then, as *samples* rather than *models*—they are not perfect. What we mean by this distinction is this: A "model" can be dangerously close to a static form, something that provides you with a formula to follow (write exactly like "this" and you'll get an "A"); by contrast, seeing the student essays as "samples" encourages you to identify what works well and what could work better—to take selectively from them according to the occasion or context. We have not corrected any spelling and grammar errors in the student essays, nor made changes to larger global concerns. This choice was deliberate; we believe that these essays provide a great opportunity to look at what worked and what can be revised. In other words, you can critically engage with the essays in a way that will help you think through writing choices, revision strategies, and different genres.

Because students from first-year writing classes at the same institution wrote these essays, the essays featured in this chapter adhere to shared assumptions and course guidelines; however, the writing represents the type of work produced in a program in which individual instructors tailor the assignments with slightly different visions or emphases. For example, some instructors may ask students to work with films and focus on visual analysis, others focus specifically on written textual analysis, while some might ask for autobiographical writing as a way to analyze identity or culture. Given this set of considerations, each student in each section will have an individualized response to that group assignment. As these selected writers have done, you will need to be aware of your own particular situation as you set out to produce writing appropriate for your class context. The point to emphasize here is that one size doesn't fit all—suit the form to the content, not the content to the form.

Specifically, how can you benefit from reading these essays? Aside from their value as a way to see what your peers are thinking and writing about, they may also prove useful as you produce your own writing. As you read the sample essays, examine the choices each author has made and consider what you might do differently or what you might try to emulate in your essays. Below is a list of questions that you may want to ask yourself as you examine each of the sample student essays:

- How does the author introduce the topic of the essay? Is it broad or specific? How does that lead into the thesis/point? Try to pinpoint examples.

- Is the thesis explicitly stated ("This paper argues…") or implied (the claim of the paper becomes clear but is not directly spelled out at the beginning)? Where is the main idea of the essay identified and how is it communicated to the reader?

- How do language and style work in the essay? Are sentence lengths and word choices effective? Are there any places where language and style break down or distract from the essay's purpose/meaning? How would you revise those sections?

- As you are reading, do you notice how the author has made transitions between paragraphs/sentences? How does the author link ideas? Are there any places that the transition is abrupt or does not exist? How might you revise the paper so that the connections between ideas are clearer?

- How does the author use quotations? How are they introduced and worked into the paper? Do you find the quotations useful in furthering your understanding of the topic?

- Does the conclusion of the essay simply restate the introduction or does it suggest any larger implications that open up as a result of the research/writing? How would you revise the conclusion? Do you think that a personal aspect might be useful for a conclusion/paper that is predominantly academic? Do you think that a statistical conclusion with suggestions for action would be helpful for a conclusion/paper that is predominantly personal?

These questions are designed to help you think through your reading/interaction with the student essays. Your instructor may want you to look at how an essay fits (or doesn't fit) a particular assignment. You may also notice strengths or weaknesses in a paper that we do not prompt you to notice, which is great! Bring this up in classroom conversations; show your peers and instructors what you noticed so that you can start to think through how you can use what you garner from a text in your own writing. This is what the student essays are about: helping you to become a stronger writer by looking at what others have done and adapting it to suit your own writing strategies for particular situations. Many of the essays included here were winners of the 2009 *Student's Guide* Essay Contest. This contest is offered every year and is open to all students in first-year writing classes. That means that *you* can enter the contest this year. All of the winning essays are included online at <http://english.arizona.edu/index_site.php?id=588&preview=1>.

Additionally, this chapter includes a four-part essay titled "Embracing Difference, Promoting Equality," written by instructors who teach first-year writing at the UA. This essay provides an instructor perspective on the first-year writing classroom, where difficult dialogues can take place, especially when dealing with texts that surround controversial issues. For example, your instructor may assign texts that will incite emotional responses that you had not anticipated having in college. You may have found yourself asking, "Why am I being asked to read this?" or "What am I supposed to learn from a text that makes me feel uncomfortable?" This essay sheds light on why instructors choose the texts they do, and it also aims to illustrate how difficult conversations can foster new, valuable understandings concerning issues of difference and inequality.

As you read this four-part essay, try to note the distinctions between the single-authored essays in this chapter and this one, which is written by four different people and thus provides four perspectives on a single topic. Not only does a multi-authored text make room for multiple authorial voices, it also weaves together different stylistic choices. Further, a text written by several authors has to maintain its organizational structure as a whole while at once synthesizing the ideas of various people.

The following chart identifies some of the characteristics of each essay. It is not intended to be all-inclusive, but if you are working on PIE paragraphs, for example, you might refer to any of the essays that are marked as "Models the PIE Paragraph." This is not to say that every paragraph in those essays is a PIE paragraph, but there should be some different examples of PIE paragraphs in all the essays with this designation. Likewise, an essay that is marked "Incorporates rhetorical analysis" will address the rhetorical situation or the strategies that an author uses. We hope that this chart will be useful to you as you begin reading the work of other first-year writing students.

	Escaping Entrapment	The Darwinian Role Reversal of Sebastian and Violet Venable	A Photographic Poet	Blade Runner vs. Freud	Bring Gold to the Middle East	Money is my Monkey Wrench	An Independent State	Ethanol: Food or Fuel	On American Hypocrisy: Disgracing our Forefathers	I Won't Always Lose at Checkers	Manhood and Imagination	Embracing Difference, Promoting Equality
Includes/analyzes a literacy narrative										✓	✓	
Incorporates literary analysis	✓	✓									✓	✓
Incorporates contextual analysis		✓	✓	✓	✓							✓
Incorporates rhetorical analysis						✓	✓	✓	✓			
Uses research		✓	✓	✓	✓			✓				✓
Incorporates reflection										✓	✓	✓
Uses the personal									✓	✓	✓	✓
Incorporates comparative analysis			✓	✓	✓							✓
Addresses a controversy						✓	✓	✓	✓			✓
Uses a single source	✓					✓						
Uses sections (headings)					✓							✓
Incorporates visual analysis			✓	✓								
Incorporates film analysis				✓								✓
Models the PIE paragraph	✓	✓	✓	✓	✓	✓						
Includes a funnel introduction	✓			✓			✓					
Includes an anecdotal introduction					✓					✓		
Addresses difference and inequality	✓				✓		✓	✓	✓		✓	✓
Uses *Writing as Revision*	✓										✓	✓

13.2 Escaping Entrapment

By Megan Peterson

There once was a time when society thought women should stay at home to cook for the family and take care of the children while the educated men went out in the real world to make a living. Before the 1900's, women were treated unfairly and considered more or less as men's possessions. Women were deemed dependent of men and therefore, an ideological prison was created for women, "the cult of domesticity," which silenced women until a few brave feminists decided to change the roles of females forever. The secretive room in Charlotte Perkins Gilman's "The Yellow Wallpaper" represents a wife's, and many other women's, escape from the entrapment of conventionality, and therefore, becoming a "new woman." As the story progresses, readers witness a naïve house wife transforming into a strong and confident individual who does not fear standing up to the superior male gender.

Bars on windows cannot keep anyone, including the narrator, from wanting to look out and wonder what is on the other side and whether or not they want to go there. Even though John, the narrator's husband, may come off as being caring, he in actuality only cares about controlling his wife and not so much about helping her recover her health. John brings his "sick" wife to a remote home because he claims to want her to recover from her mysterious illness. In actuality, John wants to seclude his wife from the outside world and have total control over her. When describing her room, the narrator proclaims, "It was a nursery first, and then playroom and a gymnasium, I should judge, the windows are barred for little children, and there are rings and things in the walls" (Gilman 245). A nursery is a place for infants that have no responsibility or authority; they are in a sense helpless. This is obviously not a room that one would think of a middle-aged woman residing in to get well. But John, holding up to the expectations of his gender, brings his wife to this room so that he is in power. As long as she resides in the room he can watch over her and control her every move, or so he thinks. Even the names that John calls his wife such as when he says, "What is it little girl" (249) shows that he places himself on a higher level then her. The wife is the infant in the nursery and the husband is the caretaker. He in a sense is her blockade from getting out of the house and into the real world because he is the babysitter: the wise one in charge who calls the shots. Being a woman during the nineteenth century meant not being able to be educated, just as an infant is new to the world and unknowledgeable. Little does John know that his wife is not as small as he thinks she is and in actuality, she possesses the strength and capability of being just as successful as her husband.

Throughout the story, the wallpaper gives the narrator strength and helps her realize that John is not the loving and caring husband that she had once thought he was. In the beginning of the story we see the narrator as a house wife who goes along with what her husband tells her, but as the story progresses we can recognize that the narrator is becoming more independent and can see right through her husband's actions and words. During her naïve stage, when talking about how she does not like her room and wants to sleep downstairs, the narrator says, "John would not hear of it…He is very careful and loving, and hardly lets me stir without special direction" (245). She wants to make herself believe that the reason why John is keeping her in the "nursery" is because he thinks she will get better and that it is in her best interest. The narrator does not consciously realize that John is keeping her in the "nursery" so that he can keep a close eye on her and be in charge of what she does and where she goes. She sees John's controlling behavior as "careful" and "loving" and yet in the back of her mind she questions his actions but does not feel capable of standing up to him. Later on in the story, when talking about not being able to sleep in the room and telling John how she feels about it, she says, "He asked me all sorts of questions too, and pretended to be very loving and kind" (253). At this point in the story, the narrator is beginning to grasp the true meaning behind John's actions and realize what he does is not out of compassion but it is a way to hold up his status as a traditional male. At this point she feels ready to take action. After years of being overpowered and told what to do by a male she is realizing that she does not need to be dependent on her husband and that she in a sense is helping him more then he is helping her because she is allowing him to feel a sense of empowerment and fit the stereotype for men.

The figures behind the wallpaper, along with the narrator, are able to find a way to escape the "cult of domesticity." Throughout the story we hear the narrator speak of odd creatures creeping around the room and being stuck behind the blindingly yellow wallpaper. "The faint figures behind seemed to shake the pattern, just as if she wanted to get out" (249). The yellow wallpaper represents John's masculine oppression over his wife and his attempt to blockade her from seeing the conventions. As the days go by when the narrator is stuck in her room, the wallpaper starts to peel off of the walls as she starts becoming more aware of John's control over her. The woman behind the wallpaper can be thought as being the woman that resides inside the narrator and her subconscious thoughts and desires to break free from the restraints that have been placed upon her for so many years. The wallpaper is covering up the outside world and once it starts to come down she is able to realize that she does not want to be an innocent infant stuck in a room being taken care of by her arrogant and oppressive husband any longer.

Once the wallpaper is torn down completely, the narrator is able to feel a sense of freedom and therefore, stand up to her husband and in essence, all men, and become a "new woman". Throughout the story the narrator struggles to find her true identity that is not defined by her husband. Near the end of the story, after the horrid wallpaper has finally been torn off the walls and the woman is set free, the narrator states, "I wonder if they all came out of that wallpaper as I did" (254). By this point in the story she has come to the realization that she can be independent from her husband and that she, like many women, can make a difference and change the roles of women in society by making the first step and standing up to her own husband. After realizing John's dominance and power over her she calls him upstairs to see that she has escaped the entrapment that he has implanted. She calls him in to see the torn wallpaper and explains, "'I've got out at last' said I, "in spite of you and Jane and I've put off most of the wallpaper so you can't put me back'" (255). She has broken free from the prison and is ready to once and for all live by her own rules. The narrator finally, after so many years, has found the courage to stick up for her self and the rest of the women that have spent their lives being belittled and treated unequally by much of society. The narrator, along with other feminists from the nineteenth century, exudes the confidence and power to leave the conventional ways of following the "cult of domesticity" and create a new role for women, a term coined "new woman." Women, after years of being considered below men and unable to do the same jobs and make the same living, were finally laying down the stepping stones for becoming known to the rest of the world as doctors, writers, lawyers, politicians, senators, and many other highly regarded positions.

Gilman's "The Yellow Wallpaper" not only represents one woman's struggle to overcome conventions and become independent, but it represents the obstacle that most women during the nineteenth century had to overcome in order for modern day women to live their lives as they do today. To think that women at one point in time were more or less their husbands' objects and personal possessions, not allowed to work, not allowed to write, and not given the opportunity to vote makes it seem truly remarkable and almost impossible that in modern day society women are able to do all of those things. At first, it seemed that John was taking care of his wife and telling her to stay inside because of the fact that he loves her and wants her to feel better but in actuality, he wants to look and feel domineering. At the end of the story, we see that he is not as tough as he thinks when his wife calls him into the room and he faints from seeing the torn down wallpaper. Everyone was placed in this world for one reason or another and to let someone else hold you back from doing what you are meant to do is a waste of a life. Everyone is entitled to his or her own opinion and own actions, male and female, and even though it may feel as though all of the odds are against you, it is your responsibility as a human on this Earth to achieve your purpose in life.

13.3 The Darwinian Role Reversal of Sebastian and Violet Venable

By Nicole Seckinger

Playwright Tennessee Williams displays his aversion to the theory of Social Darwinism in his play, *Suddenly Last Summer*, by creating characters that symbolize the fit and powerful members of society and then crafting an ironic role reversal from fit to unfit. Social Darwinism is defined as the belief that humanity is subject to the same laws of "survival of the fittest" as Charles Darwin proposed for plants and animals ("Social Darwinism," <u>Britannica</u>). Williams emphasizes his theme of Social Darwinism in *Suddenly Last Summer* by comparing the natural scene of "survival of the fittest" in the Encantadas to the lives of his characters. Sebastian and Violet Venable are described as high society, wealthy individuals who exemplify the victimizers and predators of the weaker members of society just as the birds preyed upon the weak sea turtles. Later in the play the roles are reversed as Violet is ultimately depicted as the victim when she is disfigured by a stroke and then forced to face the truth about her son's death and Sebastian is cannibalized by the unfit, impoverished children of Cabeza de Lobo who he once victimized.

Williams' contempt for Social Darwinism, exposed in *Suddenly Last Summer*, is possibly derived from his own life experiences. Williams was not one of the socially acceptable members of society because of his homosexual tendencies and outrageous themes in his writing. He was "regularly denounced as a sick, immoral, vicious fag" by many people (Vidal xxiii). Williams would have been considered one of the unfit members of society by Social Darwinists because he was not normal in a time when it "suited the designers of the moral life of the American republic to pretend that there are indeed two teams, one evil and sick and dangerous, and one good and normal" (Vidal, xxi). Since Williams was considered to be evil, sick, and dangerous by those who "have such a virulent rage for everything not in their book" he began to have hatred toward those who believed that the fit and normal people governed society (292). In his play, *Suddenly Last Summer* he reverses the roles from fit to unfit in his characters Sebastian and Violet Venable to portray his disdain for this unfair social theory that categorized him as an unfit member of society.

In order to introduce Social Darwinism in his play, Tennessee Williams illustrates a brutal scene of savagery in the Encantadas that epitomizes naturalist Charles Darwin's theory of "survival of the fittest." He then reflects the "survival of the fittest" mindset for the natural world onto his characters, Violet and Sebastian, to create an ongoing metaphor in the play. Williams describes Charles Darwin's theory of nature where the strongest species live and the weakest die when he writes, "and the sand all alive, all alive, as the hatched sea-turtles made their dash for the sea, while the birds hovered and swooped to attack" (Hawkins 25, 105). This trend can then be observed in Violet and Sebastian Venable who act as the cruel, victimizing birds who use their power and wealth to attain what they desire. Ultimately the roles are inverted and they both become the victims, or the sea turtles.

Violet Venable can be viewed as the strong, fit bird of Social Darwinism in the beginning of the play, *Suddenly Last Summer*. Thompson recognizes this comparison when she says that "a chief embodiment of this Darwinian nature is Violet Venable herself, beneath whose civilized veneer is revealed the rapaciousness of the flesh-eating birds" (110). Before Sebastian's death Violet says they were a famous couple who had the attention centered on them (Williams 111). This exhibits how her status and wealth boosted her to a high position in Social Darwinism. Williams also depicts Violet as a violent and cruel individual as she attempts to have her niece, Catharine, lobotomized in order to erase the shocking memory of Sebastian's death from her brain. She is the strong, powerful predator that uses her money and status to prey upon those who do not have the affluence she possesses. She "bribes, bullies, and beguiles all within her sphere of influence" to make sure she protects her son's name and prominence (Ford, *Fascism* 19). Violet's cruelty and savagery can also be perceived in her name. "Violet" mingles the words vile, violent, and vie, which all mirror her dominant and vindictive personality. "Venable" combines venomous, venal, venial, and venerable to match her authoritarian manner (Ford, SLS 130). Williams created this character to symbolize the ultimate fit individual in Social Darwinism but he then constructs an ironic role reversal in Violet to argue against Social Darwinism.

Despite the domineering and evil connotations to Violet's name, it can also be conflated with the word "vulnerable" because ultimately her health begins to fail and she is no longer a fit individual. Before he son's death, a disfiguring stroke changes Violet from the victimizer to the victim because she loses her ability to be useful for Sebastian (Thompson 111). She is no longer beautiful, youthful, or presentable enough for Sebastian to take her on his summer trips and use her to procure for him. Thompson examines this abuse of Violet by her son when she writes, "explicitly revealed is Sebastian's victimization of his mother, who, before her disfiguring stroke, served the same function of solicitor or pimp subsequently assumed by Catharine" (112). Violet's stroke is the catalyst for the beginning of her downfall from fit and dominant to unfit and useless. When she is forced to face the truth about her son's death by Catherine, Violet is afflicted even more severely and, weak from her extensive illness, must sacrifice Sebastian's legacy (Ford, Fascism 20). This is evident at the end of the play when the doctor acknowledges the possibility that Catharine's story could be true and Violet seems to have no influence over Catharine's lobotomy anymore (Williams 148). This is the defining moment where Violet has lost all of her power and "perishes, fortuitously stillborn, as she [Violet] exits hysterically from the stage" (Ford, *Fascism* 23). Williams portrays the slow but effective defeat of the fit individual as Violet becomes a weak and powerless member of society.

Sebastian Venable can also be compared to the victimizing, fit birds in the beginning of *Suddenly Last Summer*. He uses his prominence and influence to victimize everyone around him for his own sexual gain. Catharine describes how he used both her and Violet when she says, "I was PROCURING for him! *She* [Violet] used to do it, too" (Williams 140). Sebastian at one time used his mother to attract homosexual lovers and eventually uses Catharine to attract the young boys of Cabeza de Lobo for his own sexual pleasure and exploitation. Sebastian then victimizes and preys upon the young boys just like the birds prey upon the sea turtles in the Encantadas. Thompson examines this connection when she writes, "the devouring of the sea turtles by flesh-eating birds is reenacted initially as the loveless sexual 'communion' between Sebastian and the young boys he exploits for that purpose, a parallel in which Sebastian assumes the role of the 'cruel'" (102). Sebastian used his prominence and power to bride, bully, and beguile those around him just like his mother did (Ford, *SLS* 19). However, Sebastian also experiences the eventual reversal of roles from fit to unfit in an ironic way when he is cannibalized by the "homeless, hungry young people" of Cabeza de Lobo (Williams 141).

In *Suddenly Last Summer* Williams crafts the reversal of roles through the symbolic and ironic demise of Sebastian. Sebastian is cast into the role of the victimized sea turtle and undergo the fit retribution of being dismembered and devoured by the young boys of Cabeza de Lobo whom he had previously victimized in a sexually analogous way (Thompson 100). Williams describes the young people who cannibalize Sebastian as a "flock of black plucked little birds", which draws a parallel to the scene in the Encantadas where the "flesh-eating birds" attack the sea-turtles and furthers the understanding that the roles of fit and unfit are reversed (147, 105). Sebastian is no longer fit or predatory; instead he becomes as helpless as the sea-turtles who are savagely eaten by the predator.

Suddenly Last Summer is a culmination of Williams' view of Social Darwinism based on his life experiences. Williams creates a metaphor between his characters and the birds and sea turtles in the Encantadas to introduce "survival of the fittest" and Social Darwinism as a theme for the play. Violet and Sebastian are originally strong, fit individuals who triumph over those who are helpless and weak; similar to the ravenous birds who overtook the vulnerable sea turtles. Eventually they become weak and unfit because of illness and cannibalization. Ironically Violet loses all power over those she initially tried to control and Sebastian is made unfit by those he originally victimized. The reversal of Darwinist roles shows how Social Darwinism is not always a permanent social theory because those on top can eventually fall to the bottom.

13.4 A Photographic Poet

By Brian Rapoport

"[Frank Gohlke] is a photographic poet" ("Retrospective of Photographer"). As brilliantly stated by John Rohrbach, curator of the Amon Carter Museum, Gohlke adds a poetic nature to photography that accentuates the splendor of his craft. Imbued with a realist perspective rather than the cliché idealistic, utopian vision of nature, the Frank Gohlke photography exhibit entitled Accommodating Nature: The Photography of Frank Gohlke challenges the typical depiction of the natural world with thought-provoking rhetoric. The exhibit itself consists of beautifully crafted photos covering a plethora of subjects including but not limited to: natural disasters, mankind's effect on the environment, and banal portrayals of rural life. Although he sometimes fleshes out his photographs in full color images, the majority of the pieces remain in black and white gelatin prints, adding an old-fashioned, classic feel to the series. He also composes each individual shot in a unique style – usually varying the angle, the picture size, and even arranges pictures side by side in the same frame. As each photo intrinsically intends to display nature in its raw, realistic form, he vehemently crushes the "pastoral ideal" of nature in exchange for a more realistic, active view of the environment, as stated by the exhibit's description (Gohlke, "Accommodating Nature"). In fact, the entire display reflects and starkly illuminates the battle of epic proportions between humanity and the forces of nature and nature versus itself, although interestingly enough, he excludes humans from most of the exhibit. Through the clever implementation of unique and often unconventional technique of excluding human beings from the frame, Gohlke establishes a credible argument that reveals to man that he only possesses minimal control over nature, indicating that it cannot be domesticated by any means.

In a docile and subtle situation, the collection of photographs depicting everyday life in rural America proves man's lack of power over the natural world through credible rhetoric and argumentation, demonstrating the clash between nature and man. For example, the "Hillsboro, Texas 1978" piece in particular reflects and reiterates the central theme of his work. This work masterfully depicts a modern, ordinary two-story house completely surrounded by vegetation such as grass, trees, shrubs, and two symmetrical pillars of greenery extending endlessly into the ethereal sky. Upon first glance, it may appear as though Gohlke strays from his central theme and portrays man as controlling the natural elements that encase his home; however, deeper examination and critical analysis of the print demonstrates just the opposite. In this case, nature actually exhibits control over man, only in a discreetly subtle manner. For one, the natural grass pushes through and cracks man's seemingly solid concrete sidewalk construction, representing its sovereignty over humanity; even though humans build their concrete-based construction, they cannot thwart nature. It is also important to note that the aforementioned vegetation grows without control, strangling the man-made structure within its grasps, rather than the house, a creation of mere men, domesticating the natural world. The house's presence exposes traditional architectural conventions, which clearly conflict with the pristine order of the natural world, capturing the battle between the opposing forces (qtd. in Atherton). In order to unearth and promote the central message of this piece and the entire exhibit for that matter, he utilizes the powerful, potent strategy of weather to communicate the aim; the ominous, foreboding tone that emulates throughout the background intends to demonstrate nature's supreme reign and dominion over the creations of man. Critical to his argument, Gohlke excludes humans from this photograph, and even the house appears abandoned or unoccupied due to the lack of any possessions in the front yard. Rather than focusing directly and explicitly on humans, he fixes his efforts on the product of human creation and its minimal control over the world, narrowing the focus of the audience (Gohlke, "Re: Accommodating"). Noted for expressing the sublime aspects of nature, his lack of human presence intrinsically reflects the visage of his inspiration: the revered transcendentalist Henry David Thoreau (Gohlke "Photography and Place"). Excluding the presence of man serves a dual purpose in the composition: it humbles man from his lofty position and instills him with a reverence for a raw, realistic version of nature. In this cornerstone piece, Gohlke further accentuates the unending conflict between nature and man, with nature grabbing the upper hand in victory.

Within the second room of the exhibit, the collection of photos from the infamous 1979 tornado that ravaged through Texas once again clearly illustrates the violent conflict between nature and mankind, cleverly accomplishing it without actually including humans in the scenery. In particular, the "Aftermath: The Wichita Falls Tornado, 4503 McNeil" photograph masterfully chronicles the sheer force of natural disasters such as tornadoes. In the immediate foreground, a car, damaged by the natural force of the storm, inconspicuously sits atop a mattress and other various forms of debris on a plot of grass. Behind the automobile, a tree stands erect, devoid of leaves with debris hanging from its branches. In fact, typical to Gohlke's photography, he explores the active nature of space, rather than viewing it as an absence, with wreckage from the storm extending as far as the eye can see, capturing the sheer scope of nature's power (Gohlke "Gallery Walk"). Clearly demonstrating the active-destructive forces of nature, Gohlke shatters the utopian, idealistic version of nature that often manifests itself in the majority of landscape photography such as the work of Ansel Adams (Gohlke "Gallery Walk"). Thus, nature in all its power and splendor, despite the popular notion, retains control and victory over man-made structures, often wreaking destruction on them at will. Utilizing excellent and often unconventional techniques, Gohlke further demonstrates his point of nature's strength and adds credibility to this specific argument. For instance, he employs a rather large shot, at least four feet by four feet, to intentionally reflect the massive size of the disaster, fostering the audience with similar emotions. After staring into the depths of observation for a prolonged period of time, one easily notices that Gohlke excludes the presence of human beings in this piece in order to keep the focus on the forces of nature rather than human beings. In fact, in an email interview with Gohlke, he responded to this trait of composition in the following manner: "Human beings tend to upstage almost everything else in the image. We're social animals, which means that if there's one of us to look at, we will" (Gohlke, "Re: Accommodating Nature"). If he chose to add human life, it would in essence detract from the overall thematic significance of this work – a focus on nature; rather, keeping his audience at the forefront of his mind, he assures that the focus will remain on the sheer power and intrigue of the natural world. Not only does the absence of humans set the focus, but it also contributes to the sublime, natural sentiment that runs rampant throughout this work (Mitchell). This collection, in turn, reverberates and establishes the central motif of nature's power over man, and the utilization of credible illustration and the exclusion of "social animals" affixes unshakable veracity and potency to his argument.

Further along in the course of Gohlke's acclaimed career, he reiterates the aforementioned theme of man versus nature, conveniently excluding humans for stylistic flair, in the series chronicling his fascination with grain elevators. Specifically, the photo entitled "Grain Elevator and Lightning Flash, Lamesa, Texas, 1975" reflects that central, recurring motif. In the immediate foreground of the frame, one gazes upon the drenched, empty street that extends into the background and eventually into oblivion. Adjacent to the pavement on the left-hand side of the piece, four towers stand boldly erect, making their looming presence evident throughout the countryside. Deep within the background, ominous storm clouds lurk within the confines of the murky sky, threatening a violent strike of increased intensity at any given moment. Captivated by Gohlke's ability to depict the landscape, the viewer cannot help but notice the battle that brews between the forces of nature and meager man. As the storm approaches and begins to pelt the pavement with water, man's lack of dominion over nature reverberates loudly, with the seemingly massive man-made towers appearing frail in comparison to the grandeur and force of the natural world. Stylistically, the black and white color scheme adds to and furnishes the scenery with an ominous, powerful sense of foreboding that demonstrates nature's dominion. Critically important from a rhetorical standpoint, Gohlke again refuses to include the presence of humans within this particular portrait, which proves to be advantageous. As mentioned previously, human beings inherently love to focus their undivided attention on other humans rather than the surrounding elements, which, in Gohlke's work, function as the centerpiece of each photo. In addition to this facet, mankind can acquire more information about itself by studying the products of its presence, as stated by Gohlke in an email interview: "My primary subject as an artist is the human world, but I believe there are things we can learn about ourselves through paying attention to what we've created that we can't learn any other way" (Gohlke "Re: Accommodating Nature"). In this photo specifically, this convention of excluding humans comes to fruition, in that nature, represented by the sheer power of the thunderstorm, assails the man-made creations of humans. Through this unique element of composition, the artist successfully centers the focus of the audience on the inevitable conflict between nature and man by excluding people from the frame of his camera.

Thus, Frank Gohlke quite successfully attempts to challenge the passive view of nature in exchange for a more realistic, active view of its power. While, in his opinion, man does exert control over the environment, this control is severely limited by the forces of nature; the ensuing battle between nature and man continually manifests itself in the majority of the collections that encompass the exhibit at the University of Arizona. In the course of rendering each shot, he omits humans from each depiction in order to center the focus on the natural elements of the photography rather than frail human beings. In light of the above implications, he hopes to infuse the audience with a newfound reverence for and fascination with nature's power, knocking man off the metaphorical pedestal into a sense of humility. In accomplishing this aim, he earnestly attempts to relate nature to the audience in a realistic, normalized depiction, adding a net of perceived credibility to his visual rhetoric. Stretching the natural conventions of photography, the artist boldly explores new realms, rendering him a revolutionary in the discipline of modern photography. Rohrbach's axiom pertaining to Gohlke proves to be inherently true: his ability to render a scene seems incredibly poetic and sublime, replicating the craft of his favorite transcendentalist Thoreau.

Works Cited

Atherton, Tim. "Accommodating Nature: The Photography of Frank Gohlke." Muse-ings. 14 November 2007. Web.9 October 2008.

Gohlke, Frank. Accommodating Nature: The Photography of Frank Gohlke. Tucson, Arizona. 15 September 2008–2 November 2008. Photo Exhibit.

"Gallery Walk." The Center for Creative Photography. Tucson, Arizona. 16 October 2008. Photo.

"Photography and Place—The Photographs of Herbert W. Gleason." Frank Gohlke. 2007-2009. Web. 9 October 2008.

"Re: Accommodating Nature Exhibit." E-mail to the artist. 15 October 2008.

Mitchell, Charles Dee. "Nature Gets Restive in Frank Gohlke's Photos." GuideLive. 3 October 2007. Web. 9 October 2008.

"Retrospective of Photographer Frank Gohlke Organized by the Amon Carter Museum." Amon Carter Museum. 2007. Web. 9 October 2008.

13.5 Blade Runner vs. Freud

By Leo Yamaguchi

Technological advances are pushing the limits of what humans thought possible. But how far is too far? As our knowledge of the world becomes more comprehensive, scientists are beginning to manipulate the forces of nature by altering DNA. At the dawn of the 21st century, it is becoming a reality to clone human beings; however, this poses an interesting ethical question: what constitutes a human being? For many centuries, philosophers have contemplated this very question. In 1929, psychiatrist Sigmund Freud published *Civilization and Its Discontents* where he defined man as having the potential to destroy humanity—the prosthetic God. The intrigue of man's purpose has perpetuated through the decades and in the film, *Blade Runner*, director Ridley Scott questions the essence of man with his dystopian interpretation of the future. Scott juxtaposes human clones— or replicants— to man, which are physically undistinguishable from each other in his neo-noir film. However, Scott makes the distinction between man and replicant ambiguous to expose his commentary upon the deterioration of humanity. Just as Freud stated sixty years earlier, Scott saw the potential for the destruction of man: ethically and physically. By undermining the protagonist hero, Rick Deckard, Scott leaves the viewers struggling to distinguish the difference between man and replicant, creating ambiguity and ultimately exposing the degeneration of mankind.

Scott critiques the quintessential heroic man through the diegesis of the film and the unconventional portrayal of the protagonist. Throughout *Blade Runner*, there is a consistent theme and style towards the dystopian world that Deckard lives in. From the beginning, it is obvious that Scott intended to shock the viewers' visual senses by overwhelming them with the grand scale of Los Angeles in the near future. Ironically, the "City of Angels" is where we find our unconventional savior, Rick Deckard. With no sense of ambition or direction in life, the retired investigator seems trapped and powerless to the great corporate machine that governs all life, natural and artificial. Similarly to Freud's work, Scott implies through his film that "what we call our civilization is largely responsible for our misery" (Freud 38). A typical hero would be glorified and iconic, yet our hero seems solemn and impersonal—a fallen angel. What makes him heroic then? What makes us want to believe in him?

Scott's utilization of shot angles is a key proponent in giving us a sense of empathy towards Deckard and, ultimately viewing him as a hero. The director employs low angle shots making the city seem imposing, powerful and daunting. With the constant image of the advertising blimp spouting "a new life awaits you...the chance to begin again in a golden land of opportunity and adventure" is ominous (*Blade Runner*). It provides a false sense of hope that is unattainable and impossible to escape. However, Rick is the audiences' only hope, making him, no matter how unattractive his qualities are, the hero. Scott also makes use of high angle shots to add to the ominous aura of the film. The camera often looks down at Deckard, signifying that he is powerless and trapped by the masochistic corporate machine. We feel sympathy towards Deckard's position wanting him to succeed because society suppresses him and wants to see him fail. Scott utilizes the neo-noir style of film to create a sense of imprisonment and compassion towards a seemingly unpleasant character. Deckard is the best society has to offer—an abrasive and un-iconic figure. Society cannot even produce a charismatic, kindhearted paladin. However, it takes a slightly tainted hero to counter tainted villains. A pure hero in a tainted world would only deteriorate him, inevitably making him a victim of the machine. If the hero is already tainted, he cannot be brought down by the world around him because he is a product of it. Since he is already tainted, he cannot be tainted again. The portrayal of the "tainted" protagonist signifies the deterioration of mankind in that it is the unconventional archetypical hero that saves the day.

The corporate machine not only creates life but governs it as well. From the opening scene in the film, Scott alludes to the Tyrell Corporation as the creator and dictator of life, both metaphorically and literally. The neo-noir sky-scape is dominated by two towering buildings that illuminate the rest of the city with a dim and eerie glow. The structures are magnificent and nothing around them can compare. Freud said that "the work of civilization has become increasingly the business of men [and] the replacement of the power of the individual by the power of a community" (Freud 59) constitutes the destruction of man. The immensity of the buildings in comparison with the surrounding area symbolizes the insignificance of the individual; the individual loses its identity and is imbued with and lost in the masses. Scott immediately establishes the Tyrell Corporation as the "prosthetic God," (Freud 44) not only creating life, but dictating it as well by its imposing presence and dominance over the sky-scape of Los Angeles.

Tyrell, the CEO of the Tyrell Corporation, embodies the corporate machine and its lack of empathy and attachment towards the individual. He says, "Commerce is our goal. More human than human is our motto. [Replicants are] nothing more than an experiment" (*Blade Runner*). His creations are nothing more than an economic opportunity. The Nexus 6 generation of genetically manufactured humans was intended to invade and develop off-world colonies so that human beings could inhabit them. The replicants served as the humans' slaves. The use of slaves alone symbolizes the deterioration of man's morality at the hands of greed. Man's innately good nature is destroyed by the corporate machine because it consumes the individual and robs him of his identity. The imposing forces of society, symbolized by the towering mega-conglomerate structures, causes man to conform because "he cannot tolerate the amount of [pressure] society imposes upon him" (Freud 39). Man is left with an ultimatum: to be an individual and be lost in the masses or conform and lose identity.

J.F. Sebastian, the inventor of the Nexus model of humans, symbolizes the individual lost in the masses. The lonely genius whose only friends are artificial robots is an example of society's rejection of those who do not conform. The corporate conglomerate governs his life and dictated that he be forgotten in an underground community away from the city. His existence is lonely and depressing, but he still maintains his individuality. Is this worth it though? Is sacrificing, even a supercilious relationship with humanity, worth being exiled from mankind? Rachel, Tyrell's assistant, illustrates someone on the opposite spectrum from Sebastian who decided to conform and lose her identity instead. Rachel's situation is ironic because she discovers that she is not even a real human. She symbolizes the complete loss of identity because her identity is manufactured by the corporate machine. Tyrell Corporation not only created her, but supplied her with implanted memories, ultimately governing her life. She is not a part of the machine, "[she] is the machine" (*Blade Runner*). It is a decision of the lesser evil. The mere fact that man has to decide between this ultimatum symbolizes the deterioration of humanity.

Thought alone cannot even distinguish man from replicant. The Tyrell Corporation has "gained control over the forces of nature to such an extent" (Freud 36) that the replicants are mirror images of humans. With implanted memories, "I think therefore I am" does not even constitute one as a human because replicants can think as well. So what, if anything, distinguishes a man from an artificial being? Nexus 6 replicants were created without the capacity to empathize. However, throughout the movie, Scott challenges this aspect and juxtaposes it with man's capability or inability to sympathize. Deckard is never seen as having a companion, let alone a confidant in Los Angeles. The people, in general, are detached from reality and each other. However, the replicants join together and show compassion towards one another as evident when Batty affectionately kisses the deceased Pris. Contrary to what they were programmed to do, the replicants ironically exhibit emotion, while the humans are impersonal and seemingly incapable of affection. If replicants can express affection towards others without being programmed and humans cannot while having the capacity to, this also exposes the degeneration of mankind. According to Scott, humanity has become an emotionless automaton.

Scott emphasizes this irony through his focus on the eyes throughout *Blade Runner*. Ironically, it is the eyes that are scrutinized when trying to determine if a subject is human or replicant. The emphasis on the eyes symbolizes the ability of humans to accurately perceive and interpret reality. According to Freud, "the development of civilization imposes restrictions on [life], and justice demands that no one shall escape those restrictions" (Freud 6). In *Blade Runner*, justice would be defined by the big corporations because they do not want to jeopardize their well being. Their solution: retire all replicants. They even manipulate the terms "killing" and "retirement" to explain the termination of a replicant. By calling it retiring, instead of killing, there is less of an emotional connection with the subject, making the "killing" less emotional and senseless. Even with synthesized eyes, the replicants realize that they are being brutally abused and victimized by their creators. The humans, on the other hand, cannot understand this and see the replicants as part of the business. The replicants are juxtaposed with human characters that lack empathy, while the replicants appear to show compassion and concern for one another. Mankind cannot even see or realize that the integrity of the individual is deteriorating. Humanity does what it is told and asks no questions. Man cannot see the affinity that the replicants and humans share.

Scott leaves the orientation—man or replicant— of Rick Deckard ambiguous to emphasize the destruction of man's ethics. In the Director's Cut, Scott juxtaposes a unicorn sequence early in the movie with a latter scene where Deckard's co-investigator, Gaff, leaves an origami unicorn parting-gift for Deckard. The symbolic significance of this moment is the dramatic irony of the unicorn. Deckard never confided in anyone his daydream, yet, somehow Gaff knew Deckard's thoughts. The only way Gaff could have known what Deckard saw in his daydream was if Gaff himself knew they were implanted memories. By revealing Gaff's parting gift at the end of the movie, the viewers are forced to reconsider their perspective on the hero. Similar to Freud's *Civilization and Its Discontents*, Scott has made Deckard "become a kind of prosthetic God. When he puts on all his auxiliary organs he is truly magnificent" (Freud 44) and indistinguishable from the genetically manufactured clones. Are man and robot innately different? Maybe not in the literal sense, but metaphorically, is man any different from a replicant designed for a specific task and to follow orders? Just like the replicants, the individual is left powerless to the corporations and the economic machine that drives society. In this way, man and machine are not so different. Another interpretation of Deckard's daydream is that the unicorns show that the characters, whether human or replicant, share the same thoughts and recognize their affinity. This shows us that humans and replicants' are innately the same "people" because we are capable of having the same dreams. If anything, the replicants' ability to show compassion and sympathy against all odds makes humans look bad since Scott portrays humanity as impersonal and cruel. In the last scene of the movie, Roy Batty, the militant leader of the replicants, has the opportunity to end Deckard's life. However, Batty chooses to save his life instead. Before Batty's imminent death he delivers his final words:

> I've seen things you people wouldn't believe. Attack ships on fire off the shoulder of Orion. I watched C-beams glitter in the dark near the Tannhauser Gate. All those moments will be lost in time, like tears in rain... Time to die.

The soliloquy symbolizes the possible perpetuation of man's deterioration. If man does not change his ways then all the moments in time will be forgotten. With important moments in time forgotten, there is no way that humans can learn from their mistakes and the big corporate machine will take advantage again and leave the individual stripped of his identity. Even the replicants were captive to the great machine and are left to die in its grasp. Man shares a natural affinity with replicants in that they both suffer from the same corporate machine.

The ambiguity that Scott leaves between man and replicant forces the viewer to distinguish for themselves what defines man. In 1929, psychiatrist Sigmund Freud published *Civilization and Its Discontents* where he defined man as having the potential to destroy humanity. To him man had the possibility of becoming a sort of prosthetic God, which would inevitably lead to mankind's demise. Scott's social commentary in his film reveals the possible consequences if man does not maintain a strong sense of individuality. If individuality is lost, Scott saw the self destruction of mankind as well. By clearly identifying what man is, humanity has hope and can avoid its immanent fate as symbolized in the neo-noir dystopia, *Blade Runner*. However, Scott does provide hope for a brighter future. In one of the last scenes in the movie right before Roy dies, he and Deckard are "purified" by the rain. The rain symbolizes the washing away of the past and a new beginning. With man ready and willing to start over, mankind can find happiness and avoid a dystopia.

13.6 Bring Gold to the Middle East

By Christine Filer

Introduction

Aspire Tower's 4,000 LED lights brighten the sky in a captivating sight until they are suddenly extinguished. One of the most recognizable athletes in the world takes the stage in an envelope of darkness, until his presence is immediately engulfed in spotlights. He holds in his hand one of the most historical and universal symbols to grace this planet; the Olympic torch. Thousands of athletes, Qatari citizens, tourists, and spectators chant, clap, and cheer in an indefinable roar. Walking with pride and grace, he approaches the giant Olympic torch and to the anticipation of thousands of onlookers, lights the torch. What was a dull roar becomes the loudest conglomerate of cheers that anyone in attendance will ever hear in his or her lifetime. Tears stream down faces as emotion and adrenaline pump through the crowd. An unforgettable night would only be the beginning of the 2016 Olympic and Paralympic Games in Doha, Qatar.

Dating back to Ancient Greece, the Olympic Games have long been a part of Western Civilization, having drastic impacts on the city and country in which they were hosted. Doha, Qatar has applied to host the 2016 Olympic and Paralympic Games for a multitude of reasons. Without a doubt, commercialism, culture clash, housing crises, and poverty were not among Qatar's reasons for bidding. While opening its country to the world would result in many drawbacks for Qatar, these pale in comparison to everything the country would gain. Automatic fame, wealth, and a more central position in the world are simply three of the accomplishments Qatar would earn as a result of hosting the Games. Not only would the Olympics in the Middle East be outstanding for Qatari citizens, but also for the athletes who will be participating, those who will be in attendance, and the citizens of the rest of the world. The 2016 Olympic and Paralympic Games should be performed in Doha, Qatar.

Without a doubt, one can make an argument for the Olympics to take place in Doha. However, what about the rest of the bid locations for the 2016 Olympic and Paralympic Games? Baku, Azerbaijain; Chicago, United States of America; Madrid, Spain; Prague, Czech Republic; Rio de Janeiro, Brazil; and Tokyo, Japan would all be excellent choices for the Olympics. After all, that is why each city and country placed their bid and applied to host the Games. Even so, only Doha, Qatar is the right location for the 2016 Olympic and Paralympic Games.

Thesis

What better time is there to bring such a large scale event to the Middle East? With more and more attention placed on the region each day, it is important for the area to also experience (in front of the entire world) a part of the tradition that is believed to have been reserved solely for the West. The Middle East consists of more than the War on Terrorism and locations to drill for oil, and it is vital for the current citizens of the world to take note of that for possibly the first time. Hassan Ali Bin Ali, Chairman of the Doha 2016 Olympic Bid agrees with this, as he believes that Doha's hosting the Olympics would present, "the entire world with a unique opportunity to witness positive change by embracing the spirit of unity so inherent in the

Olympic movement" (Doha 2016, Why Doha 2016?). The Olympics have the power to transform not only a country, but the world.

Mexico's 1968 Olympics forever changed the way that the world regarded the country. In the perspective of the average world citizen, Mexico went from "a backward, *mañana* republic" to "a brisk, ambitious nation ready to take its rightful place in the twentieth century" (Johnson 25). The tipping point in the entire way the world views Mexico was the 1968 Olympic Games. Without them, it is quite possible that Mexico would still be seen as a country undeserving of a spot in the future, only as a country left behind in the dust. Officials present for the Games "firmly believe that because word of their efficient Olympic efforts was transmitted around the world through television," this change in perspective was allowed to occur (Johnson 25). Television is still around forty years later, and would no doubt have the same effect on the way the world thinks of Qatar. It is quite probable that the world's perspective would be changed and then shaped by the success of the Olympic Games in Qatar; resulting in a much more accurate view of Qatar than is available to the average citizen today.

Not only would the Olympics change the way Qatar is seen, bringing the 2016 Olympic and Paralympic Games to Doha would have a drastic impact on the financial state of Qatar. Businesses and even mere residents would benefit from the surge in tourism. Gerd, in research for the FIFA World Cup 2006, mentioned such things in his report as an, "upgrade of the national transportation system," and, "new alignment of Germany as a modern and hospitable destination in international tourism," that would improve Germany as a whole (10). If those were results of the FIFA World Cup in Germany, the impacts in Qatar due to the Olympics would be ten times greater. According to Solheim, Doha needs a revamped transportation system to allow for more timelier and convenient travel (Interview). Germany's transportation system was not that bad off to begin, if that country can improve their transport, Qatar's would most likely be unrecognizable to previous users. Not to mention, Germany was already a part of the tourist sector. Qatar, truly, is not a popular destination for those desiring to travel. Becoming one would result in a great increase in Qatar's national revenue for years to come. This is especially important to Qatari citizens as they continue their efforts to shy away from oil and move closer toward a lasting, dependable, and successful economy.

When it comes to financing the 2016 Olympic and Paralympic Games, Doha will not have any trouble. Thanks to the royal family's support, Doha will have within $20 billion to spend toward hosting (Kolatch). Putting such capital into the Olympics would surely result in a monumental pay-off for Qatar after the Games.

Much of the economic boom would be jumpstarted in preparation for the Olympics, as with any major event, and would result in an even better event. Qatar has already experienced this with their anticipation for the Asian Games in 2006, revolutionizing Sports City. Aspire Tower, now the tallest building in Qatar, cost $183-million alone, in addition to the stadium, roads, and hospital specializing in orthopedic care built before the Asian Games (Brown). Part of a series of public projects composing the 320-acre Sports City, the Aspire Tower impacted Qatar's economy and would provide quite the tourist attraction for Olympians and fans. Thanks to a display of 4,000 LED lights wired inside the frame, at night the tower is capable of exploding, "in a series of colors and designs that produce exactly the effect they should: shock and amazement," which could not be more perfect for the Olympic Games (Lubell). Just imagine the castle in Walt Disney World's Magic Kingdom at night. The beautifully changing colors, the captivating lights, and the way both combine to create an unforgettable, inspirational sight for each and every guest. The Olympics, kick-started with a display of 4,000 LED lights in Aspire Tower, would leave a long-lasting impression in the minds and hearts of those watching. Such a beautiful sight would no doubt result in greater tourism and profits for Qatar.

Fame and riches set aside, the most influential effect Qatar hosting the Olympics would have would be a total change of mind throughout the world. According to Bacon Pierre de Coubertin, "The Olympic movement tends to bring together in a radiant union all the qualities which guide mankind to perfection," (Johnson 23). One does not have to complete hours of research to come to the conclusion that the Middle East is not currently viewed as a safe or successful region of the world. Despite the state of Doha and Qatar and how well off they are financially, the majority of the rest of the world has no idea. Hosting the 2016 Olympic and Paralympic Games and hosting them well, would bring together a multitude of positive perspectives of Doha. It is about time that the rest of the world realized that not every Middle Easterner is a terrorist. As with Mexico in 1968, the Olympic Games are broadcast throughout the world and have the power to change the thoughts of people from the Far East to the West). How refreshing it would be to not only have a Middle Eastern country be a tourist attraction, but to also have positive connotations with citizens worldwide.

Doha, Qatar should be chosen to host the 2016 Olympic and Paralympic Games. Sure, Qatar is rapidly turning into a more and more commercialized country, if only to belong in today's world. And, obviously, hosting the Olympic Games would result in countless great effects for the country itself. Take the tourist into account though. Not only would the average spectator receive the treat of watching Aspire Tower light up at night in a show of great grandeur, but Qatar has more to offer than an arena in which to host the Olympics. Picture Palm Tree Island for example; a calm, relaxing, beautiful afternoon spent on the beach. For the typical traveler wishing to escape the hum-drum of the daily grind, does it get any better than that? Doha, in 2016, would have the best of both worlds: serene and gorgeous vacation spots in addition to the greatest sporting event in the world. The two together would result in the perfect trip for any spectator or tourist. In addition to the ways it could impact Qatar and the world, as well as the way the world views Qatar, the Olympics in Qatar would be greatly beneficial for those wishing to attend the event. Doha, Qatar should be chosen to host the 2016 Olympic and Paralympic Games.

Antithesis

Even so, some feel as if bringing such a Western tradition to the Middle East would not be a positive endeavor. Former Doha resident, Kristina Solheim, brings this perspective to light in explaining that the Asian Games resulted in quite the culture clash as she felt that Qatari culture was thrown out the window in order to play host to a variety of other cultures (Interview). The Doha 2016 Olympic and Paralympic Bid Committee feels that Qatar hosting would "bring the Olympic flame to the Arabic-speaking world for the first time, extending the Olympic ideals to millions of new hearts and minds" (Doha 2016). However, nothing is said about the culture of Qatar being brought to the rest of the world, only the contrary. This thought is reinforced by Susan Brownell, in describing the Olympics in Beijing and how the West assumes, "that any cultural exchange with China should be a one-way exchange in which China learns from the West, not a two-way dialogue" (2). One could easily infer that if this is the way the West is reacting to China hosting the Games, Qatar playing host would result in a similar, if not worse, mindset toward cultural exchange. Therefore, having the 2016 Olympics in Qatar would not be, as Avery Brundage described, a great "social force" or "a revolt against Twentieth Century materialism" (Johnson 24). The 2016 Olympic Games would merely import other countries' goods and ideas into Qatar.

Synthesis

At the same time, is this decision such a monumental one? Count Henri de Baillet-Latour, former president of the International Olympic Committee doesn't believe so, as he explained that, "The Olympic Games are not held in Berlin, in Los Angeles or in Amsterdam. When the five-circled Olympic flag is raised over a stadium, it becomes sacred Olympic territory and theoretically and for all practical purposes, the Games are held in ancient Olympia," where they first began (Johnson 23). Perhaps the bid process itself is too extreme. After all, it can be assumed that no matter what city or country is chosen to host the Olympics, that they will spend a great deal of money, employ hundreds of people, and take months to prepare to host the Games as they should be hosted. With such work going into an event, it will be prosperous and successful. When a country is placed in the world's eyes in a positive light, it will then be seen positively. If before it was seen in a negative light, a transformation will occur and the country will now be seen in a much more positive way. It would be nice for Qatar to have these effects for themselves. However, based on Baillet-Latour's thoughts, one could believe that the country where the Games will be hosted is insignificant (Johnson 23).

While he makes a plausible argument, Baillet-Latour is a bit mistaken, as location is key. The location of the Olympic Games is a place that will be on the tongues of people throughout the world for years, both in anticipation of the Games and again in retrospect. This instant buzzword carries numerous connotations with it, comprised of both people's predispositions to what the location is like and what sort of job they are doing of hosting the Olympics. If Doha wins the bid, the 2016 Olympic and Paralympic Games would be epic. As IOC President Avery Brundage stated, "The Olympic Movement is a Twentieth Century religion. Here there is no injustice of caste, of race, of family, of wealth" (Johnson 24). There is no place in the world right now, other than the Middle East that would benefit as strongly from an event of such equalizing power. From terrorist attacks at Gaza Strip crossings to the tension between Israel and Palestine, from the Americans' invasion in Iraq to Iran's nuclear activities, the Middle East could certainly use an event of such caliber. There is nothing else out there that has the power to bring together so many diverse countries and peoples in peace, if only to compete or watch others compete in sports contests. The Olympic Games have the power to unite people and lead them to put away their differences for awhile. If brought to the Middle East, Olympic gold would result in a level of harmony that is, for lack of better words, golden.

Alternatives

Without a doubt, hosting the 2016 Olympic and Paralympic Games will have a great effect on both the city and country where they are hosted, no matter where that location might be. Therefore, while Doha would be transformed, might the same be said for Baku, Chicago, Madrid, Prague, Rio de Janeiro, or Tokyo? Is so, then Qatar might be an excellent choice for the Games, but there could be a better one out there.

The United States (Chicago) appears to be the best possible choice for the Games to be held. With a near flawless bid application and much experience in hosting, USA should be unanimously voted for (Chicago 2016). However, the United States last hosted the Summer Games in Atlanta in 1996 and the Winter Games in Salt Lake City in 2002. Does the country truly deserve to host the Games once more? It would be more beneficial to the world, including the USA, for the Olympic and Paralympic Games to be held elsewhere. While Chicago would put on a good show, nothing more would come out of USA hosting the 2016 Games.

Madrid, Spain, seems to be the next obvious choice. Nevertheless, one of the country's main reasons for bidding is to reach "unity of institutions and business sector" (Madrid 2016). If Spain would like to host the 2016 Olympic and Paralympic Games, one had better hope that their government and businesses can cooperate and communicate with each other. To place one of their central aspirations of hosting the Olympic Games on such, as well as to present Madrid the honor to host the Games, is absolutely preposterous. Spain's bid deserves to be immediately disregarded, at least until their country is in check.

The world's economy is dependent on oil; however, this should not impact the IOC's decision on who to award the honor. Baku, Azerbaijan is an oil city, which is proven by their Olympic bid itself, stating that "the exploitation of the natural resources, primarily crude oil and gas, has defined the identity of Baku," rather than any other factors (Baku 2016, 7). Unfortunately, Baku's attempts to limit their focus on oil are not as strong or as complete as Qatar's. Thus, the country perpetuates the world's dependence on oil, even while numerous other nations are making the necessary steps towards a sustainable Earth. Most of 2016's Olympic bids include great explanations on how the Olympic and Paralympic Games, if hosted in their country, would be "green" and limit the planet's destruction. So, why should a country that is directly contributing to the Earth's demise be granted the honor of the world's attention?

Prague (Czech Republic), Rio de Janeiro (Brazil), and Tokyo (Japan) should not even be considered as possible hosts by the IOC. The Czech Republic does not honestly wish to welcome the Olympic and Paralympic Games into their nation, they are aiming to develop "130 sport centres in 75 Czech cities," rather than impact the Olympic Games, spectators, or the world in any way (Praha 2016). Rio de Janeiro is looking forward to hosting the FIFA World Cup in 2014; it would be far too difficult for one country to take on both events in a matter of two years. Finally, Tokyo hosted the Games in 1964, a mere eleven events ago. There is no particular reason why Tokyo should be granted with such an honor for the second time in less than fifty years.

The Olympic Games are more than a simple sporting event, with all their glory and power, they deserve to be hosted in the most ideal location. Chicago, Madrid, Baku, Prague, Rio de Janeiro, and Tokyo are not right for the 2016 Olympic and Paralympic Games. Even by making the simplest arguments, it is quite clear that Doha is better suited and a better option for the 2016 Games.

The Choice

Conclusively, the 2016 Olympic Games belong in Doha, Qatar. While each country undoubtedly has much to offer to both the Olympic and Paralympic Games, Doha is the best possible choice. Admittedly, Chicago's organization is superior, Madrid's layout would be beautiful, and Baku's location is even more unique than Doha. Even so, the Olympic Games are a monumental event hosted for the entire world to see. The best possible choice in 2016 for the athletes, the spectators, the host city and country, the rest of the planet, and the Olympic and Paralympic Games themselves is Doha, Qatar. Bringing Olympic gold to the Middle East would change the world forever.

Works Cited

Ahlert, Gerd. "Hosting the FIFA World Cup™ Germany 2006: Macroeconomic and Regional Economic Impacts." *Journal of Convention & Event Tourism* 8.2 (2006): 57–78. Print.

Baku 2016 Olympic and Paralympic Bid Committee. *Baku 2016*. Baku: Baku 2016 Olympic and Paralympic Bid Committee, 2008.

Brown, Jeff L. "Tower Lifts Olympic Torch to New Heights." *Civil Engineering* 77.4 (2007): 10–11. Print.

Brownell, Susan. *Beijing's Games*. United States of America: Rowman & Littlefield Publishers, Inc., 2008. Print.

Chicago 2016 Olympic and Paralympic Bid Committee. *Chicago 2016.* Chicago: Chicago 2016 Olympic and Paralympic Bid Committee, 2008.

Doha 2016 Olympic and Paralympic Bid Committee. *Doha 2016.* 2007. Web. 30 Apr. 2008.

Doha 2016 Olympic and Paralympic Bid Committee. *Doha 2016.* Doha: Doha 2016 Olympic and Paralympic Bid Committee, 2008.

Johnson, William O. *All That Glitters Is Not Gold.* New York: G. P. Putnam's Sons, 1972. Print.

Kolatch, Jonathan. "Doha, Qatar, pursues the 2016 Olympics." *Wall Street Journal*: 12 Dec 2007. Print.

Lubell, Sam. "Sports City Tower." *Architectural Record*: 1 Aug 2007. Print.

Madrid 2016 Olympic and Paralympic Bid Committee. *Madrid 2016.* Madrid: Madrid 2016 Olympic and Paralympic Bid Committee, 2008.

Praha 2016 Olympic and Paralympic Bid Committee. *Praha 2016.* Questions and Answers. N.d. Web. 30 Apr. 2008.

Solheim, Kristina. Personal Interview. 23 Apr. 2008.

13.7 Money is My Monkey Wrench

By Parker Owan

Does money buy happiness? If it doesn't then why do advertisements on TV beg to tell you otherwise? And if it does then why is the phrase "money can't buy happiness" thrown around so much? Kasser in his essay, "Mixed Messages" effectively addresses the dichotomy of materialism prevalent in American society, and presents logical research that successfully accomplishes his goal. The conclusion he draws from his research is that increased tendencies of valuing materialism result in deprivation of vitality. Kasser succeeds in providing an in-depth analysis of materialism in American culture through original research and studies, and he focuses on the opposing views on the subject that have so subtly taken refuge in the exact same culture. Many of his primary arguments are focused on either proving a result to the reader or explaining a scientific method or research style. Some arguments he uses effectively are found in his descriptions of specific testing, which at first glance might seem simply explanatory, but the feel Kasser projects to the audience is extremely effective in producing a desired objective.

The text itself is very work intensive, and Kasser endeavors to make many claims regarding materialism's impact on human psychology. His first argu-

287

ment regards the dichotomy involved in our materialistic culture. Everywhere you look—the television, billboards, poster boards, storefronts—capitalism is telling you to buy something. As Kasser says, "Happiness can be found at the mall, on the Internet, or in the catalogue." (SOL, 503). Kasser portrays the materialistic-centered culture found in America and other Western cultures. However, Kasser also realizes that Western philosophy and religion shun the use of materialism to produce happiness in someone. In the words of Kasser, "Sages from almost every religious and philosophical background have similarly insisted that focusing on attaining material possessions and social renown detracts from what is meaningful about life." (SOL, 502).

Kasser initially gives insight into himself by establishing his credibility and stating his background on the subject of studying culture mindsets. His credibility is established on three levels; the first is the fact that he conducted all of his own research for the essay. His insight into the studies discussed in his paper was higher than a paper that would emphasize third party work.

Kasser explicitly addresses members of American society in his essay, as is evident by his statement found in his initial premise, "Although behavioral and evolutionary theories largely dominated American academic psychology in the last century" (SOL, 504). Another excerpt from the text emphasizes the point that this essay is directed solely to American culture, "Even though Americans earn twice as much in today's dollars as they did in 1957, the proportion of those telling surveyors from the National Opinion Research Center that are "very happy" has declined from 35 to 29 percent." (SOL, 505).

However, there is a catch. While in Kasser's mind this research essay is directed toward American capitalism alone, one particular statement he makes later on in the essay drives me to believe that it could be applied far less sparingly. "Notably, this cluster of goals also was found in students from both Russia and Germany, suggesting that the coexistence of money, fame, and image values can be found in cultures less consumeristic than the United States." (SOL, 510). Clearly, the duality of materialism can be applied to more nations than the United States, and this is essential to Kasser's thesis since it is applicable to humankind in general.

Kasser carries his research in the essay through the vital premise that both dipole "messages"—"materialism is flawed," and "materialism is the key to happiness"—coexist in Western culture. This is a clarification of his primary argument that focuses the attention of the paper to a concentrated, scientifically-testable subject. As Kasser so perfectly states, "It seems that whenever we inquire about the value of materialism, we receive conflicting answers." (SOL, 503). This is the paramount of Kasser's argument: that both of these messages may exist in the same culture, but only one of them can be true since they are opposing forces at work in the same society. The fact that he so carefully chooses the method in which he backs his main argument up demonstrates the effort and credibility of his entire essay. This primary argument is fundamental to the premises of the research he refers to in the remainder of his essay, and he clearly and effectively defines his point.

Kasser uses the majority of his essay to carefully explain his research and its corresponding results in a detailed manner about studies performed on college students regarding, what Kasser calls, the "Aspiration Index." The "Aspiration Index" is, in and of itself, an argument for the essay because the idea behind the index is novel and inclusive. He even states the first one he used did not work as well as he had hoped, so he developed a new one that worked much better, producing more accurate and precise results.

The first major point that Kasser reaches as a result of his research is that "The more materialistic values are at the center of our lives, the more our quality of life is diminished," (SOL, 513)—in a way stating that materialism is the monkey wrench of Western popular society. Research regarding the first "Aspiration Index" successfully ties this to his main argument. His initial conclusion is reached using an index which had users rank the order of importance of financial success aspirations. Clearly, this is relevant to the premises of his argument, and he portrays his research in an unbiased, scientific fashion. This is one of the many things that Kasser does well about this essay. He frequently refers back to earlier statements, which could be confusing to some readers, but in the long run, it is the most effective way to build and support his argument. Because the subject is very complicated, Kasser must try to refresh the reader's memory to the most important point in order to keep the reader focused. However, it is not too Kasser's advantage to dumb down the level of writing since his audience is most-likely educated and immersed in the work force. He successfully recognizes this and structures and writes his essay accordingly.

He continues later on to say that "These relationships have been documented in samples of people ranging from the wealthy to the poor, from teenagers to the elderly, and from Australians to South Koreans" (SOL, 517). What is interesting to note here is that Kasser no longer limits the extent of materialism to Western civilization but to humanity in general, "Australians to South Koreans" (SOL, 517). This logical order of events is what lucratively ties Kasser's work together and brings his research to a concise and consistent conclusion. While it is scientifically incorrect to call any result a completely conclusive finding, Kasser does say that all of his findings show reliable trends demonstrating a correlation between material goals and dissatisfaction with life itself. His primary question has been confirmed by his work, and this is extremely essential to the legitimacy of the paper since Kasser initially posed a question that he sought to answer.

Kasser's argument is solid and he progresses through his premises to reach his final conclusion. When there is not enough data, he tells the reader, and then explains how he performed more research to get more data. The flow between points assessed by Kasser is logical in its construction. One of the best examples of construction of premises in this essay is Kasser's constant reference to previous research or even previous statements made in his essay. It helps in tying together the complex subject matter addressed by the essay, and Kasser finds a suitable method for referring the reader to previous research. Possibly the most convincing aspect of "Mixed Messages" is the use of scientific terminology and abbreviated, but non-compromising explanations all backed by a simple, concise progression through arguments. He presents his arguments clearly and succinctly, while retaining their scientific aspect, a trait difficult to project well to an audience. Kasser's initial question, "Does money buy happiness?" is answered through the question, "Do people who take unbiased and controlled surveys tend to answer that they find more happiness in materialistic goals or intangible goals?" The scientific aspect of the paper is much more specific, and he tends to effectively translate the science into understandable terminology.

13.8 An Independent State

By Amin Mahmoud

Palestinians and Israelis have been going through war with one another for the past 60 years. Each claim that they have the right to own the land. They both are fighting to own the land for themselves and each thinks they have the right to own it. In order for Palestine or Israel to be considered a sovereign state, both Palestine and Israel must meet certain criteria (Crawford). According to international law an independent state must have met four requirements: effective and independent government control, it must be a certain area that contains defined borders, the control of a permanent population, and the ability to be involved with foreign relation (Becker). According to Max Weber, the definition of a state is an entity which has made the successful and exclusive claim to the legitimate right with borders to the use of violence. In light of this definition of independent state, let this paper examine the claims both the Palestinians and Israelis make to support their arguments for an independent state. This paper will challenge if both/either entities has the right to own the land and be called an independent state.

In 1947 the UN general Assembly passed Resolution 181. This resolution divides historical Palestine into two different states: One Arab and the other Jewish (Pipes). One could argue that this resolution proves that Palestine gained international legitimacy then, and deserved to be called an independent state. However, Palestinians and Arabs refused to accept this resolution as they considered it unfair, and instead on May 1948 several Arab countries (Lebanon, Syria, Jordan, Iraq, and Egypt) along with the Palestinians waged war against Israel to try to capture the entire land. This war resulted in the defeat of Arab armies and the establishment of an independent state of Israel on 1948 (Pipes). This event became well known as Israel's War of Independence. During this war, thousands of Palestinian fled their land and became refugees. Israel's War of Independence made a huge change for Palestinians and instead of creating a new state of Palestine, the recognition of a Palestinian state was pushed back instead of moving forward.

According to the Jerusalem Center of Public Affair, Palestine must meet the criteria for statehood in order to be recognized by the international community as a sovereign entity. The entity must fulfill the standards and must show that it does. This article states "Only if the Palestinians entity satisfies the traditional criteria for statehood by exercising independent and sovereign governmental control...over a permanent population in a defined territory over which it has possession, can its recognition as a sovereign state be considered" (JCPA). Palestinians meet several criteria to become recognized as a state based on international law. Palestine is a nation, and this is one of the important things to have when forming a state both in fact and in law (George).

The four requirements must be met by an entity before it can be called an independent state. First the effective and independent government control. Palestine must be able to control the territory it will govern, also referred to as "territorial sovereignty". With respect to having government order Palestine fulfills this requirement; the Palestinian Authority took over the leadership position and responsibility of the role of the government of Palestine in 1994 as a result of the Oslo peace accord. Currently, Mahmoud Abbas has taken over this position of being the leader of Palestinians (George). Therefore the entity already has a government formed, which is a parliamentary democracy. Second requirement is that it must be a certain area that contains defined borders. The perspective territory for the Palestinian state will include the West Bank, and the Gaza strip. The current state of Palestine territory includes Gaza Strip, East Jerusalem as the capital, and the West Bank. The land itself comes out to be 6217 Square Kilometer in area (CIA). The third requirement is the control of a permanent population. In regards to population, the decision on population will be the permanent residents of the Gaza strip and the West Bank who consists of majority Palestinian Arab (George). Gaza strip contains 1.44 million people living in the area, and the West Bank has 2.80 million people. The Arab-Palestinians have a dense population in these areas making up the majority in these areas. Both areas have one government which controls them that is the Palestinian National Authority. The last requirement is the ability to be involved with foreign relations. It is important that Palestine's neighboring countries recognize it as a state. There are over 100 states that have already recognized Palestine as a state (Crawford). Therefore over 100 states do have formal relations with Palestine.

If the Palestinians meet all these conditions to have an independent state, what is preventing them from declaring this state? The only thing that prevents the Palestinians from declaring their state is the Israeli occupation. Israel occupies Palestinian land and people by force since 1967. This includes the West Bank, Gaza strip and Jerusalem and the inhabitants of these areas. It controls their will and denies their right to self-determination. Therefore, the Palestinians have not been able to declare a viable independent state of Palestine. The opposing side of Palestine's recognition as a state, comes from the belief the entity does not meet the standards to be a state. According to Crawford, it is hard to imagine Palestine as a state, because Israel already has a state in the same territory (Crawford).

The Jewish people claim a right to historical Palestine. The Jews have lived in Palestine thousands of years ago. In early 1900s Jewish groups started to move back to historical Palestine during the British mandate. Israel believes that they have the right to claim the land because they have an old, sacred history there. Jews went through bad situations during World War II, where they were killed and treated terribly. Jews decided that they wanted a land to live in, and chose Palestine because they used to live there centuries ago. The Old Testament (Torah) says that the land originally belongs to Jews. Jews were exiled and returned over 3000 years ago. So in better terms Jews used to live there before the Palestinians did. According to the Jews they have the right to come back to their homeland after being exiled from it by force. Jews follow the Old Testament, and believe what is written in it, the same way Muslims believe what is written in the Qur'an. Therefore Jews believe they have the right to own the land since they believe they lived there before the Palestinians did.

Let us discuss whether Israel meets the criteria of an independent state. According to international law a state must fulfill four different requirements to become an independent state as mentioned above. Israel has a government that is effective and has control over everything to do with their land. Israel have areas that contains defined borders, it actually has all the land except for the Gaza strip and the West Bank. It has borders with other countries like Jordan, Egypt, Lebanon and Syria. The control of a permanent population, Israel's population according to the CIA fact book is 7,112,359. Israel controls over 7 million people, and provides safety to them and rights (Strawson). Having Israel recognized by many countries is something positive. Israel has foreign relations with almost all North and South America, Europe and Asia. Israel is the state that protects the borders from any threats, or attacks (Crawford). Israel has authority over their areas. Israel is also authorized to conduct foreign affair relations (Crawford).

What constitutes a problem to the legitimacy to an independent state of Israel? Occupation of some parts of Palestine by force and those parts are the Gaza Strip (until 2006), East Jerusalem and the West Bank. Israel imposes its will over the inhabitants of these areas Israel occupies. Also Israel lacks recognitions of the Palestinians and the majority of the neighboring Arab countries except for Egypt and Jordan. Before Israel can enjoy a peaceful independent state with their neighbors they will have to address and solve the occupation problem first.

The formation of a Palestinian state has been in progress for decades, and this is important because it shows improvement. As of today, there have been many attempts, once in 1948, and another time in 1988, and in 2005. (Pipes) On November 15, 1988 the Palestinian president at the time, Yasir Arafat declared an independent state of Palestine in Algiers as the leader of the Palestinian liberation Organization (Pipes). The Palestinian people have created their own national identity over the years (Pipes). There have been various failed attempts for peace agreements including the 1993 Oslo Peace Accords, the Camp David 2000 Summit, and 2002 Road Map for Peace. The common theme for these agreements has been in favor of the Israelis, and unfavorable to the Palestinians. According to BBC News, the most recent peace agreement is the Road Map for Peace, with the objective to create a final agreement between the Palestinians and the Israelis, which was presented by President Bush (Kessler). The Oslo Accords focused on peacemaking, like the previous agreements; "The Government of the State of Israel and the Palestinian team representing the Palestinian people agree that it is time to put an end to decades of confrontation and conflict" (The Avalon Project). In this agreement, it specifically recognizes that there is a political body which represents the Palestinians, and their help is needed in order to stop the violence. The next line in the agreement is "recognize their mutual legitimate and political rights, and strive to live in peaceful coexistence and mutual dignity and security to achieve a just, lasting and comprehensive peace settlement and historic reconciliation through the agreed political process" (The Avalon Project). This phrase implies that both the Israeli political body and the Palestinian body are legitimate, and can co-exist with each other in security and settle for both sides to be content. Both the Palestinians and the Israelis agreed to these terms, and yet Palestine is not considered a state. Why would the state of Israel sign agreements with the Palestinians if they do not recognize them as a state? Israel's actions speak louder than its words, by acknowledging Palestine, to the point where each agreed to maintain the stability of peace.

From the above analysis, it is obvious that the current situation requires great attention from the United Nations, and the world community to decrease the strain among the Arabs and the Jews which are basically the Israeli's and the Palestinians. This cooperation will help the political process of the new Israeli state, and help the Palestinians feel welcome in their homeland as well. The entity of Palestine, unfortunately does not meet standards for statehood. There are many arguments on whether or not the entity meets the requirements, but the approval of the UN, Israel and the US will be essential for such a state. If there was cooperation among all of the sovereign nations, I believe that Palestine will one day meet its full potential in becoming a state. A two state solution is the best solution for Israel and Palestine. Having a two state solution will decrease the amount of crime between both the Palestinians and Israeli's. Of course many Palestinians will disagree for having a two state solution because they believe that it is an unfair solution, but I am sure many will agree to live a peaceful life. Israel on the other hand might not agree on a two state solution, but it will sure benefit them for having a peaceful life along with the Palestinians. A hypothetical situation would be me coming to my relative house and demanding that the entire house be for me, and no one else, and they can have the kitchen. This is not a fair agreement, and this is how many of the Palestinians feel about the Palestinian-Israeli conflict which I have spoken to. The Palestinians entity does not meet the criteria to some, but not to all. Both states can meet the criteria, but both lack the recognition of each other.

Works Cited

"A Performance-based Roadmap to a Permanent Two-state Solution to the Israeli-Palestinian Conflict." *BBC News.* 30 April 2003. Web. 20 October 2008.

CIA World Fact book. "West Bank." October 2008. Web. 2 Nov. 2008.

——."Gaza Strip." October 2008. Web. 2 Nov. 2008.

Crawford, James. "The Creation of the State of Palestine: Too Much Too Soon?" *European Journal of International Law.* 27 July 1999. Web. 14 October 2008.

George, Forji Amin. "Is Palestine a State?" *Expert Law.* June 2004. Web. 15 October 2008.

Israel-Palestine Liberation Organization Agreement: 1993. *The Avalon Project.* October 1996. Web. 20 October 2008.

"International Recognition of a Unilaterally Declared Palestinian State." *Jerusalem Center for Public Affairs.* Jerusalem Center for Public Affairs, n.d. Web. 15 October 2008.

Kessler, Glenn. "Talking Points Aside, Bush Not a First." *Washington Post.* 5 October 2005. Web. 13 October 2008.

Pipes, Daniel. "Declaring Statehood: Israel and the PLO". 1989. Web. 20 October 2008.

Strawson, John. "Zionism and Apartheid: The Analogy in the Politics of International Law." *Engage Journal.* Engage Journal, n.d. Web. 13 October 2008.

13.9 Ethanol: Food or Fuel

A Speech by Ameya Neelam

Ethanol is not the next big thing. It is the reason for lack of food, higher corn prices, drops in the economy and an overall degradation in the fuel industry. I agree with Jean Ziegler, the United Nations Special Reporter on the Right to Food, called for a five-year moratorium on biofuel production to halt the increasing catastrophe for the poor. He proclaimed that the rising practice of converting food crops into biofuel is "A crime against humanity," saying it is creating food shortages and price jumps that cause millions of poor people to go hungry. What does this tell us about ethanol? It definitely is not one of the solutions for the energy crisis we are facing today.

Ethanol does not solve problems regarding increase in the price of corn, increase in the cost of common commodities like milk and meat, excess carbon monoxide in the atmosphere; instead it is the reason behind all of the above.

Ethanol production from corn consumes large quantities of unsustainable petroleum and natural gas. Even with the most-optimistic energy return on investment claims, in order to use 100% solar energy to grow corn and produce ethanol (fueling farm-and-transportation machinery with ethanol, distilling with heat from burning crop residues, using no fossil fuels), the consumption of ethanol to replace current U.S. petroleum use alone would require about 75% of all cultivated land on the face of the Earth, with no ethanol for other countries, or sufficient food for humans and animals. Several of the outstanding ethanol fuel issues are linked specifically to fuel systems. Fuels with more than 10% ethanol are not compatible with non Ethanol85-ready fuel system components and may cause corrosion of ferrous components. Ethanol fuel can negatively affect electric fuel pumps by increasing internal wear, cause undesirable spark generation, and is not compatible with capacitance fuel level gauging indicators. It is for the same reason that ethanol is not used in aircraft engines.

According to an April 2008 World Bank report, biofuels have caused world food prices to increase by 75%. In 2007, biofuels consumed one third of America's corn harvest. Filling up one large vehicle fuel tank one time with 100% ethanol uses enough corn to feed one person for a year. Thirty million tons of United States corn going to ethanol in 2007 greatly reduces the world's overall supply of grain. The use of corn to produce fuel has pushed the U.S. government to slash the amount of food aid they give because more of the corn that it has is being poured into ethanol. The higher demand has caused prices to rise as land in the United States is being transformed from soy land into cornfields. Prices of soy are increasing, as well as Australian wheat and fresh vegetables. The increased use of ethanol as fuel has resulted in the quick growth of corn at the same time. Since this cannot go hand in hand, a lot of money has been invested for the fast growth of corn. In order to retrieve the same money spent on growing it, the prices of corn are being increased. This proves that ethanol is highly inefficient and unreliable.

Coming to the human side of a lack of food in the world market it can be said that the use of ethanol has a lot to do with the increase in prices of every food item possible because it has some form of corn present in it. There are many countries even today which face situations concerning lack of food it is, not only because they are not able to afford to it but also because most of the raw food supplies are used to produce fuel. So when food isn't begin bought on a regular basis but instead is used to produce fuel it makes the whole sale markets face huge losses. When such huge markets face losses it requires less labor force. Less labor force affects the economy and this is how the economy drops. Clearly ethanol has proved to be incapable of solving any of the pressing problems concerning the economy or the environment. It is nothing but an added burden. Ethanol's unreliability has diminished the quality of food and fuel. Fuel is the biggest necessity in the United States since every machine needs some sort of fuel to function. Therefore it boils down to whether or not the country is willing to pay for the continued usage of ethanol as a fuel and ignore what it does to the rest of economy or stop it from being used as an alternative fuel for good and concentrate on standardizing the costs of food so that lower and middle people are able to afford a decent meal.

The present scenario shows, people who can't afford a decent meal everyday, are now struggling even harder to get through a week as the prices are constantly escalating. The congress is definitely being put under some pressure to try and make ethanol production come to a halt. This means there are a few people who believe that it involves government subsidies and marketplace interference. The corn based ethanol doesn't seem to be fulfilling its use as a renewable fossil fuel. It looks like the government officials leave no choice for the people when it comes to providing them with what they want. Ethanol is being used as a fuel and yet it doesn't seem to fulfill any energy needs. It is believed that it does not in anyway help keep the environment clean. It is a misconception that ethanol does not produce carbon dioxide or will reduce the amount of carbon dioxide in the atmosphere that normal fossil fuels do. This means that drivers are technically releasing twice the amount of carbon dioxide. This naturally is not safe for the environment. Apart from that it is known to dissolve impurities in water, which means it, cannot be transported through pipelines instead, it requires trucks and freights. This arrangement makes the cost of distributing shoot up.

Hence the pressure on growing corn every year goes up by ten fold. Unfortunately this pressure is causing a lot of damage to the water surrounding the gulf. The algae and nutrient pollutants produced are making the water bodies unclean and unfit for any sort of growth such as fish and water plants. This affects the oxygen levels in water. This might result in the decline of seafood consumption.

Finally I would like to conclude by saying that ethanol cannot and must not be continued to be used as an alternative fuel. It is obvious from the above, information complete with statistics to provide evidence about the disadvantages of using ethanol. Not only does it fail to be a good alternative fuel but is also responsible for the average American family to not be able to afford a pound of beef without thinking twice. There is absolutely no question of saving. The corn used to feed the cows has become so expensive because of its importance in the production of ethanol that dairy product prices have increased by three fold. One cannot think of making more fuel when there are thousands of people starving all over the world and, their food being taken away only to be used for something so controversial. Ethanol is being used far away in other countries to fill up tanks during war but is anyone bothered about those people who are in the war without their fill in the stomach? Their lives are at stake already because they don't have enough food. Is this what the future holds in store for everyone? The only way to put a stop to all of the above is to completely shut down the use of ethanol once and for all. The only thing it does is to make the higher authorities question whether saving a life is as worth while as using a machine. I repeat ethanol is not the next big thing and will cease to be.

13.10 On American Hypocrisy: Disgracing our Forefathers

A Speech by Thomas Wilson

At 8:46 in the morning, on the eleventh day of September in the year 2001, the World Trade Center's northern tower was essentially bombed by a Boeing 767 at the 94th floor. Exactly sixteen and one half minutes later the southern tower was hit by a second Boeing 767, causing twice the horror involved with the first. Both towers crashed to the ground. Just under 3,000 people were killed. In the days that followed the nation looked for support from our leaders to ease their troubled hearts and fears. Within weeks the US had declared war on Al Qaida, and all that harbored their members, and this included Afghanistan. In the weeks following 9/11 the allied forces captured dozens of suspected terrorists and suspected terrorist supporters. Three of these suspected terrorists were British nationals who had immigrated to England from Pakistan, and were visiting Afghanistan as part of a wedding trip. Simply because of where they were located and because they spoke English they were detained by British forces and eventually shipped to Camp X-Ray in Guantanamo Bay. They were detained without trial for 2 years until they were released and declared innocent in 2003. During their time at Camp X-Ray they endured multiple forms of torture including starvation, sleep deprivation, hooding, and stress positions from US military personnel that have been documented in the film *Road to Guantanamo*. Their story is a prime example of the how measures taken in the name of 'war' can prove to violate natural human rights.

When we hear the word 'Torture', what do we think? Do we think witch hunts, Holocaust, Stalin, dark ages, or Prisoner of War? Does the word torture hold any positive connotation? Does America, a nation that claims an ideology against violations of human rights, come to mind? Torture is morally wrong by any governing body. Since the United States began the war on terror, more and more contention has risen concerning human rights. It is common of presidencies, during a time of war, to retain certain freedoms of those seemingly involved in the conflict. The United States government has extended its reach due to this War on Terror in many ways. One disturbing infringement of human rights is the Bush administration's endorsement of torture, an obviously immoral act, to try and gain information from US detainees. What is moral and what is immoral does not always dictate how a government will act, but in the case of the United States it is also unlawful to violate human rights.

This nation is founded upon a set of moral principles. Citizens of the United States benefit from the Bill of Rights, which never allows cruel and unusual punishment, which of course includes torture. It also gives the rights of due process, a fair trial, and protects the idea of 'innocent until proven guilty'. These rights are inalienable to all human life, and although they don't directly apply to non-citizens our founding fathers said they were universal. We cannot simply abandon these rights due to a person's place of birth. The America I know and love, the America my ancestors died for does not and would not put provisos on when to apply the bill of human rights, whether the human is American or not. If those who support prisoner abuse feel that this is not a compelling enough responsibility to cease torture, than perhaps a legal responsibility will sway them. In 1949 the United States and many other nations signed on to the third Geneva Convention, which took place in response to World War II. In an effort to limit violations of human rights, and curb the atrocity of war, the civilized world set limits and boundaries to how prisoners of war would be treated by their captors. Whether or not a person is a declared citizen of an enemy country or a terrorist who claims to be separate of a country, they are still protected from any form of physical or psychological torture. Also it provides that nothing that degrades a human can be used as a tactic of interrogation either. Yet we have numerous senators in the United States Congress, the very people who should respect our treaties most of all, that feel that a suspected terrorist should not be granted these rights. For example, an argument was put forth that abuse of suspected terrorists is degrading and therefore wrong, and Republican Senator John Thune of South Dakota said "when you talk about humiliating or degrading or those types of terms, in applying them to terrorists . . . people in my state would [not] be real concerned that we might be infringing on [the terrorists'] sense of human rights". Aren't human rights unconditional? Consider, if you will, that the human mind feels that torture is indeed an injustice and degrading. If you were to walk into a room where a person was handcuffed and naked with a bag over their head, and a man was restraining a snarling Doberman Pincer just inches from the person's body, making them run up and down the room from the dog, would you feel ok? Would you not feel violated and disturbed, if you didn't know for certain that the person had done anything wrong, would you feel that it was justified? The United States military has done this and many other degrading things to detainees in the name of Anti-terrorism, under the direction and endorsement of the Bush Administration. In many cases we haven't even been able to prove their guilt; only ten detainees have ever been officially charged with a crime! Our military has taken these people from their homes and denied them due process and trial for months and years on the idea that they may be associated with terrorism or Al Qaida. In America a man can kill a man in broad daylight on national television, and he is going to receive a lawyer, speedy trial, and due process even though there is documented proof that he killed the other man. If a guard beats him up or mistreats him that guard could be charged with a crime, but as long as we are in another country with non-citizens we can treat a SUSPECTED terrorist with a lack of human dignity? Our nation is built upon a belief that to reach our goals we must be justified upon moral and legal grounds; it is the very idea that sparked the American Revolution and founded our constitution and bill of rights. We must be true to the foundation of our legal system; our supreme court has said that torture is wrong. When Dick Cheney's aide, Lewis 'Scooter' Libby, was charged with perjury and obstruction of justice, President Bush was very quick to say that "in our system each individual is presumed innocent and entitled to due process and a fair trial". All the while President Bush has withheld due process from over 400 US detainees, and more and more stories of torture and misconduct have risen to the surface. Of course, there are still those in our government who are fighting to eliminate torture from our interrogation methods. 21 year Republican Senator John McCain has been against cruelty as long as it's been an issue. As many of you already know Senator McCain was himself a prisoner of war for 5 and half years in Vietnam. Now regardless of your personal opinion of McCain, consider this please. He has 21 years of working in congress so he must have an understanding of the principles of just government, and has served military experience in wartime where he was indeed tortured by the Vietcong. If he feels that it is illegal, immoral, and also unreliable to use violence or maltreatment as a means of interrogation, then find me an individual who is more qualified to make a contrasting argument. When an armed man in a military uniform twists and pushes your arm in such a way that it feels like it is on the verge of breaking, and he keeps continually asking you the same question while making it a little more painful each time, wouldn't it make sense that you would say whatever it takes to relieve the pain and save your arm? How is this reliable? When you force someone to say what you want to hear, without ensuring reliability, should you base your military intelligence off of it? The answer is no, it makes no sense that degradation is an effective way of extracting the truth.

There is another hypocrisy that our government is approaching in this war on terror. It has been said that this war is a war on an idea, and to fight something like terrorism that has no national borders or main headquarters is indeed fighting an idea. Then our just reason for this war is that those who fight terrorism are the opposite of terrorist. If terrorism is our enemy and we don't want to be associated with it, then we must do all we can to keep a moral high ground, and be an example to the world of freedom, justice, and harmony. When the public sees videos and images of insurgents in the Middle East terrorizing, torturing, and executing coalition soldiers and news reporters, they see what is considered so evil about these terrorists. So if part of what defines America's hate towards these terrorists is how they treat human life to get what they want or to make their point, then do we not have a responsibility to fight that action, too? It is childish and morally immature to say "they started it" or "an eye for an eye". Republican Senator Saxby Chambliss of Georgia said "It certainly irritates me to no end to think that we have to continue to do what's right at all times when the enemy that we're fighting is going to be cruel and inhuman to American men and women who wear our uniform [if] they might fall into their hands." Think about what he said: are we to base our treatment of prisoners on how they would treat us, on how a terrorist would treat us? This mentality is ignorant and barbaric. If a schoolboy is punched in the face by another schoolboy at recess and the second boy waits and punches him back later at lunch time, aren't they both wrong, is anything accomplished? Doesn't the second boy lose his right to be mad, his moral high ground, because the principal will suspend both boys for breaking the rules?

This is essentially what our torture of detainees is. Let me share with you something that I was taught by my father, and although you don't have any reason to trust his opinion know that he is a hard worker, loves his country, and is usually a conservative. My father turned to me one day when we were debating this very subject and said "Thomas while we are fighting this war on terror, if you stoop to level of a terrorist and use their tactics against themselves, you have lost the war on terror." And I would argue you have even joined their ranks. In using terrorist tactics you support terrorism as a justified tool in war. The moral and legal principles this nation was founded on do not and should not change due to a state of so called war. The America that our troops are fighting for and have fought for does not have moral or legal grounds to torture prisoners of war. There is no just means for abuse, and it fails to ensure reliable intelligence because it lacks accountability. There is no good reason for governments to torture. Let me end with a quote from our authority on the subject Senator McCain. "It's not about the terrorists, it's about us. The battle we are in is about things we stand for and believe in and practice and this is an observance of human rights no matter how terrible our adversaries will be."

13.11 I Won't Always Lose at Checkers

By Randolph BreitReed

My mum always told me that you cannot ignore a problem, thinking that avoiding it will solve it. Bringing focus and attention to the problem is what begins the path to a solution. Like most kids, at a young age I figured everything my mum said was nonsense. She was never a fan of T.V or violent video games (I don't blame her) so we frequently played board games on the weekends. My mom kicked ass at checkers. I have always set incredibly high standards for myself. I probably timed myself to see how fast I could get out of my mother's womb during birth. So, when I sat down to play checkers with my mother for the first time and was brutally beaten (at checkers), I threw the checker board across the room and stormed away, leaving her in the living room, angry with my bad sportsmanship. "You can't expect to be perfect the first time, Bo," is what she told me. I took this to heart and have realized since then that everything takes practice, including my writing.

Writing started for me just like it did for everybody else—in school. I wrote horribly. The worst part was I typed slowly, which meant that not only did the teacher suffer through it, I did too. I remember some of the essays I foolishly handed to the teacher: those research papers you didn't bother to do any research on, thinking you could get away with it, trying to confidently illustrate the friendly relations Iraq and Iran have always had.

My dad was an English professor and I know for damn sure I worried the heck out of him. All he did was read and talk about Twain and Faulkner, Victor Hugo's *Les Miserables*, and that one local writer he always claimed to be on good terms with. But there I was, making funny faces in front of the bathroom mirror with a pair of underwear stretched around my head. I would not have even touched a book if my room hadn't been the "A" through "C" section of my father's library. He spent more time in my room than I did.

In the first year of high school, however, I learned something I hadn't known before. It wasn't something I intended. Besides, I don't think that's how revelations work. I learned that the boring literature assigned in high school was only a minute fraction of the material that was available to me. I started to read and my dad stopped gritting his teeth in his dreams at night. I read the simple stuff first, flipping through Calvin and Hobbes, and then worked my way up to "harder reads" such as Hawthorne and Steinbeck's *East of Eden*.

With the time I had, I read as much as I could. My dad shoved a new book in my hands every week, but they just piled up on the end table in my room. Like my typing, I read slowly so I couldn't fly threw books like the rest of my family did. In spite of this, I think that because I read slowly my attention was drawn to detail that most people didn't catch. I read further into the text with intrigue. As I read more and more I came across quotes, sentences, paragraphs, excerpts, and novels that inspired me and morphed the way I viewed the world. I envied the authors of these works of art. I craved their power. I wanted to have the same influence on people that they were having on me. I turned to writing.

When I first started I didn't know what or how to write. For direction I used the structure and style of the essays, short stories, and novels I had already read to come up with my own ideas. More often times than not, I kept the basic plot but naturally, I dumbed it down and made a few changes here and there. However, it wasn't long before I realized it was too hard to write about something you didn't care for. A piece of writing without feeling has no appeal. They are just words on paper. I understood that I no longer needed to use others' inspiration to fuel the fire of my own. All the inspiration I needed was between my ears, underneath the skin and bone of my thick skull.

Writing stories and practicing my writing throughout high school contributed indefinitely to my writing for academia. Not only did writing outside of school add to my performance, the determination and work-ethic I obtained at home benefited it as well. It taught me that I cannot expect to write an "A" quality paper in one sitting—or even five sittings. I am lucky to have learned that "falling in love" with my writing only interferes with its progress. The process of revising my work is a necessity I am fully aware of. Contrary to popular belief, revising your work becomes more important as you become a better writer as opposed to less important. There is always room for improvement, which is clearly evident in the essays I write for college.

The first thing I noticed about myself in college was the close-minded attitude I had towards my writing. I came from a disoriented high school with low expectations so I was often the only student in my class to receive an "A" on an English essay. As a result of my frequent superiority in English, I was convinced my writing would always be the best. Luckily, I realized I was wrong, way wrong. The first essay I wrote for English was a textual analysis of a short story in the class text, *Writing as Revision*. I read the story once, wrote the essay once, then handed it in to the teacher without completing a single revision. What was a revision anyways? My essay was handed back and to my surprise, I did not receive an "A." This was when I came to realize how much work and persistence was truly required to write a great paper. The view I have of my writing now is astonishingly more critical and open-minded. Realizing the royal position I had in high school will seldom be the case in the future helped open my eyes to other problems I ignored in the past. One of the most important of which is listening to a second opinion.

My triumphs in high school never gave me the chance to consider the perspective of one of my peers. I never had a reason to listen—and so I didn't. Yet, like the change in my attitude, my experiences in English 101 showed me the value in having a peer read my work. Other students brought many things to my attention that I would have failed to see otherwise. They pointed out the unbalanced distribution of my arguments as well as my passive voice and the abundance of extraneous wording. For example, in my first essay titled *A Dirty, Dark Bodega*, four of my body paragraphs are half the size of my introduction. Similarly, I also had multiple paragraphs that covered three quarters of the page. As it could easily be predicted, the small paragraphs carried less support and relevant analysis of the text, where as the large paragraphs were packed with an overwhelmingly excessive amount of superfluous detail.

The extraneous detail that was spread generously throughout my paper was often the result of the extensive use of what I initially thought was "style." After having several people tell me my so-called style was "really not necessary," I removed it from the text. One example of this is in my introduction where I wrote "The younger individual has seen fewer years and as a result, they have less information to decipher the complex codes they encounter in their lives." "What codes?" is the question my peers advised me to answer. I originally felt that deciphering complex codes made it sound like I knew what I was talking about, and because of that, I wrote it despite the fact that there is no mention of codes in the text. I realized I did not have an answer to the proposed question and therefore, I changed the sentence to "The younger individual has seen fewer years and as a result, they have less information and experience to interpret the obstacles they encounter in their early lives."

While it was necessary to take irrelevant information out of the paragraphs that were too large, I also needed to add relevant support in places where it was lacking. The small paragraphs I had in my essay were too simplistic, too bland, and were poorly supported. A sentence that illustrates this is as follows: "Unlike the younger waiter who whines about his delayed departure, the older waiter is considerate of their needs." This sentence shows very little specificity as to which "needs" the older waiter is considering. Adding detail and support in the later part of the paragraph provided clarification to an otherwise open-ended claim. In the attempt to supply the reader with this particular clarification I added "The old man on the other hand appears to have found his purpose in life and proves to be content with his retreat to the café. He has more time than the younger waiter to devote to caring for others. The younger waiter's rude and inconsiderate behavior towards the old man is only a mere by-product of his narcissistic personality." This addition, I believe, created not only a large paragraph, but also one that carries more specificity, variation in diction, and sentence structure.

Despite the frequent reminders I receive, I feel that I have a few habits that have yet to be broken. The more noticeable of the two are varied verb tenses and passive voice. Neither of the two is particularly threatening, however, they interfere with the strength and flow of my paper. Further, they are both flaws in my writing that extend from my time in grade school to my first semester of college. As a result of this, they're pissing me off. Yet, as is the case for most, if not all problems I encounter, practice and perseverance will rid me of this habit and accordingly, I will take another step towards being a better writer. I currently feel more confident in my writing and am certain that the revisions I made were tremendously beneficial to the quality of my paper. However, as I have learned, there is always room for improvement. I think I'll go write some more.

13.12 Manhood and Imagination

By Adam Azoff

Today, when I reflect upon the influences that shape the writer and type of communicator I am, several contributing factors come to mind: teachers, parents, my culture, and books I have read, have in some way impacted the way I write and communicate. Despite a long-term presence of such influential factors, I found myself lacking in imagination when it came to writing creatively. In fact, my entrance to high school seemed to initiate this loss of creative power along with the childhood innocence that once permitted me to envision a world of fun and excitement. I could no longer find myself in a world where heroes always conquered the forces of evil, where I could be at one moment on a space ship traveling through far away galaxies or where I could perhaps serve as the pilot of a jet airplane gliding through endless clouds the next. It was not until I regained this ability, and discovered the power of language and its affects, that I began communicating in a way that permitted me to express myself completely.

As a kid, I would spend most of my day imagining. While playing, an activity which influenced nearly every facet of my life, I pretended to be an astronaut, dinosaur, or spider man swinging through the monkey bars, and always made sure my action figures fought against each other in long epic battles. At this age, my mind was free to wander. I could meander through my childlike thoughts and beliefs because they were not yet contaminated by the harsh realities of the world. I did not yet know to fear death; I was not yet aware of the pain and suffering of the people in Rwanda; I was not aware of the obesity epidemic that was sweeping through the United States. The innocent thoughts that marked my day were purely mine. There were no obstacles in my life at this time- everything seemed to lay before me with luck and simplicity. I thought everyone got along with each other; there were no differences to fight over and nothing to complain about except vegetables. Just like the happy dog playing catch at the park, I was fully content living in each moment with my thoughts, longing for infinite days of imaginative playtime. An end, though, was inevitable.

When piecing together my distant childhood memories, it is difficult to distinguish true recollections from impaired ones, but I do have an approximate idea of when, where, and why I lost my imagination. When I was five, my parents brought me to the holy land of Israel, where we visited family members who for the majority of my young life were either unknown or very distant. One noticeably absent figure from the family was my Grandpa who by then had been dead for five years. Realizing that he was actually dead and would never come back was a crude awakening for a child who always believed death was only a temporary state, as it was for the characters on cartoons. After accepting that I would never meet my Grandpa in this lifetime, a flurry of questions came over me. What happens after one dies? How does it feel to die? Why do people die? I became so infatuated with questions whose answers varied so greatly that I forgot what it meant to pretend. The veil of fear that covers our society's indecision and inability to discuss these concerns blinded me. The death of my Grandpa made life seem serious, too serious for me to have anytime left for imagination.

It was not until my Bar-Mitzvah, when Judaism's rite of passage deemed me a man, that I learned how not to live in constant fear of death. Instead, I began looking optimistically forward to life. However, having a veil lifted from my sight did not necessarily mean I fully regained my vision. I still remained cautious and unimaginative in some areas of communication, particularly in my writing. This transition nevertheless had a significant impact on my perception of communicating with others. According to the Jewish calendar, it is the day I turn thirteen, and all my Bar-Mitzvah training would be put to the test. After spending months learning the words and latent meaning behind every passage, I was excited for this opportunity. When I stepped into the holy synagogue, the small sanctuary was already reeking of the robust scent of sweaty rabbis and family members praying to their god. I was nervous, as unfamiliar family members with high expectations were among the audience, peering down on me like a hawk searching for a meal amongst the distant ground. As I recited the words of the sacred Torah it had a profound effect on the large congregation and me. Every word that left my lips resonated throughout the spiritual atmosphere and I slowly felt elevated from my physical body. Now, above the others, I recall seeing my mother, with proud tears running down her slender cheeks, and the rest of my family as they listened to every word closely. It seemed as if god itself was reciting the same passage. After the services, I asked my rabbi if what I had experienced was at all normal. It felt too powerful to be true. He responded that in a moment of clarity and intense elation, one might experience the world differently, as if an outsider looking in on one's own life. Religions of all sorts share this unique ability to elevate the meaning of life but, as my rabbi warned me, "being elevated is a two-edged sword." I then knew what it all meant. Words and communication have a strange power associated with them that I experienced during my bar mitzvah. Something about what I said and how I said it created emotional feedback, and in some ways, gave me the authority to control some of those feelings and emotions.

Surely, in the wrong hands, this power can be used to cause great evil or it can be used to accomplish remarkable feats. Hitler utilized the power behind language to attract followers for a cause that, to most morally cognitive individuals, was absolutely horrific. Martin Luther King Jr. conversely used the power of language to fight racism and to bring more opportunities for African-Americans. This power is precisely what my rabbi meant by a "two-edged sword". Buddhist philosophies stress that speech should never be overlooked or taken for granted, all speech should be kind, truthful, useful, and said with genuine compassion because you never know in what way your words will impact the listener. The most insignificant little statement might deeply move the mind of another. Through this increased understanding of the importance of communication and new answers to questions regarding the meaning of life and death, I headed into high school.

What I was not able to do during my first few years of high school was find a solution to how, in the midst of structures such as the five-paragraph essay and guidelines regarding what to exactly write about, I could convey myself creatively. Although I understood that the purposes of these structures are to help organize ideas, I was unsure if one should be required to have a certain limit or quota on the amount of ideas presented in a paper. In some cases, I recall being required to support a specific claim. I did not realize it at the time, but looking back, it is evident the writing I was obliged to complete muffled my imagination. The five-paragraph essay is like training wheels on a bicycle, it is helpful for getting one started; however it eventually prevents further growth and development if never taken off.

During my sophomore year English class, I had to write a five-paragraph essay on a book called *"The Lord of the Flies"*, written by William Gerald Golding. The book captures what may happen when a group of British school kids are stranded on an island and have to govern themselves. The tale reveals a lethal and unsuccessful outcome. The underlying moral, one may argue, suggests that society governed by man is savage, uncivilized, and usually fails. My assignment, therefore, was to discover why the school kids became so savage and how such behavior relates to our culture. The problem arose when I desired to write about how their behavior was to be expected. It was, perhaps, normal and not a reflection of our culture. I thought this contradicting opinion would actually make a unique and interesting paper. According to my teacher, the "major" would not support my required thesis and I was forced to give up the idea all together. I took this criticism personally, and thought of myself as being inept to understanding scholarly writing styles. I found that all my writing was always a regurgitation of some already established idea. I felt trapped, like a bird enclosed in a cage, and I was ready to break free and fly away from the grasp of inadequate high school expectations. I wanted to soar above the writing standards, but I needed someone to let me free!

Going into my English class for the first time my junior year, I walked in as an overconfident, popular, football player blinded about my inability to express on a piece of paper. I walked out at the end of the year with a "D", a new sense of morality, a mentor, and as a much more creative writer. My mentor's name is Mrs. Frank and the grade I received at the end of the year absolutely did not reflect the amount of knowledge I learned throughout the year, but actually revealed to me how during high school I had never been challenged. For the first time there was an individual willing to critically judge and objectively analyze my writing, which resulted in realization that my writing had many areas with spacious room for improvement. Always patient, she would selflessly devote her time to the enhancement of her student's education whenever called upon by being knowledgeably informative and supportive, despite the fact that she seemed to be the busiest person on the planet. I started reading books because she showed me the beauty of writing. I began listening to more meaningful music because she revealed to me music's unique ability to convey a powerful message. I even started becoming more critical about what I watched on television because she brought to light the media's use of subliminal messaging in advertisement. In other words, I looked up to Mrs. Frank and learned so much from her because she was someone I could always communicate with about anything.

With her relaxed and comforting voice, she showed me how to free my mind from the constraints of the five-paragraph essay. She did this by teaching me how to find my own voice and still incorporate the important aspects of the writing structure: thesis, conclusion, and body paragraphs, which all serve a critical purpose in organization. I learned to make my writing more relatable and entertaining by adding imaginative imagery, detailed diction, and interest creating devices. My writing soared to an entirely higher level, separated from my previous mundane writing style. It was now free flowing. Most importantly, my relationship with Mrs. Frank, a product of our unique communication, inspired me to discover an invigorating sense of self.

My own thoughts found their way onto paper, and by being able to express myself I felt liberated. With these new perspectives and abilities, I found that writing is only a different form of communication which should not stray far from my casual speaking voice otherwise it could seem unnatural or even incorrect at times. Not worrying about whether my writing fit into a particular structure or if I could support my claims by what other people already said, I soon found myself writing freely. The thoughts came from inside me, and I was finally able to imagine again! Similar to when I was able to imagine childhood dreams, I was now able to write my manhood dreams with an integrated combination of creativity and concern for detail.

I pack up my experiences with me now and travel to a new stage of my life, college. Just as the difference in level of writing from elementary school to middle school, and from middle school to high school, the transition from high school to college is one of many differences and challenges. As a beginner on this new scene, I have only received a small taste of the University of Arizona's writing curriculum. I feel as though I need to elevate my writing to meet these new expectations, and prove myself worthy of being in this position. For instance, as an anthropology major, my writing must become more factual and analytical. Comparable to the limiting feeling I received at first from writing five paragraph essays, having to write with an analytical style can feel constraining. I believe I can surpass this challenge. If I am able to utilize what I have learned from my past experiences, the rites of passages that have allowed me to be where I am, I will hopefully manage to elevate my writing again by integrating imagination with technicality. I envision that when I am older I will be able to enhance the awareness of cultural diversity and, somehow, impact the world positively using communication.

I do not feel my potential as a writer has been met. I realize my ability to become a better writer is essential for overcoming the challenges presented by college and life. With the impact of my eleventh grade English teacher and my Bar Mitzvah, along with other influences on my understanding of communication, I feel confident in accomplishing my future goals. In my writing to come, I envision myself creating articles in magazines or perhaps columns in newspapers- writing that is noticeably not in five-paragraph essay format. With a learned analytical style integrated with mature understandings, vivid imagination, and detailed word choice, I feel I can utilize the power of language to make the world a better place in whichever methodology of communication I employ.

13.13 Embracing Difference, Promoting Equality

By Esmé Schwall, Crystal Fodrey, Kindall Gray, Lisa O'Neill, and Julie Lauterbach-Colby

I: Dissonance and Disturbance

By Esmé Schwall

My students read bell hooks' provocative essay titled "Seduction and Betrayal," and I was excited to hear their reactions. In the essay hooks indicts the films *The Bodyguard* and *The Crying Game* for seducing and betraying the audience. According to hooks, both films promise to portray relationships that transcend divisions of race, class and gender. But ultimately, she writes, the promise of transcendence is thwarted by the films' endings in which the relationships don't work, and the status quo of racist, heterosexist hierarchies is restored. I knew students would disagree with some of hooks' claims, and be uncomfortable with some of her rhetorical strategies, but I also anticipated fruitful and engaging conversation about her essay.

As soon as class began, however, my enthusiasm turned to dismay and discomfort. The conversation felt rigid and hostile. Students said things like, "She's racist" and, "Why do 'they' always complain about race?" Hoping to rescue a discussion that had gone negative and sour, I screened a clip from *The Bodyguard* I felt was bound to convince students of the relevance of race to the film. The scene explores a domestic scene between Frank Farmer (Kevin Costner), who is white, and Rachel Marron (Whitney Houston), the black woman with whom he is romantically and professionally involved. In the scene, Frank's father pulls out a chess board and motions for Frank to join him in the game. Frank asks his father, "Am I black or white?" His father responds, "Son, you know you're white." I thought for sure this scene would invite a consideration of the racial implications hooks observes in the film, but in response students yelled out, "Oh, please," and, "It isn't about race! It's about chess." I felt myself getting defensive, wanting to protect the claims of an essay I didn't write and the views of a person I'd never met.

My discomfort was confusing, not least of all because the same lesson had gone over so well with another group of students. While my second class resisted even acknowledging race as a valid lens through which to view the film, my earlier students had found that the inter-racial relationships in both films are steeped in the imagery of danger.

Why did these two groups of students respond so differently to the same texts and class format? Why was one class ready to discuss possibilities and interpretations of the essay and the films, while the second class left me feeling emotionally drained and defensive? Why did the students in the second class sound so hostile and exasperated—even offended? And what was my job as the teacher?

In retrospect, I can see that **cognitive dissonance**—a kind of mental friction—had everything to do with bell hooks, my students, and myself. We experience cognitive dissonance when something new rubs up against an often subconscious expectation or assumption about the world. In "Seduction and Betrayal," hooks doesn't use the term cognitive dissonance, but certainly this is a way of explaining the conflict she felt when her expectations about the films (that they would finally show interracial and inter-class relationships that worked!) were disrupted by the reality of the films (the relationships were doomed from the start, reinforcing the stereotypes and hierarchies she had hoped the films would challenge). The students in my second class experienced cognitive dissonance as a result of bell hooks' cognitive dissonance. Their experience of the world was being challenged by hooks' experience of the world, and they didn't have a place to store this contradictory information. Then, my students' cognitive dissonance ignited my own cognitive dissonance. I had made assumptions about what the students would find interesting or worth talking about, and then my assumptions about my students collided with the reality of their perspectives.

It turned out that naming and acknowledging cognitive dissonance was helpful during future class discussions about controversial texts. Letting students know ahead of time that they might experience cognitive dissonance, and then using that discomfort to access possibilities of interpretation, became a helpful practice. Students wrote successful essays in which the concept of cognitive dissonance helped reveal and resolve tensions within texts. It turned out that confronting the dissonance directly was more fruitful—and even more comfortable—than ignoring it or wishing it away.

II: Critical Consciousness in the Contact Zone

By Crystal Fodrey

Why do teachers sometimes ask you to read about, write about, and discuss issues of difference and inequality in composition classes? It's *not* to make you intentionally uncomfortable, although experiencing cognitive dissonance is not a bad thing because it can help you challenge preconceived cultural ideas that you may have never thought to challenge before. We do it because the subject matter can be intellectually stimulating and eye opening, which can lead to interesting writing topics for you to explore. We do it so that you might become more open-minded and sensitive to issues that affect your fellow classmates and other members of the UA, Tucson, national, and global communities. We also do it because gaining this type of critical consciousness can help you attain the mental tools you need to use the power of your literacy to help *em*power the disenfranchised, the illiterate, the powerless.

One way teachers, myself included, foster an environment conducive to the development of critical consciousness is to treat the classroom like a thirdspace and/or a contact zone. Thirdspace is defined as "a space where issues of race, class, and gender can be addressed simultaneously without privileging one over the other" (Soja 5), and contact zones are "social spaces where cultures meet, clash, and grapple with each other, often in contexts of highly asymmetrical relations of power" (Pratt 34). In my classroom, that means that we often analyze texts—from essays to documentaries to spaces on campus—that highlight issues of cultural differences and inequalities, and we share experiences through reflective writing and class discussions, critically analyzing the texts in question.

In one class, for instance, we wrote about and discussed how power is unequally distributed in some of the spaces my students regularly inhabit. This led to a heated discussion about who should have power and why some groups, like members of sororities and fraternities, have more power than others in certain spaces. Some students who did not participate in Greek life for ideological or socioeconomic reasons described their views of fraternity and sorority houses as "cult-like" or exclusionary. This prompted several sorority and fraternity members to defend their organizations, explaining the ways that the houses stand for strong traditions, values, and commitments to service, despite their exclusionary status. After this fruitful discussion during which students exposed and analyzed spatial inequalities, I explained the concept of a contact zone to my students and asked them to list some benefits and challenges of having our class function in that way. Here's what they came up with:

Benefits

- creates an opportunity to meet new people in a way you might not be able to in other classes

- "really" get to discuss and debate things

- get a more inside view of other cultures represented in the class

- gain a wider knowledge about many cultures

- develop better communication skills

- clear up misunderstandings about different cultures

Challenges

- students may feel left out or offended

- someone could harshly disagree with someone else's point of view

- people are more open; therefore it is easier for them to get made fun of

- similar/same cultures group together, leaving others alone

- it's hard to be open about controversial issues around strangers

In the discussion, one student noted, "the whole world is pretty much a contact zone, so why should the classroom be any different?" Yes, communicating in a classroom contact zone, like communicating anywhere that cultures meet, clash, and grapple with one another, can sometimes create tension, but as long as you have an open mind and take time to reflect on the issues that cause you cognitive dissonance, usually the benefits will far outweigh the initial discomfort. The experience will give you the opportunity to emerge from the class not just a better writer and critical thinker but also one who is more attune to the world around you.

Works Cited

Pratt, Mary L. "Arts of the Contact Zone." *Profession* 91 (1991): 33–40. Print.

Soja, Edward W. *Third space: Journeys to Los Angeles and Other Real-and-Imagined Places*. Oxford, UK: Blackwell, 1996. Print.

III: Beyond Political Correctness: Using Language that Honors Everyone

By Kindall Gray and Lisa O'Neill

Our job as instructors of writing often involves facilitating discussions among students about controversial subjects like race, class, gender, and sexuality while also redirecting offensive comments which might violate the Code of Academic Integrity and maintaining a positive, safe environment in the classroom. These types of comments are inevitable when discussing controversial issues, and often unintentional on the offender's part, as students new to college do not always know what is appropriate and what is not. That being said, offensive comments have the potential to shut down conversation. For instance, they can turn students off who feel judged or offended or they can cause the student who made the comment and has been reprimanded never to share their views again. In other words, it's all pretty shaky ground for us as teachers. We have to handle these situations gracefully and swiftly in order to encourage an open, safe space and prevent a classroom environment that is stifling. The question is: how do we as teachers do that? Let's look at a real-life classroom scenario in order to illuminate the situation.

Kindall: I watch a film with my students that deals with homosexuality and gender issues called *The Crying Game*. My students seem surprised by the material but not offended. After we watch the film, we have a discussion regarding the complicated questions the text poses. Quickly, the conversation turns to the more superficial aspects of the film, probably due to the difficult nature of the subject matter. Subconsciously, I'm glad it turns superficial; perhaps it's less awkward that way. Though I love to challenge my students' preconceived notions about the world, I'm also a human being, and I get nervous just like anyone else.

Finally, one of my students speaks up and addresses the elephant in the room: "Well, I think the movie was really surprising," he says, "because even though the man in the film doesn't think he's gay, he is still in love with a man dressed up as a woman. There's no denying that. He loved him before he knew he was a man, and he loved him after. This makes the viewer question their ideas about sexual preference, doesn't it? I mean, it shows love isn't always about gender. That's what it showed me, anyway."

His comment impresses me, and immediately, the rest of the class joins in. One student's candidness makes everyone feel comfortable discussing the true questions the film poses. Many agree with their outspoken classmate, and believe the movie does challenge our ideas about attraction and human love. Some of them find this disturbing; others find it plain interesting.

In the middle of this conversation, a normally quiet student announces, "The dudes in the film are immoral fags. I'm a Christian, and that's what I believe."

The room falls so silent you can hear a pin drop. I look from the student who made the inflammatory comment to the students around him. I sense that perhaps the other students don't agree with him, or feel embarrassed and/or offended by his comment, but no one speaks up. As the instructor, I have to handle this the right way, in order to set not only the tone for the rest of the conversation, but for the rest of the semester.

So, now I ask you: What would *you* do as the instructor? What would resolve this situation, in your eyes? Or, what might you do if you were another student in the class?

Let's consider a few things before we rush to a solution: the scenario was *not* totally negative. In fact, the scenario showcased how classroom discussions can take off when a single student puts their guard down. Disagreements can result from many things, some positive. For instance, we all have differing experiences, values, beliefs, and knowledge-bases, and because of this can learn from eachother, even through disagreement. If everyone censored themselves in the classroom, the scenario I described wouldn't have occurred at all. That means the rich conversation would be lost.

But is it possible for every student to be heard—even those whose comments might offend others? What if students framed their opinions as *inquiry*—or as questions instead of as judgements? For example, the gentleman offended by *The Crying Game* could have said, "As a Christian, I had problems with the characters' homosexuality and even with the discussion we're having.

My religion views homosexuality as immoral. Did anyone else struggle with the subject matter of the film?" Then, he would have not only responded openly and honestly about his reactions to the text, but he also would have done so in a way that honored the other voices in the room. Furthermore, his question would have *invited* discussion of relevant ideas rather than shutting it down.

We shouldn't avoid disagreements about difficult subjects, because that would mean losing opportunities to learn about the world around us, but we *should* try to make our classroom conversations open and beneficial to all. As teachers, we do not want a self-censoring classroom, but one that moves beyond political correctness. "Politically correct" terminology is rooted in the desire of people in positions of power to avoid offending certain groups. By using "African-American" instead of "black" or "differently-abled" instead of "handicapped," these leaders hope to reframe language so they will not upset anyone. While they worry about the words themselves, we want to consider what lies beneath them. For instance, when we examine a text that challenges our assumptions, we must realize that the person sitting next to us may have experienced similar feelings or situations to those addressed in the text. Just by the nature of our own background and upbringing, we may be confronted with pieces that hit close to home about our own gender, race, income level, sexual orientation, familial background, culture, or hometown, among others.

Our hope as teachers is that we not only use inclusive language in the classroom to honor the complexity of each person's experience but that we also approach classroom discussions with an open mind and an attitude that is receptive to other people's experiences. Let's look at a scenario where classroom dynamics shut one student out of the conversation.

Lisa: We had just finished watching Spike Lee's *When The Levees Broke*. I was excited for students to discuss issues that Lee brings up about the United States government's response after the levees broke in New Orleans. However I found many of my students were defensive. While they were saddened by the film, many of my Caucasian students, the majority race in the class, remarked that race didn't have anything to do with the response after the levees broke. They felt that Lee, in his role as director, had skewed this information to suit his own interests. Some of my students implied or said outright that Lee had searched for news footage only of African-American people so that it would appear that the government's response to victims of Hurricane Katrina had to do with race.

I left that day deeply disappointed because I felt our discussion had simply dismissed complicated issues. I was also disappointed because I knew there were other opinions that were not being voiced. In her short writing assignments, one of my African-American students felt Lee was justified in implicating racism through his film; she wrote that the government's response to Katrina would have been different if the majority of those who'd remained in the city had been white.

I knew this student's voice would add another perspective to the dialogue, but I didn't want to put her in an uncomfortable position, so I decided, the next day, to read anonymous excerpts from several students' writing. I began by reading hers: "I feel that if the hurricane would have hit a city that was predominantly white then the President and the government would have made sure those people were rescued and had aid."

Immediately, one of my outspoken Caucasian students said loudly, "Well, that's just ridiculous." And instantly, my chest tightened. In my attempt to include the viewpoint of my silent student, I had made her more vulnerable and even more excluded from the conversation. I used this moment as a time to regroup as a class, asking that we be respectful of each other's opinions. I encouraged students to voice their differing opinions, but I reminded them that words like "ridiculous" or "stupid" were not respectful. I asked the student who disagreed to talk more specifically about why she had that reaction. Only later did I realize I could have asked her to reframe her opinion as a question. For example, "I'm not sure that's true. What about class? Poor white people were displaced, too. What do you all think?"

None of this is easy. We are complicated individuals, with complicated belief systems and ideas that we bring to any text we read and any conversation we participate in. How can we make these conversations beneficial? This is the question that comes up again and again, and the question itself seems to be at the heart of cognitive dissonance: with cognitive dissonance comes conflict. But we as teachers believe that it is our differing opinions that make the conversation educational and worthwhile.

IV: "The Text is Simply One-sided" or "There is Only One Way to Look at This Text"

By Julie Lauterbach-Colby

Based on the challenges discussed above, you may ask yourself if the endeavor to engage more fully with a text is a worthwhile notion. I would answer, "Absolutely." In the classroom setting, but also within the broader lens of life and everyday decisions, we must allow ourselves the ability to open-minded-ly and holistically approach a text's meaning and implications. In this sense, we must first come to honor the complexity of a given text. This section will help you to begin taking classroom discussions and applying those ideas to your own writing. Your unanswered questions or concerns about a text will then become clearer as you try to engage them in writing.

Most students come to college with a mental framework that operates on a scale of extremities. Many believe that there is a right and wrong answer to any given question and that their job is to figure out the correct response to receive a passing grade.

In truth, we all operate, to one extent or the other, within our own modes of ideology; our beliefs shape the way we look at and perceive any given text, whether that text be a short story, film clip or sculpture—or even another writer's response.

That said, with even our first glance at a text's title or opening paragraph, we begin to make neat and tidy assumptions about the text's meaning that we will carry with us throughout our entire reading of the piece. This primary reaction helps us categorize and organize the text. For instance, you may feel comfortable answering questions such as, "What was the story about?" or "What did the photograph look like?" because these are summary questions you answer in your everyday life: "How was your day? What happened?" Usually these questions have a simple, concise answer, one that can be weighed on a "right" or "wrong" scale. Many times, however, these assumptions only go so far; the analysis of such a text then remains only surface-level, or reactionary. You may have heard similar comments as to the ones below from some of my students: "The father in Sherman Alexie's story "Because My Father Said He was the Only Indian to See Jimi Hendrix Play 'The Star-Spangled Banner' at Woodstock" was a liar and a drunk."

Such statements are, to be sure, appropriate starting points. When reading or encountering a text for the first time, you may find that it is natural to conjure up some sort of primary reaction to the piece. Perhaps you were struck by some character in the story, or were disturbed by one image or detail. However, these claims and ideas for a text should never stop here. In Greg Smith's essay on film, "'It's Just a Movie': A Teaching Essay for Introductory Media Classes," one of the foundational points made is that there is a reason for every minute detail within a film. Nothing can be written off as accidental or dismissed as arbitrary. Is it safe to assume that with most texts the same principle applies? I think so. The authors make conscious and deliberate choices in their work. Each choice can be seen as a layer and each layer as a testament to the text's complexity.

You may be asking yourself, "Well, how can I dig deeper into a text's meaning?" At this point, a close reading of a text proves useful, as do the intuitive primary questions of textual analysis: *how?* and *why?* By asking and genuinely seeking answers to these questions, you will not only find yourself deepening your understanding of the text, but thinking differently about the world in which you operate. In other words, you will begin to turn your reactions into *inquiry*. Start to ask yourself, "How can I change this reaction, what I'm feeling, into a more provoking question or inquiry?" or, "How can I write about this feeling in a way that might allow me to push my own initial thoughts about the text?" By practicing this idea, we automatically reengage and re-open the conversation for other ideas to be shared and discussed.

For example, let's take a comment made by a student concerning the wife in Karen Brennan's short story "Floating." In the text, Brennan presents her readers with a female protagonist who believes that she has the ability to levitate within her own home. Her new-found ability to float occurs simultaneously with a mysterious, secret and dead "child" that the woman keeps in a dresser drawer, and hints at a disintegrating marriage. Outside her home's four walls she is constrained to the ground. The student's response, after reading the story, was simply, "Well, that woman was just crazy."

How would you have responded? As readers, we have to ask ourselves deeper questions concerning the text: Is the woman indeed crazy; is she hallucinating; are there other ways of approaching this character's situation?

We might then be compelled to search for other possible meanings: why is this woman only able to float within her own house; how does such a constraint lend weight to the domestic woman's plight; what are some reasons for the baby's presence in the story; why can't the woman communicate properly with her husband; why can't he see that she is able to float; how might a woman's interpretation of this text differ from a man's? The list of questions and inquiries continues. The important point is to see that by asking these questions, by engaging in the material, you will begin a personal investigation. With that investigation comes a personal investment. Such careful study will help to enrich your ongoing conversation around the text, as well as provide you and your peers with a more firmly-rooted understanding of yourselves and the larger world.

A
Writing Tutors

The University of Arizona offers many resources where students can receive extra help with their writing. Some are open to all students and are free of charge; others are restricted and charge a fee. The following descriptions will help you find the center that is right for you.

The Writing Center

All writers benefit from extra readers. You can find such readers in the Writing Center, sponsored by the English Department and administered by Writing Program GATs. It is open to all University of Arizona students at no cost. The Writing Center is neither a remedial writing program nor an editing service. It is a place to talk about ideas and get feedback and guidance from peers. Specially trained peer consultants who are experienced writers with majors from across the curriculum can help you at any stage of your writing process: confronting your recurrent fear of a blank screen, interpreting an assignment, brainstorming ideas, organizing notes to write a first draft, explicating your instructor's comments, generating a revision plan, or editing a final draft. They can also help with writing tasks, such as lab reports, applications, and personal writing.

You can sign up for half-hour conferences by visiting the main location at Bear Down Gym, room 102, Monday through Thursday, from 10:00 a.m. to 4:00 p.m. Additionally, the Writing Center is open from 10:00 a.m. to 2:00 p.m. on Tuesdays. You can also call the Writing Center at 621-3182 to set up an appointment. The Writing Center's homepage is located at <http://english. arizona.edu/index_site.php?id=287/>. Speak to your instructor or call 621-3182 for details about exact consultation times and locations outside the main location.

Writing Skills Improvement Program (WSIP)

The Writing Skills Improvement Program was established over twenty years ago to assist minority and economically-disadvantaged students to improve their writing skills and achieve academic success at the University of Arizona. Eligible students can register directly at the WSIP office at 1201 E. Helen Street. A personal tutor will work with each student for the entire semester as needed at no cost. The WSIP also serves the academic community at large by offering a free series of Weekly Writing, General Education Writing, and Graduate Writing Workshops. The Weekly Writing Workshop is especially valuable to all students taking composition classes and covers many aspects of academic writing. The program offers a number of services to their target population, as well as to any student who desires to improve his/her writing skills on a space-available basis (preferably referred by a writing instructor). For more information visit the WSIP at 1201 East Helen Street, access their website at <http://web.arizona.edu/~wsip/>, or call 621-5849.

Strategic Alternative Learning Techniques (SALT) Center

The Strategic Alternative Learning Techniques (SALT) Center offers enhanced services for students with learning disabilities and attention deficit disorders. One of the only programs of its type in the nation, it provides students who qualify with individualized academic support, learning and career workshops, tutoring in writing and a variety of other subjects, and a computer lab. Students must apply to the program through a separate application. A limited number of scholarships are available. For more information about fees and scholarships, contact SALT at (520) 621-1242 or visit their website at <http://www.salt.arizona.edu/>.

B

Campus Resources and Internet Addresses

Campus Resources			
Arizona State Museum	1013 E. University Blvd.	621-6302	http://www.statemuseum.arizona.edu
Campus Health Service	1224 E. Lowell Street	621-6490	http://www.health.arizona.edu
Center for Creative Photography	1030 N. Olive Road	621-7968	http://www.creativephotography.org
Dean of Students	Old Main 203	621-7057	http://dos.web.arizona.edu
Disability Resource Center	1224 E. Lowell Street	621-3268 (V/TTY)	http://drc.arizona.edu
English Department	Modern Languages 445	621-1836	http://english.web.arizona.edu/
Department of Multicultural Programs and Services	Old Main, Level One	621-1094	http://dmps.arizona.edu/
Museum of Art	1031 N. Olive Road	621-7567	http://artmuseum.arizona.edu
Oasis Program for Sexual Assault and Relationship Violence	Highland Commons 1224 E. Lowell St.	626-2051	http://www.health.arizona.edu/webfiles/hpps_oasis_program.htm
Office for International Student Programs and Services	915 N. Tyndall Ave.	621-4627	http://internationalstudents.arizona.edu/
Strategic Alternative Learning Techniques (SALT)	1010 N. Highland Ave.	621-1242	http://www.salt.arizona.edu
University of Arizona Poetry Center	1508 E. Helen St.	626-3765	http://www.poetrycenter.arizona.edu

Campus Resources Cont.

University Learning Center	Old Main 201	621-4548	http://www.ulc.arizona.edu
University College	ILC 103	621-7763	http://www.universitycollege.arizona.edu
Veterans' Affairs	Modern Languages 347	621-9501	http://vets.registrar.arizona.edu
Writing Center	Bear Down 102	621-3182	http://english.arizona.edu/index_site.php?id=287
Writing Program	Modern Languages 380	621-3553	http://english.arizona.edu/index_site.php?id=36
Writing Skills Improvement Program	1201 E. Helen St.	621-5849	http://web.arizona.edu/~wsip

Important Internet Addresses for First-Year Writing

Computer Centers on Campus	http://www.oscr.arizona.edu/labs/instructional/index.html
Purdue University Online Writing Lab (OWL)	http://owl.english.purdue.edu
University of North Carolina at Chapel Hill Writing Center Handouts	http://www.unc.edu/depts/wcweb/handouts
University of Arizona Home Page	http://www.arizona.edu

UA Student Policies, Procedures and Codes includes:
  Code of Academic Integrity
  Code of Conduct
	http://dos.web.arizona.edu/uapolicies

UA Libraries	http://www.library.arizona.edu

C

Computing Centers on Campus

All computing centers are free and open to students. The following labs have open access to all students. Take your university ID and a storage device (disks, flash drives, and so on) to store your information. Call the labs for hours or check the schedule at <http://www.oscr.arizona.edu/locations/hours>.

Electrical and Computer Engineering (ECE) Room 229	621-8534
Engineering 318	621-3206
Information Commons Main Library, 1st Floor	621-6441
La Paz Residence Hall S107	626-2434
McClelland Park 102	626-0403
Nugent 102	626-2714
Old Main 201	621-4548

For the most up-to-date listing of computer centers and services on campus, see the Office of Student Computing Resources website at <http://www.oscr.arizona.edu>. You may also call or visit the 24/7 help desk in the Martin Luther King, Jr. Student Center, Room 207, at 626-TECH.

D
ESL Resources

While college-level writing can be intimidating for all students, writers whose first language is not English face extra challenges. Writing an essay in a different language and within a new culture is challenging. Knowing how to use the resources available to you will help you make the best of your experiences in your writing course, in the U.S. academic community, and even in U.S. society. As an ESL student, you should use not only your teacher's help but also the information in this section, in addition to Appendices A, B, and C. In the sections below you will find tips from instructors who teach ESL writing, tips from students who have taken ESL writing, and a list of resources that may be helpful for you.

Tips from ESL Instructors

Get to know the people in your class; you will have the opportunity to form friendships with people from all over the world. Take advantage of this because it is a rare and wonderful opportunity.

— Selena Mahoney

It is important that you pay close attention to the comments your instructor writes on draft(s) of your paper, but remember that instructors normally focus on the large elements of a paper (e.g., the thesis statement, paragraph structure, etc.). It is your responsibility to go beyond those comments, which are only a starting point for revision.

— Estela Ene

Use the [Bear Down and other] writing centers and native English-speaking students to help you with your writing. Also, go to your teacher's office hours. My students who used the writing centers and came to office hours showed significant improvement over the students who tried to do everything themselves.

— Selena Mahoney

Tips from ESL Students

Write in a journal every day. These journals will help you to become more fluent.

— Oscar de Ita

I think that the most important thing for an ESL student to be successful is understanding the requirement of each writing assignment since each country may have different standards for its college students. So to understand what is required in colleges in the U.S. is a key that affects our performance in these writing courses.

— Yuzhen Huang

Discuss with friends what you want to write about. They may provide you with ideas or points you never thought of to use in your essay.

— Wenyang Tan

Read as much as you can to improve your vocabulary and grammar.

— Ismiza Shukor

Read more. Write more. Ask more.

— Wing See Ng

Always ask questions.

— Olubusola Olatoregun

Resources for ESL Students

On-Campus Resources

- **The Office of International Student Programs and Services** serves as the representative and advocate for international students here at the University of Arizona. They can provide information ranging from visas to international programming. Their web site may be found at <http://internationalstudents.arizona.edu>.

- **The Center for English as a Second Language (CESL)** has served ESL students at the University of Arizona for over thirty years. They offer both Intensive English Programs throughout the year, as well as Evening

Programs that focus on reading, writing, speaking, and listening. While CESL classes are not offered for University of Arizona credit, many students have found CESL courses to be useful in sharpening their English skills. See their home page at <http://www.cesl.arizona.edu>.

- **The Writing Center** (also see Appendix A) can help you at any stage of your writing process: confronting your recurrent fear of a blank screen, interpreting an assignment, brainstorming ideas, organizing notes to write a first draft, explicating your instructor's comments, generating a revision plan, or editing a final draft. They can also help with writing tasks, such as lab reports, applications, and personal writing. Approximately 50% of the people who come to the Writing Center for help speak and write English as a second language. Tutoring at the Writing Center is free. See <http://english.arizona.edu/index_site.php?id=287>.

- **The Writing Skills Improvement Program** (also see Appendix A) is a free service designed to assist minority and economically disadvantaged students to improve their writing skills and achieve academic success at the University of Arizona. The WSIP also serves the academic community at large by offering a series of Weekly Writing Workshops and Summer Institutes for Writing. They offer a number of services to their target population, as well as to any student who desires to improve his/her writing skills on a space-available basis. Many of the tutors at WSIP have worked extensively with ESL students. See <http://wsip.web.arizona.edu>.

- **Private Tutors** may be a good choice for students who require help with large projects. One possible source for fee-based tutors is from students enrolled in the University of Arizona Master's program in English Language and Linguistics (EL/L) or the PhD program in Second Language Acquisition and Teaching (SLAT). To request a tutor from these programs, contact the administrative assistants from those programs:

  o English Language and Linguistics (EL/L)—Elaine Lim, Modern Language 456, 621-7216, email: maesl@u.arizona.edu

  o Second Language Acquisition and Teaching (SLAT)—Shaun O'Connor, Transitional Office Building 208, 621-7391, email: shaun@u.arizona.edu

Online Resources

General

- Dave's ESL Café   http://www.eslcafe.com

- Linguistic Funland   http://www.linguistic-funland.com/tesl.html

- E.L. Easton   http://eleaston.com

Writing

- Purdue OWL   http://owl.english.purdue.edu

- Advice on Academic Writing   http://www.utoronto.ca/writing/advise.html

- Univ. of Wisconsin Writer's Handbook   http://www.wisc.edu/writing/Handbook/

Grammar

- The Internet Grammar of English   http://www.ucl.ac.uk/internet-grammar

Dictionaries

- The Newbury House Online Dictionary   http://nhd.heinle.com

- Merriam-Webster Online   http://www.m-w.com/dictionary.htm

E

The Essay and Cover Design Contests

For the past 29 years, the Writing Program has held an essay contest for students enrolled in the first-year writing courses. Not only does the contest give instructors the chance to read the year's best essays and students the chance to share their best work, but also prize-winning essays often become samples for future students (as you can see in Part IV of this *Guide*). Even if your essay doesn't win a prize, the editors might ask your permission to print it in the next edition of the *Guide* or on the online *Guide*.

This year's essay contest winners were selected from more than 75 entries. Some of the winning students' essays have been reprinted in this edition of the *Guide*, and you can find all the winning essays online at <http://english. arizona.edu/index_site.php?id=588&preview=1>. The essays were separated by type, and each type was judged based on specific criteria provided by the Writing Program course directors. The editors of this book then distributed all the essays to the judges to rate the top essay in each category. These judges were experienced writers and instructors familiar with the first-year writing courses.

Entering the contest is easy. Go to the Essay Contest Instructions online at <http://english.arizona.edu/index_site.php?id=585&preview=1> and follow the directions described there to submit your essay via email to the Guide Editors. Essays are accepted year-round and entries are judged around the middle of each Spring semester. (This year's deadline is listed online with the instructions.)

Winner of the Annual Cover Design Contest

In addition to the essay contest, the Writing Program also holds an annual cover design contest, and the winning entry is chosen as the cover of this *Guide*. The winner of the contest is also asked to create art for the headings of each chapter and section. We invited students from across the university to participate in this year's contest. We allowed everyone in the English department to have a vote in selecting the cover. The editors thank all contestants and those who voted in the contest. **This year's winner is Colin Darland.** We also wish to acknowledge the work of **Fiona Foster**, the runner-up in this contest.

The Annual Jan Lipartito Historical Remembrance Writing Contest

The Jan Lipartito Historical Remembrance Essay Contest was established in 1998 to honor Jan Lipartito's contributions to the Writing Program and to encourage students to integrate historical research and reflection into their writing. Jan worked as adjunct lecturer and Teaching Advisor in the Writing Program for many years before retiring in 1999. She researched the "public and private" records of World War II and integrated her concern for remembering the Holocaust into her teaching and service work. The Historical Remembrance Essay Contest award is given to noteworthy essays that include historical reflection, personal memoir, or formal historical research. **This year's winner is Amy Markantes, who wrote the essay "A Freeing Passion" for Angela Miller's English 101 course.**

The Hayden-McNeil Difference and Inequality Student Essay Award

The Hayden-McNeil Difference and Inequality Award was established by the University of Arizona Writing Program's Difference and Inequality Committee in 2008. This award recognizes student writing that either explicitly or implicitly brings readers' attention to issues of difference and inequality in the classroom, the individual's experience, the campus, or the world at-large. A candidate's essay should demonstrate an awareness of the D&I Committee's main objectives (described at <http://english.arizona.edu/index_site.php?id=472&preview=1>), even though the essay may not have been written with those objectives specifically in mind. **This year's winner is Christine Filer, who wrote the essay "Bring Gold to the Middle East" for Jeremy Frey's English 102 course.**

Students in all first-year writing courses may enter these contests. Entry forms are online at <http://english.arizona.edu/index_site.php?id=585& preview=1.> Deadlines and entry procedures for the contest are the same as those for the *Student's Guide to First-Year Writing* Essay Contest mentioned previously. All essays are judged on the clarity and originality of the thesis, the persuasiveness with which the thesis is defended, the effectiveness of the organization, and the clarity of expression.

Winners of the Annual First-Year Writing Essay Contest

Additional thanks to the judges: Alison Betts, Connie Bracewell, Denise Burgess, Rosanne Carlo, Erica Cirillo-McCarthy, Amy Cook, Greg Grewell, Ashley Holmes, Ron Lorette, Aretha Matt, Angela Miller, Amy Parziale, Jessica Shumake, Jack Skeffington, Susan Thomas, Elise Versoza, Ashley Warren, Andrew Winslow, and Amanda Wray.

English 101+

First Prize—Literacy Narrative: **Adam Azoff,** "Manhood and Imagination"— Instructor, Yingliang Liu

English 101

First Prize—Textual Analysis: **Megan Peterson,** "Escaping Entrapment"— Instructor, Angela Miller

First Prize—Reflective: **Randolph BrietReed,** "I Won't Always Lose at Checkers"—Instructor, Kristin Mock

English 102

First Prize—Persuasive Essay: **Christine Filer,** "Bring Gold to the Middle East"—Instructor, Jeremy Frey

English 103H

First Prize—Text-in-Context: **Melanie Moussazedeh,** "Inadvertent Sins in Dante's Inferno and Boccaccio's Decameron"—Instructor, David Buchalter

First Prize—Textual Analysis: **Leo Yamaguchi,** "Blade Runner vs. Freud"— Instructor, Jean Goodrich

First Prize—Visual Analysis: **Brian Rapoport,** "A Photographic Poet"— Instructor, Jeremy Frey

First Prize—Text-in-Context: **Nicole Seckinger,** "The Darwinian Role Reversal of Sebastian and Violet Venable"—Instructor, Jessica Shumake

English 104H

First Prize—Reflective: **Erin Chute,** "Aria: A Beginning, Middle, and Beginning"—Instructor, Patrick Baliani

English 109H

First Prize—Research: **Elizabeth Casavant,** "Sketching History"—Instructor, Debra Gregerman

Index

About the Editors

Marissa M. Juárez (left) is a PhD student in Rhetoric, Composition, and the Teaching of English at the University of Arizona, where she has taught courses in freshman composition and business and technical writing. Since arriving at the UA, she has been a member of the Writing Program's Difference and Inequality committee. In her scholarly work, Marissa explores the Afro-Brasilian martial art of capoeira as a form of bodily communication where practitioners engage in a "conversation" with each other through bodily movements, expressions, and gestures. Drawing upon theories of rhetoric, performance, space, and race, she looks at how practitioners of the art form use their bodies to challenge discriminatory ideologies and build coalitions. Outside of school, Marissa enjoys playing capoeira, spending time with family and friends, and exploring the landscape of the Southwestern U.S.

Marlowe Daly-Galeano (center) is a PhD student in the Literature Program at the University of Arizona, where she is also working toward a graduate certificate in Women's Studies. She is particularly interested in nineteenth-century American literature by and about women. She enjoys teaching courses in first-year composition, literature, and women's studies. Currently she teaches English 101. Her newest non-academic interest is finding ways to support local and sustainable farming practices. Marlowe also enjoys reading about food (as well as cooking and eating it), singing, hiking, doing yoga, hanging out with her family, and taking walks with her awesome dog, Marvin.

Jacob L. Witt (right) is a PhD student in Second Language Acquisition and Teaching at the University of Arizona. Before arriving at the UA, he earned an MA in Communication Studies at the University of Northern Iowa, where he studied immigration metaphor in political rhetoric. Since arriving at the UA, Jacob has earned an MA in English Language and Linguistics and taught English 101, 102, and 108. He currently enjoys studying ESL composition, Linguistics, and Japanese. In his spare time he enjoys gardening and spending time with his family.